Muriel Feiner

The Bulls, The Bullfighters and Their World

Club Taurino of London

Publications of the Club Taurino of London

Walter Johnston *Brave Employment* (1997)
The Law and Regulations for Taurine Spectacles (1999)
Club Taurino of London Handbook (2004; revised and enlarged 2009)
Tristan Wood *Dialogues with Death* (2006)
Ivan Moseley and Tristan Wood *The English and the Bulls* (2009)
Iain Richardson and Jason Bowyer *Stopped Clocks* (2012)
José Miguel Arroyo and Pablo Aguado, trans. Brian Harding
Joselito. The Real Deal (2015)
Ivan Moseley *... to die in the skin of a rich man* (2016)

Printed by Short Run Press, Exeter
Copyright © Muriel Feiner/Club Taurino of London

ISBN 978-0-9932716-2-5

Club Taurino of London
PO Box 58515, London SW13 3AF
United Kingdom

I dedicate this book to the Fiesta, the bullfighting world, and to all its participants and followers, who have furnished me with such wonderful experiences.

To my father who, perhaps without knowing it, instilled in me a profound love of Spain and its culture without having left his native Brooklyn.

To my husband, a Spanish matador, who afforded me an extraordinary introduction into this exclusive world.

And to everyone, who can look upon other cultures, religions, traditions, customs, ethnicities and lifestyles, with curiosity, deference and even passion ... because they will make the world a better place.

Contents

Dedication	i
Contents	iii
Foreword	vii
Introduction	ix
Understanding bullfighting: strictly for the uninitiated	xi
Acknowledgements	xiv

Chapter 1. The Bull	1
The Bull-breeder	1
The legendary: Eduardo Miura	3
The popular: Victorino Martín padre (Sr)	12
Victorino Martín García	17
The up-and-coming: Pablo Mayoral	23
The *Mayoral* or Ranch Foreman	28
Julio Presumido (of the Victorino Martín ranch)	29
The Veterinary Surgeon	32
José Pedro Gómez Ballesteros	33
Chapter 2. The Bullfighters	39
The Matador de Toros	39
The veteran: Antonio Chenel *Antoñete*	39
The current star: Enrique Ponce	51
The struggling contender: Raúl Galindo	61
The *Novillero* or Novice Bullfighter	65
The Bullfighting School—*La Escuela Taurina*	65
Fernando Cantos	68
The Rejoneador or Bullfighter on Horseback	70
Three generations of Rejoneadors	72
Álvaro Domecq y Díez	72
Álvaro Domecq Romero	77
Antonio Domecq y Domecq	80
The Banderillero	82
The veteran: Julio Pérez El Vito	83
The veteran: Antonio Chaves Flores	89
The contemporary: Arcadio Ferrón *Curro Cruz*	95
The Picador	99
The veteran: Domingo Rodríguez *Rubio de Quismondo*	100
The contemporary: Luis Antonio Vallejo *Pimpi*	106
The Comic Bullfighter: Manuel Pérez Luque *El Chino Torero*	112

Chapter 3. The Matador's "Inner Circle"	118
The *Apoderado* or Manager	118
Manuel Flores *Camará*	118
The *Mozo de Espadas* or Sword-handler	125
Gonzalo Sánchez Conde *Gonzalito*	125
The Bullfight Tailor	132
Justo Algaba	137
Chapter 4. The Bullring	142
The Impresario	142
Seville: Diodoro Canorea	143
Small towns: Víctor Aguirre	146
The President of the Corrida	151
José Manuel Sánchez	151
The Bullring Surgeon	157
Dr Máximo García Padrós	157
The Bullring Chaplain	163
Father Mariano Frías	164
The Bullring *Mayoral*	169
Florencio Fernández Castillo *Florito*	169
The Bullring Caretaker	173
Alfonso Alonso and Manuel Alonso	173
The Horse Contractor	178
José Salcedo	178
The Bullring Musicians	183
The director of the band: Lorenzo Gallego Castuera	184
The drummers and buglers	187
José García Vázquez, Alonso Gallardo, Jesús Rubio and José María Silva	187
The Taxidermist	190
Justo Martín Ayuso	190
The *Taquillero* (Ticket Office Manager)	194
Iñaki Veiga	194
Miscellaneous Sales Personnel	199
Blas Romero *El Platanito*	199
Manuel Cicerone	199
Félix Reyuerta	200
Simón Rodríguez	201
Chapter 5. On the sand	203
The *Alguacilillo*	203
Teodoro Martínez Meca	203

The *Monosabio*	207
Luis Durán	209
Fermín Vázquez	211
The *Arenero*	213
Cesar Palacios	214
The *Mulillero* (Muleteer)	219
Juan Anchuelo	220
José Antonio Tamayo	222
The *Puntillero*	225
Agapito Rodríguez	226
Antonio Medina	229
The *Torilero*, *Chulo de Banderillas* and Carpenters	229
Marcelino Saboya (Torilero)	231
Francisco Sanz (*Chulo de banderilleras*)	232
Sergio Sánchez-Monje (Carpenter)	233
Victor Ruiz (Carpenter)	235
Jesús Pérez (Bullring employee)	237
Chapter 6. The Taurine Media	239
The Journalist and Bullring Critic	239
The veteran: Rafael Campos de España	239
The contemporary: José Luis Ramón	243
The Bullfight Photographer	247
Francisco Cano *Canito*	249
The Bullfight Cinematographer	255
José Hernández Gan	257
Radio and Television	264
Matías Prats Cañete	264
Chapter 7. The Aficionado	270
Mariano Aguirre Díaz	271
José Luis Moreno-Manzanaro	273
Salvador Valverde *Salva*	274
Glossary	277
Bibliography	285
Books in Spanish	286
Books in English	287

Foreword

A number of years ago, a senior colleague of mine remarked that the best teachers are rarely "naturals", people to whom everything came very easily, but more often people who themselves had to make an effort to learn about the matter in hand, and can therefore help the student through the same process more sympathetically. I didn't fully appreciate the wisdom of his remark at the time, but his thoughts have often come back to me. They return when I mix with young musicians, for example, among whom it is clear that the best performers are not always the best teachers, and vice versa.

They did so once again when Muriel Feiner asked me to introduce her book. She is the ideal person to guide us through all the aspects of the *mundillo taurino*—the little world of the bulls—which she makes clear are more numerous than we might have imagined. Because she was not born into a taurine family: she was no pampered daughter of a *ganadero* with thousands of hectares, brought up on an exquisite *cortijo* in Andalusia, nor a girl whose father left their modest apartment in the suburbs of Madrid every weekend to place the banderillas for an unknown *novillero* one third his age, whose dreams of becoming a *figura del toreo* were as certain to be shattered as his own had been, decades before. Although those two ways of being involved with bullfighting are so different, each means that you see the "little world" from inside; you are an insider.

Muriel started as an outsider. Not even that: she started as someone who felt a duty to see a bullfight even though she was convinced that she would hate it. (One could observe that her feeling that duty was a sign of that openness of mind that led her to conclude once that duty had been fulfilled that not only did she not hate it—but that she couldn't get enough of it!) Her nationality, her religion, her background as a young woman in Brooklyn were so foreign to the bullfighting world, that she was, not just an outsider, but a rank outsider. However, through her enthusiasm, her determination, her personal skills and her talents with words and camera, her hard work as an organiser (and let's not forget, being an American), she became an insider. Those years of progression from a wary spectator to a highly respected *taurino* (sorry, Muriel, but *taurina* just doesn't sound right in the macho world of the bulls), the wife of a matador, make her the ideal guide not only to the glamorous side that the average outsider can readily appreciate, but also to the workings of the system.

Ivan Moseley

Introduction

There is an extraordinary group of people who make it possible for the incomparable bullfight spectacle to take place, with all its pomp, pageantry, tradition, dramatic excitement and splendour. Each one of these participants, be he or she noteworthy or apparently trivial, has a very specific and direct role to fulfil in order to make the celebration of this unique artistic display possible at the poetically legendary "five o'clock in the afternoon". Some of their duties and responsibilities are more dangerous, artistic, indispensable, difficult or laborious than others, but one thing is clear: without each and every one of them, fitting together like tiny pieces in a mammoth puzzle, it would be impossible to present a complete and harmonious whole and stage this highly artistic and remarkable encounter between man and beast: the bullfighter and the brave bull.

The Bulls, the Bullfighters and their World endeavours to explore the roots, the orchestration, the development and the celebration of the bullfight in detail, through the testimony and confessions of the players in this "three-act drama" presented on an exceptional stage: the bullring. The players themselves introduce us to their personal—and in some cases hitherto unknown—world, which forms a part of a Spanish tradition dating back many centuries. It is necessary to begin our "quixotic quest" well before the prophetic hour when the trumpets sound and the drums roll, with an expectant crowd of aficionados in their seats, waiting for the *alguacilillos* or mounted constables to initiate the traditional *paseíllo*, the opening parade. Nor will our probing journey end when the *mulilleros* or muleteers drag out the last bull, whose final destination will be the butcher's shop.

I want to offer a deep, intimate view of the corrida, with a systematic search "behind the scenes", to discover all of the diverse facets of a spectacle to which the common spectator or even the seasoned aficionado cannot obtain easy access. The fundamentals of the profession, along with the secrets, mysteries and tricks of the trade of the Fiesta in general, will be revealed in direct interviews with its protagonists, through their explanations, confessions, testimony and entertaining anecdotes about their own lives and experiences. They feel that the bullring is their second home— or maybe their first—and most of them have spent the greater part of their lives involved in the bull world, due to their *afición* and *devoción*. They all concur when they say that they cannot conceive of their lives without their taurine activity, which in many cases may be only minimal or sporadic, but it nevertheless constitutes as vital a part of their existence as their daily sustenance.

The in-depth study of the respective roles of these individuals furnishes us with fascinating details, nuances, skills and revelations as expressed by those who come together to form one large family, made up of heroes big and small, from the matador to the *arenero* (sand-sweeper) or the muleteer. They share one common goal and one common passion: a love of this unique, ancestral and grandiose art, and they all contribute their "grain of sand", their courage, their skill and their devotion to making this beautiful and exciting Fiesta possible. My goal is on one hand to pay tribute to this exceptional "taurine humanity", whose members and participants live their passion and dedication to the utmost, and, at the same time, to use their individual stories to enhance our own understanding of the bullfight.

I hope readers will find the experiences and anecdotes of these protagonists entertaining, moving or enlightening, bearing in mind that they are only representative of the vast number of individuals who love and live for the Fiesta and are directly responsible for having conserved this extraordinary Spanish art and tradition until the present day.

Muriel Feiner

Understanding bullfighting: strictly for the uninitiated

Bullfighting is perhaps best defined as a centuries-old art form, daring and exceptional like no other. Although Spanish in origin, it is practiced not only in its "mother country", but in several Latin American countries, in southern France, and in an incomplete form, without the kill, in Portugal, as well as in the United States (mainly in California and Texas). Associations of enthusiastic aficionados are located all over the globe, from London to Milan, New York to Chicago, and Stockholm to Tokyo.

The purpose of bullfighting is to create art by pitting man's skill, intelligence, grace and bravery against the unrestrained fierceness of a unique species known as the *toro bravo,* or fighting bull. The domination of this naturally wild animal by the mere flowing folds of the red cloth in the hands of the bold, courageous matador, as he executes elaborate manoeuvres in the very face of danger, is something which can be easily comprehended and appreciated by those who are capable of overlooking the quite superficial but also necessary blood-letting in the course of the fight.

I have always tried to avoid becoming embroiled in useless arguments in defence of bullfighting, because I feel it is a matter of taste and because one must respect other people's opinions. Those who find it indefensible will certainly not be drawn to read this book in the first place, so I will assume that the reader is either an aficionado or open-minded and inquisitive enough to have already overcome any initial prejudices against Spain's "Fiesta Nacional".

It may be helpful to provide for the uninitiated a thumbnail sketch of what the bullfight is all about. The English translation of the *corrida de toros*—the bullfight—is clearly a misnomer, for it gives the idea of a sport, which it is not. It implies a struggle between two equal adversaries, in which man is naturally expected to come out the 'victor', although this may not always be the case. The corrida is a confrontation between man's intelligence and sensitivity and the bull's basic animal nature, and the final objective is to create an unparalleled and dramatic work of art. For centuries, this remarkable creative manifestation has proved capable of inspiring artists of many nationalities and disciplines: painters, sculptors, writers, poets, composers, dancers ... as exemplified by such brilliant individuals as Nobel-prize winning authors Ernest Hemingway, Camilo José Cela, Mario Vargas Llosa and Gabriel García Márquez; poet Federico García Lorca; painters Goya, Picasso, Dalí, Manet, Sorolla, Zuloaga; sculptors Fernando Botero, Mariano Benlliure, Humberto Peraza; composer Georges Bizet, with his opera *Carmen*, contemporary flamenco dancers Joaquín Cortés, Antonio Canales and María Carrasco, and an endless list of other artists. However, there is another aspect which makes this art truly unique: it is the only one in which the artist can lose his life.

In bullfighting, the simple cliché "it takes two to tango" is evidently true; there can be no glorious taurine achievement without its bull or its bullfighter. It should be stressed that the bull in the corrida is not a typical Guernsey, but a very distinctive species of imprecise origins: some say it migrated from the Ural Mountains and crossed the Pyrenees to settle in the Iberian Peninsula, while others believe it originated in northern Africa. This pedigree bovine breed differs enormously from its domesticated milk- and meat-producing brethren in that it is an untamed animal, known to charge anything that moves.

The Spanish *caballeros*, mounted noblemen, were the first to challenge this wild beast from horseback in order to display their valour and horsemanship in the early Middle Ages. The famous warrior El Cid offered similar heroic performances in the 11th century, and the conquistadors, such as Hernán Cortés, did the same, transporting the fierce livestock—God only knows how!—across the Atlantic to the Americas with them, as a means of diversion. This is how the Spanish bullfight spectacle spread to the New World and gained deeply rooted popularity in most of Latin America.

The great Spanish writer José Ortega y Gasset, who had studied the taurine phenomenon in depth, once said, "You cannot understand Spain, its culture, or its history, without truly understanding the corrida, because every facet of Spanish society is clearly represented in the bullring".

When the first Bourbon king, Felipe V, ascended to the Spanish throne at the beginning of the 18th century, his refined French education made it difficult for him to comprehend this compelling spectacle, which, nevertheless, continued to delight his subjects. His overt disdain led to the gradual withdrawal of the aristocrats from direct participation in the Fiesta, but as the corridas had already become highly popular and firmly established among the plebeians, a new profession came into being to carry on the daring tradition: the matador on foot, who emerged from the ranks of the peasants or serfs who had served the mounted noblemen in the ring, remaining close by in order to rush in and draw away the bull should the rider fall from his mount and be left at the mercy of the beast. This bold new figure, who faced the animal with only a short cape and a sword in his hands, became the new hero during the second half of the 18th century.

In those early years, the prime purpose of the bullfight was to kill the bull, while providing a new and thrilling form of public entertainment; and, of course, the meat was certainly put to good use afterwards. Over the last two and a half centuries, the corrida has evolved into a far superior art form, the purpose of which is to dominate the animal, with bravery, skill, grace and art, achieving the ultimate domination at the "moment of truth". It should not be forgotten that the animal's destiny has not changed with the passage of time and, once dead, its meat is still sold for human consumption.

The corrida is now a tightly controlled and regulated spectacle, in which each of its three "acts", the work with the large pink cape and the picing in the first act; the placing of the banderillas, metre-long barbed sticks, by a man without a cape, in the second; and the all-important *faena* using the *muleta,* the smaller, red cloth leading to that crowning "*momento de la verdad*" with the sword, in the third and final act, have all taken on paramount significance, recognition, skill and purity, which are closely examined and appreciated by an increasingly knowledgeable and demanding public. This audience is not seeking to be entertained, in the sense of amused, rather it wishes to be moved by a profound expression of art.

Plato wrote: "Beauty is in the eyes of the beholder" and many a bored spectator has been known to fall asleep at the opera or ballet. I feel fortunate to be able to appreciate the depth and beauty of this extraordinary Spanish Fiesta, this drama in three acts, which Federico García Lorca called: "The most vital and poetic treasure Spain has to offer".

Postscript: I hope that, with this panoramic perspective of the Fiesta and the Glossary, the reader who is not an aficionado will be able to obtain a greater understanding and appreciation of this spectacular art and the exceptional individuals, who, through their dedication and afición, have made its survival until the 21st century possible.

Acknowledgements

In Spanish they say: "*Ser agradecido es de bien nacido...*" I couldn't come up with an appropriate counterpart in English and the best I could find was: "Gratitude is the sign of noble souls". I cannot thank Ivan Moseley enough for all he and the Club Taurino of London have done to make the publication of this book possible. It was never meant to be a translation of *Los Protagonistas de la Fiesta,* Parts I and II, published initially in Spanish in 2000 by Alianza Editorial, because the truth is that my first intention was to write this book in English. What better way to explain the Fiesta in all its depth and splendour than by following the human thread throughout the different stages of the corrida? It was a highly gratifying and enriching experience because I met some truly wonderful people, to whom I am extremely grateful for sharing their time, their passion and their experiences with me; each one was a *figura* in his own right. However, after publishing *La Mujer en el Mundo del Toro* (1995), with Alianza Editorial, my editor Francisco Cortina asked me to write another book and he loved the idea of having the development of the corrida narrated by its participants.

This is the reason many of the people interviewed in the book are now, sadly, deceased, but rather than update the personalities with more current ones, I preferred to maintain these people who, each in his or her own field, proved to be particularly exemplary, emblematic and noteworthy.

Chapter 1. The Bull

The Bull-breeder

We must begin our journey into the world of bullfighting with the bull-breeders, because without the brave fighting bull, there can be no Fiesta. In order to be a good aficionado, one must be familiar with the *toro bravo*, its origins, its characteristics, its particular breeding, its *encastes*, and the broad and unusual vocabulary, used to describe this noble animal, the fundamental cornerstone for the true glory and grandeur of the Fiesta.

The code of practice for bullfighting, the *Reglamento Taurino*, modified for the last time at national level in 1996, created a stud book, a register for Empresas Ganaderas de Reses de Lidia, supervised by the Ministry of Justice and Interior, in which the four associations of bull-breeders must record every one of the animals born into the herds of their members. The four different breeders' associations: La Unión de Criadores de Toros de Lidia, the most senior, founded in 1905; Asociación Nacional de Ganaderías de Lidia; Ganaderos de Lidia Unidos; and Agrupación Española de Reses Bravas, are considered collaborating entities with the Spanish Ministry of Agriculture, and represent approximately 1,100 brave bull ranches in Spain, France and Portugal. Each association groups its member ranches according to locations: the Central region, Salamanca, Southern Spain (Andalusia and Extremadura), Portugal and the recently incorporated France. The cattle fought in the roughly 5,000 *festejos*: *corridas de toros*, *novilladas*, *festejos de rejoneo*, *festejos populares* and other assorted and minor taurine events celebrated each year, came from ranches whose number increases every year, an encouraging indication of the current good health of the Fiesta.

The origins of the brave fighting bull seem to be found in the ancient aurochs, which wandered into Spain through the Pyrenees and in cattle that were brought across from North Africa. Man has always felt fascinated by this brave, noble and *encastado* animal and anxious to display his courage, strength and intelligence before it, records of which date back to the ancient civilisations of Crete and Rome. However, it was at the end of the 17th century that Spaniards began to show a special interest in selectively breeding the wild bulls according to the specific conditions required for fighting (the *lidia*), and thus the six main fundamental *castas* or breeds were created from which all the brave fighting bulls have descended. These *castas* are as follows: 1. The Jijona, founded by José Sánchez Jijón and characterised by a large bull, with a big-boned structure, highly developed horns, very dangerous tendencies, and for the most part, black or red hides. 2. The Navarra, concentrated in the north of Spain, which were smaller in size and weight, but highly aggressive, strong and resistant, making them very dangerous despite their short horns. 3. The Cabrera, represented today by the famed Miura ranch, which were large, long-necked animals, with thick horns, very agile and quick to learn, thus making them the most feared *toros* in history. 4. The Gallarda, which belonged, curiously enough, to an order of monks in Andalusia, and were handsome, bulky animals, with well-developed neck muscles and curly grey hair, embodied today by the Pablo Romero or Partido de Resina ranch. 5. The Vazqueña, founded by Gregorio Vázquez in Utrera, a town outside Seville, which were animals noted for their attractive appearance: impressive physical form, large horns, bravery with the horses and above all their highly varied hides: black, white, red, grey, *berrendo* (black and white) and *sardo* (cream). 6. The Vistahermosa, from which roughly 90 per cent of today's bulls are derived, created by the Conde de Vistahermosa and noted for their attractive appearance and relative manageability. Subsequent mixtures of bloodlines have resulted in a wide variety of ranches.

It must be remembered that the *ganadero*—the breeder—has a hard job, for he has to cross brave bulls with brave cows and does not see the results of his work for at least four to five years. It is generally believed that it is the cow which transmits the bravery to their offspring, while the seed bull is responsible for the animal's physical appearance, but as they say in taurine and in any pedigree cattle-breeding circles: two and two never add up to four.

One seed bull can customarily impregnate about twenty-five or thirty cows a season, and the calves are born nine months later. The *mayoral* or ranch foreman clips a metal plate, the *crotal*, to each calf's ear, bearing a number which will help to identify him until the *herradero* or branding is carried out, following weaning, when the animals are roughly eight to ten months old. In the course of the *herradero*, the animal is branded with several characteristic markings: on the right rump, the particular brand of the ranch, and below that the initial of the association to which it belongs: "U" for the Unión, "A" for the Asociación, "E" for the Agrupación and "L" for the Ganaderos Unidos. Large numbers are branded on the flank to identify each individual animal, and finally on the right shoulder the last digit of the year in which it was born (in order to assure that no illegalities are committed in regard to its age when it is fought).

The *herraderos* also offer the perfect opportunity to vaccinate the animals, rid them of parasites, and make the identifying cuts on the animals' ears characteristic of each ranch. When they are two and a half years old, the *tienta* or *tentadero* of cows is held to test their bravery: if they do well in the ring on the ranch, they will become mothers of brave bulls; if not, they will be sent to the slaughterhouse. If a seed bull is sought, the male calves used to be tested in an open field by a man on horseback, in what has today developed into a sporting activity, called the *acoso y derribo*. Most *ganaderos* today select seed bulls according to their "family history"; they may also test them in a *tienta*, but facing only a man or horseback, and usually none on foot.

When the bulls are three and a half years old (for *novilladas*) or four to six years (for *corridas de toros*), they are grouped into lots of six to eight and embarked in special crates which are transported on a lorry to the bullrings where they will be fought, where they must arrive at least twenty-four hours in advance of the corrida.

The current *Reglamento Taurino* specifies the minimum weights for bull to be fought in the various categories of bullrings (see p. 48).

The Legendary: Eduardo Miura

Seville, 1942. Breeder of brave bulls. Divisa (colours): green and black in Madrid; green and red in provinces. Antiquity: April 30, 1849.
Ranch: Zahariche, Lora del Río (Seville)

The legendary bull ranch of Eduardo Miura officially celebrated its 150th anniversary in 1999, although the current owner, Eduardo, together with his younger brother Antonio and their sister Reyes, the mother of matador Eduardo Dávila Miura, is anxious to clarify that the ranch really dates back to 1842. (The custom in Spain is for a person to use two surnames: his father's surname followed by his mother's, thus Eduardo's father is Señor Dávila and his mother is Miura.) "That was when my great-great-grandfather bought his first brave cows, although we made our formal presentation in the Madrid bullring on 30 April 1849, the date of its official antiquity." Eduardo, an agricultural engineer, is very proud of the family background: "It is the only ranch which has been *lidiando* [sending bulls to be fought] under the same name for all this time".

The Miura ranch is distinguished from the other ranches for many reasons, and not just its long history. It is the only one which has two different *divisas* or coloured ribbons: green and red in the provinces and green and black when they are fought in Madrid. Many people have thought that the red was changed to black in the capital as a sign of mourning for the tragic death of matador *Pepete* in that city on the horns of a Miura bull on 20 April 1862. This, however, is not the case; prior to that time the Miuras had to change their "colours" in the Spanish capital so as not to clash with those of a more senior *ganadería*, that of Antonio López.

Three generations of the Miura family

There can be little doubt that the Miura ranch is synonymous worldwide with brave bulls, and Eduardo is aware of this: "Miura is no longer just a surname, it is as distinctive of brave bulls as Ferrari is of sports cars or Vuitton of luxury leather goods. In fact, the name has been used as a trademark with its specific connotations for a wide variety of items, both with and without family authorisation. At the beginning of the 20th century, my great-grandfather allowed a friend from Cazalla de la Sierra to use it for his anisette and brandy. There is also Miura rice, which has nothing at all to do with us, Lamborghini launched a Miura model in Brazil, and there is even Miura tabasco sauce in Mexico and Miura jeans in Chile ... and all this marketing of 'our name' without our permission is beginning to annoy me. A hundred years ago it did not matter that much but now a trade name is important. The owner of the Heinz Company once said that the ketchup didn't matter; it was the product name that counted. We are devoted to our bull ranch but who knows if one day someone in our family would like to market something else using our name?"

The Miura ranch has also been associated with tragedy, for the Miuras have killed more professional toreros than bulls from any other ranch. Eduardo does not like to talk about just how many fatal victims there have been: "It is not the kind of statistic I like to record". According to the history books, we can cite the following: matadors José Rodríguez y Rodríguez *Pepete* (Madrid, 20 April 1862, the bull *Jocinero*), Mariano Canet Llusio (Madrid, 23 May 1875, *Chocero*), Manuel García *El Espartero* (Madrid, 27 May 1894, *Perdigón*), Domingo del Campo *Dominguín* (Barcelona, 7 October 1900, *Receptor*), the *novilleros* Faustino Posada (Barcelona, 18 August 1907, *Agujeto*), and Pedro Carreño (Ecija, Seville, 21 May 1930), Manuel Sánchez Criado (Seville, 15 August 1894, the *puntillero* of the Seville ring) and, of course, Manuel Rodríguez *Manolete* (Linares, 28 August 1947, *Islero*). "It is a part of our legacy and I cannot deny it, but you also have to take into account our long history. Another ranch with a long and equally tragic background is Duque de Veragua. I guess we stand out more because our bulls were responsible for the deaths of leading matadors such as *Pepete*, *Espartero* and *Manolete*. As our bulls were very popular in the early 20th century, in the 300 corridas fought in Spain in 1917, 200 animals, between *toros* and *novillos*, came from our ranch. Furthermore, the death rate of toreros was very high at that time, before Dr Alexander Fleming discovered penicillin and that 'miracle drug' finally became available in Spain. I can assure you that if our fame was based solely on the fatal gorings inflicted by our bulls, our ranch would have long since disappeared. Our animals are brave and they charge perhaps more violently than other ranches, but that makes for an interesting corrida."

What makes the Miura bull so outstanding? "They have a special, feisty nature. They are not 'stupid', but sharp and aware of everything going on around them, and that is what we look for when we breed them. However, it does not make our job easy because when we approach them just to fill their feed bins, we have to take great care, as they are easily ruffled. A bullfighter who faces them has to possess a profound knowledge of the art and the experience and valour to put it into practice, because our bulls do not allow for many mistakes ... they learn quickly."

To explain so many deaths, aficionados have claimed that the Miura bull has a longer neck than other bulls or even an extra vertebra, a suggestion which Eduardo rejects and considers absurd. "My ancestors established their basic 'recipe' for raising bulls more than 175 years ago. The goal of bullfighting at that time was for the bull to put up a brave fight with the horse and with the man. Today bullfighting has changed and the purpose of the matador's work is to create a work of art, but we still seek to raise strong, agile, athletic animals and not just to fatten them up to make them look good in the eyes of the spectators. Our bulls do have a bigger frame and so they can carry more kilos and yet prove to be strong, resistant and powerful animals."

The Miura bulls are also considered to be more intelligent than most of their counterparts and can easily leap over fences to attack their prey. "I have to admit that our bulls are rather unruly and indomitable and get angry very quickly. I am not saying they are braver in the taurine sense of the word than the rest, but they are indeed different, complex and temperamental. In fact, they fight a lot among themselves. They are like bees in their nest; if they are left alone they are fine, but if you move in on their territory, watch out!"

A look back at the history of the Miura ranch is like reviewing the history of bullfighting itself and it would be almost impossible to imagine the bullrings without this emblematic brand. Miura wisely comments, "I know everything in life has its beginning and its end, and we have already been around for 175 years, but I hope we will be around for 150 more! Who knows? We like to consider ourselves 'marathon runners' and it makes me sad to see how other legendary ranches, with more than 100 years of history, have disappeared. Nothing lasts forever, people come and go, but I think history and traditions are important".

The reputation of the Miura ranch has been so formidable that the famous toreros *Bombita* and *Machaquito* went on strike in 1908 and refused to fight these bulls until they were paid double their ordinary fees. The issue went to court, but the Miura family won the case.

It is still considered a major event when a matador is announced with the Miuras, yet if we look back in history, the great Juan Belmonte fought an average of ten Miura corridas a year. According to Eduardo, his great-grandfather sent his bulls to all the top *ferias* (taurine fairs) and the leading matadors had no choice but to fight them. "The fact is that although there were a lot fewer ranches then, the aficionados insisted on the *figuras* fighting Miuras, because it was the bull ranches which really bestowed the 'diploma' of matador on the toreros. Now, the public grants the 'title', but I am not sure on what criteria they base their decisions."

A well-known story is that when the ranch foreman told Eduardo's great-grandfather that Juan Belmonte had dared to touch the tip of the horn of one of his bulls in a *desplante*—a gesture of defiance—in the course of a corrida in

Seville, Miura became so devastated that he burst into tears. "I am sure that it must have made him very upset, but I doubt to that extent. However, it happens that when Belmonte was scheduled to fight for the first time with the great José Gómez Ortega Joselito and in order to demonstrate his courage, he specifically requested the Miura bulls."

Are there many figures today who make the same gesture of facing the feared Miuras? "There are some, but I can say that Manuel Benítez *El Cordobés*, José Miguel Arroyo *Joselito* and Vicente Barrera did not and José Tomás has not. However, Paco Camino did so twice, as did Santiago Martín *El Viti* and José Mari *Manzanares padre*; Sebastián Palomo *Linares*, who cut two ears and was carried out through the Puerta del Príncipe during the Feria de Sevilla of 1970. Even the highly artistic *Rafael de Paula*, [an unpredictable gypsy], fought one Miura corrida! I know my bulls have a bad 'temper', but let's not exaggerate. Of course, the toreros will look for an easy way out unless the aficionados demand some brave and noble gesture from them. Bullfighters have to be looked upon with respect and awe and the spectators in the bullrings cannot be allowed to feel that they would be capable of doing what the bullfighter does in the ring. The same thing is true of any sport. A spectator must not think he can run with the football like Beckham or drive a racing car like Schumacher."

Oddly enough, Eduardo's favourite torero, and his father's, was the very artistic Pepe Luis Vázquez (who died on 13 May 2013) and he was the one who directed the ranch's *tentaderos*, testing the young cows. This is surprising, considering the fact that Vázquez was known for his exquisite style and not precisely for his courage. "Pepe Luis possessed an exceptional understanding of the bull's behaviour and extraordinary technique. His son, Pepe Luis *hijo* [Jr], is a reflection of his father's sensitivity and intelligence both inside and outside the ring. There were also sentimental reasons: my father made his début as a *ganadero* in the Feria de Sevilla in 1941, the same day that Pepe Luis made his first appearance as a matador."

Pepe Luis Vázquez Silva, the matador's son, continues to take part in the *tentaderos*, which are carried out behind closed doors, in an intimate manner, and, unlike the custom of many other breeders, there are no guests, no women present, and no meal afterwards. "We consider the testing of the animals as work, not play. What we do, however, is invite the toreros who *lidiar* our corridas to the *tentaderos*, as compensation for what they must face in the ring; at least the feisty nature of even the young cows serves as a good training session for them."

What are the criteria followed in the selection of the animals? "We test the young cows to see if they will make good mothers, based on their behaviour in the ring. The calf has to charge the horse several times and then follow the *muleta*—the small red cape used in the *faena*—well so that the matador can triumph. You could compare it to a student taking a test: he has to be able to respond rapidly and correctly; if he hesitates, he hasn't really learned the lesson. One thing is certain, though: we want a bull with *casta* and temperament, not a stupid, docile *manso* that doesn't have a mind of its own."

Like all breeders, Eduardo is concerned with the weakness of the *ganado* (cattle) often observed in the ring nowadays and complains that the general public is demanding much larger and very bulky animals, whose weights are not appropriate for their morphological frames. "On top of that, the *faenas* are becoming increasingly longer and more elaborate, and in order to follow the cloth the bulls are obliged to make almost anti-natural movements, which their anatomy cannot support. This explains in part why bulls sometimes stumble and fall during a bullfight, but rarely in *corridas de rejoneo*, in which the animals charge the horse with their heads held high, thus avoiding excessive stress to the neck muscles and skeleton. In my grandfather's time, the bull spent maybe three minutes in the ring, whereas today the public expects long, artistic *faenas* lasting ten minutes or more. A whole corrida a hundred years ago lasted roughly an hour and a half at most, today it is closer to two and a half or even three hours."

Don Eduardo accepts the fact that the Fiesta has changed over the years and he is not opposed to evolution, within certain limits: "We *ganaderos* supply half the players in this public spectacle and we have to accept that if the Fiesta has evolved over the years, so must the bull. The bulls a century ago were fiercer than they are today, but now the public wants a slow-charging, noble animal".

Eduardo and his brother Antonio are indeed proud of the legacy they received from their father. "'Work hard every day. The secret to success in any profession is hard work.' He instilled in my brother and me a sense of devotion and love of the bulls and he made us understand that everything we have and what we are, we owe to these animals. We are the heirs to a world-renowned brand name." When I asked if his son Eduardo hijo liked the bulls and ranch life, he replied, "Of course! Besides, no one would think of asking the Crown Prince of Spain if he wants to be king some day. That is expected of him".

Life on the ranch is not easy. It starts very early in the morning, transporting the sacks of feed out to the animals and riding around the range to check on the stock. Theseare difficult and dangerous animals and many a *ganadero* has suffered serious injuries when unexpectedly

Don Eduardo at Zahariche ...

encountering an angry bull, but this is considered all in a day's work. "The *mayoral* or *conocedor* is responsible for instructing the *vaqueros* [literally "cowboys"—the ranch-hands], but he always waits for us to show up. That was the way it was with my father and my grandfather. We don't have the luxury of punching a clock, we work the hours we have to work and set the pace side by side with the rest of our ranch hands. We also inherited from our father the custom of doing everything personally; on other ranches, it may be the foreman who keeps the books and feeds the animals, but not with us. We are very lucky about one thing; we really form one big, happy family here in Zahariche. All our *vaqueros* were born on the ranch and some of our employees can trace back to four generations. It is a job that is passed on from father to son: us as the breeders and them as the *vaqueros*. Our current foreman is José Mateo, the son of Antonio Mateo Rodríguez, who died tragically in 1998 when he was thrown from his horse. We are pleased that everyone living here feels that the ranch is their home and that they are not salaried employees. I think I inherited a slightly paternalistic attitude from my father in the sense that I worry about their happiness and well-being and if someone has a problem, I like to help them solve it. That is our 'business philosophy' and we think that it is the only way things will go well. Furthermore, it is not easy to find qualified people who want to work on a ranch because it can be a 24 hour-a-day job, whereas nowadays people just want to sign in at nine in the morning and clock out at five in the afternoon. Anyone who raises animals knows full well that they have to eat every day and can get sick on Friday night or Sunday morning and you have to take care of them."

... and in the Las Ventas bullring

Don Eduardo recognises that he is different from the typical Andaluz. "I love to read and be well-informed about everything that goes on and, contrary to most people in Andalusia, I don't like flamenco, I don't like to go tapas-hopping and I don't like the Feria [April Fair in Seville]. I just like to ride around the ranch and see the bulls."

And he doesn't like to *torear* either. "My sister's son, Eduardo Dávila Miura, is the first torero in our family. No-one ever fought in our family, not my grandfather, my father, my uncle, my brother or me, not even in the small ring we use for the *tentaderos*. When Eduardo told us he wanted to be a torero, we were not exactly delighted with the idea ... to say the least! It is a very difficult profession and we feared that his surname, Miura, would prove a serious handicap. In the end, we are all very proud of what he has accomplished."

The alternativa (the taurine "coming of age") of Eduardo Dávila Miura (right), with Raúl Gracia El Tato as "godfather" and Javier Vázquez as "witness"

Don Eduardo is a man who admits to certain contradictions. He is romantic and pragmatic, traditional and highly respectful of his heritage, but very much a man of his times and was among the first *ganaderos* to post his web page on the internet. He loves the bull, which he calls the "main player in the Fiesta", and yet he has never picked up a cape or *muleta* in his life. And even more surprising he admits that one of his favourite toreros is *Rafael de Paula*, a very artistic but erratic gypsy, about whom he relates the following story. "The female impresario Lola Casado, an intelligent and truly admirable woman, organised a *mano a mano* [a corrida with only two matadors] with our bulls in Sanlúcar de Barrameda between *Rafael de Paula* and *José Martínez Limeño*, a highly skilled and capable matador, who faced many of our animals. The bulls proved difficult and *Limeño* received a minor goring in his leg. Paula went running to the infirmary even before *Limeño* did, terrified that he would have to kill the rest of the corrida all by himself. *Limeño*, very responsible and brave, returned to the ring and eventually cut an ear, but *Paula* did not fare as well. When it was all over, back in the hotel, *Paula* went to see how *Limeño* was feeling and said to his friend, 'God willing, I will never ever fight another Miura corrida in my life!' He hesitated for a moment, and then added solemnly, 'And even if God wants me to, I won't!"

The popular: Victorino Martín padre (Sr)
Galapagar, 1928-2017. Breeder of brave bulls. Divisa: Blue and dark red. Antiquity: May 29, 1919. Ranch: Las Tiesas and Monteviejo, Moraleja (Cáceres)

If an emblematic, highly successful ranch has emerged in the last half of the 20th century, it is indeed that of Victorino Martín. Victorino, the most popular of *ganaderos*, commanded the highest prices for his animals and was the only breeder to have had a bull, *Belador,* pardoned in Madrid to date, on 19 July 1982.

To what did he owe his success? "There's no special secret. It's simply a matter of making a careful selection in the breeding and the *tentaderos* in order to attain what you want to see in the plaza. Unfortunately, you have to wait four long years to see the results and discover if you are on the right track or not. The bull has to be complete: brave enough to charge the horse and then submissive to the *muleta*."

Victorino Martín overseeing the vaccination of his bulls,
in the presence of a representative of the Guardia Civil (bottom right)

One of the problems of late is the widespread weakness of the bulls, but this is not something that plagues the Victorinos. "Thank God," he said. "I think it's due mostly to a lack of *casta*. If a bull appears in a debilitated state and you have done your very best to feed your stock, exercise them and keep them healthy, then what is failing is the *casta*, which is the driving force responsible for keeping them going."

Roughly 22 seed bulls and 300 brave cows graze at Las Tiesas and Monteviejo, Victorino's ranches in Cáceres province, and it is his son, Victorino *hijo*, who clarifies what the family is seeking in their animals. "We think the bull must be noble, but we also raise an animal which is determined to 'go down fighting'. Our bulls are of a pure Saltillo strain, and this breed is noted for its temperament and its *casta*. It is an intelligent, quick animal, which learns the rules of the game before the matador even realizes it. We have tried to temper it slightly because no one wants to witness a tragedy in the ring, but we also want to see the matador facing a worthy enemy."

Victorino Martín *padre* was born and raised in the country. First he bred beef cattle, although his dream was always to possess his own *ganadería brava* (a ranch raising fighting bulls). When he was well over 80 years of age, he travelled to almost all the rings in which his bulls were fought—at least 15 *corridas* a year from the *ganadería* which bears his name and another half-dozen from his second strain, Patas Blancas—but he was happiest at home on his ranch in Extremadura. "I love to spend the day riding across the fields and supervising everything. Here, in the country, there is no stopping. I get up at seven in the morning if not earlier. Breakfast is plain biscuits, coffee and an orange, which tides me over until three in the afternoon when we stop for lunch. Then it was back on the horse and out to the fields again." He displayed incredible vitality for his age and such skilled horsemanship that he could have become a rejoneador. "I never wanted to fight either on foot or on horseback. I only wanted to be a bull-breeder, and I am more than satisfied with that!"

Victorino *padre* and his brother Adolfo (father of the current *ganadero* Adolfo Martín) were involved in breeding everyday cattle when the opportunity arose for him to buy a left-over string of animals from the Juliana Calvo ranch. He had done business with the ranch foreman before, buying sheep and calves for their butcher's business. Calvo wanted a mere one million sixty thousand pesetas (£8,000), which Victorino did not have at the time, but as there were no other buyers and he was known to be a man of his word, the rancher agreed to payment by instalments. Victorino believed in th**is breed of bulls, and slowly but surely he sorted and weaned out the good from the bad, buying more and more lots of the same bloodline as they became available. Nevertheless, his name did not appear on the bills until five years later, when he felt that his own stock selection was beginning to take effect. Everything began to fall into place after 1965, when the bulls were fought under the name of Martín and a "rags to riches" bull-breeding story began.

He first began to attract attention during Madrid's Feria de San Isidro of 1968, when the top matadors Manuel Benítez El Cordobés and Sebastián Palomo Linares quarrelled over the corrida of the most popular bulls of the moment, those of Francisco Galache. According to Victorino hijo, "My father has good business sense, and he announced to the press that in order to resolve the problem, he would offer a corrida of his six-year-old bulls free of charge to these *figuras*, and make a considerable donation to the Red Cross to boot. Needless to say, neither matador wanted to fight my father's animals and they quickly reached an agreement about the Galaches!"

At the beginning of June that same year, disaster struck the family. A seed bull in a very bad mood because it had been in a fight with another animal attacked Victorino, and inflicted nine gorings on him, several of which could have been fatal. When his family finally discovered him lying on a riverbank, near death, they rushed him to the hospital, and it took him nine long months to recover. It is not just the torero who risks his life before the brave bulls, because many such accidents have occurred to bull-breeders and *vaqueros* as well. These animals are difficult and dangerous to handle and, in fact, Victorino hijo suffered a similar accident in 2005.

With Victorino padre lying in the hospital for weeks on end, the family began to face serious financial difficulties, not only in paying the medical bills but also in covering their everyday needs. Their main source of income lay in three corridas of six-year-old, fully-grown, impressive animals that nobody wanted! Finally, a friend, Manuel Aleas, went to the Madrid bullring impresarios and explained the family's tenuous financial situation, the many operations they had to pay for, and the dire situation of Victorino's wife and two children. When the impresario Juan Martínez visited the ranch and saw the animals in the country, he reportedly exclaimed, "Those are not bulls, they are elephants with horns!" Nevertheless, he decided to buy a corrida for a "low season" Sunday-afternoon corrida on 18 August 1968, for which he engaged three "modest" toreros. The results were totally unexpected: these beautiful, awesome animals, strong, noble and defiant, impressed not only the bullfight journalists but the general public to the point where the impresario immediately purchased the remaining two corridas, which were fought with great success in terms of public attendance and the bullfighters' performances. And that is how the Victorino legend began: with a major catastrophe and then a not-so-minor miracle.

But Victorino Martín's audacity did not stop there. Once he had recovered from his injuries, he was determined not only to raise stock which embodied his concept of what a brave, intimidating bull should be, but also that the bulls should be of an importance equal to that of the toreros. If the other breeders were always paid the same amount: 350,000 pesetas (£1,600) per corrida, he demanded more: 500,000 (£2,500), which meant a smaller purse for the impresario. He provided another great corrida in August 1969, but as he stuck to his guns about his price, Victorinos were not included in the big Feria de San Isidro in May 1970.

Then the matador Andrés Vázquez appeared on the scene, a "torero's torero", who had fallen somewhat out of favour with the crowds, but a brave matador, nevertheless, who knew the technical aspects of the art to perfection, and was thus capable of dominating the Victorinos. With Andrés Vázquez's help, Victorino padre was finally able to break the monopoly of the impresarios. In 1972, the prestigious Corrida de la Prensa, attended by King Juan Carlos, was announced as a mano a mano between Antonio Bienvenida and Andrés Vázquez, while the public and press demanded that the bulls be Victorinos. Finally, the impresarios gave in, the ring was packed, the toreros cut ears, and the ranch was awarded the prize for the best corrida of the San Isidro cycle. Victorino sighed with relief. "I have at last proved the true worth of my bulls with a great triumph in Madrid!"

Victorino's branding irons

From this point, Victorino bulls became a "must" in all the major fairs in Spain and France, and the overall effect on the Fiesta could not have been better. The public began to expect and to demand well-bred bulls with their horns intact, the correct age (at least four years old) and well-developed muscular structure. Victorino Martín's booming career as a bull-breeder reached its culmination in the "Corrida del Siglo" (Corrida of the Century), held on 19 July 1982, when his *Belador* became the very first—and to date only—bull to have its life pardoned in Las Ventas, due to the extraordinary bravery and style it displayed before its matador, José Ortega Cano, on an unforgettable afternoon which began at seven in the evening and ended at midnight when *Belador* was finally coaxed back into the corrals, to be treated by the veterinary surgeons and eventually returned to the ranch.

Victorino *padre* restated his position: "Our ranch will remain true to its standards, with the normal ups and downs that affect all living things, animals and people alike. Our lives revolve around the integrity of the bull and the Fiesta and we will defend our beliefs to the end".

This is the story of a bull ranch, which has truly become legendary. Victorino Martín may be one of the few ranchers who became rich with the bulls. "The only people who earn money from the *campo* [fields] are the football players", he joked, "and so we have to raise beef cattle, other livestock and crops just to survive".

The *ganadero* adored his life on the ranch raising bulls, and even the tension when they are being fought in the ring, although very often the spectators were more intent on watching the reactions of the breeder in the stands than the performance of his animals.

The toreros who have best understood these animals over the years have been Andrés Vázquez, Miguel Márquez, Luis Francisco Esplá, Pepín Liria, Manuel Caballero and Manuel Jesús El Cid and, of course, Francisco Ruiz Miguel, who took part in 86 corridas of Victorino bulls. Not all toreros are capable of fighting them, nor do they understand them, and according to Victorino, "most do not even want to fight them, but they do so at least once in their careers as a token gesture of courage".

Victorino complained that he was very busy having bought a new strain of bulls, fought under the name of Monteviejo, nicknamed "Patas Blancas" (white feet), because of their black and white "*pinto*" hides. "We actually bought the stock because we have the grazing land, but we don't want to have more than 300 Victorino cows, from the Albaserrada strain, in order to produce between 12 and 15 corridas a year. We also have a lot of beef cattle, but there is no fun in raising them, so we are busy trying to recover the purity and bravery of this Barcial strain from Salamanca. We bought 83 cows and one pure Barcial seed bull. Even though we want to maintain the purity of the stock, we did use a Victorino as *semental* (seed or stud bull), as an emergency measure until, little by little, we have enough Barcial bulls to maintain the strain. We know it's going to take years before we begin to see the results of our work."

Although Victorino Martín *padre* spent most of his time on the ranch, he loved to go to the cinema, the theatre and to travel. He thoroughly enjoyed a trip to Turkey and made a lot of friends, although he spoke only Spanish. He mumbled, "What a pity they wouldn't let me organize a corrida in Istanbul!"

Victorino Martín García
Madrid, 1961. Bull-breeder, veterinary surgeon and retired bullfighter

Victorino Martín *hijo* remembers the first time he had to face a brave bull. "I was four years old and we were living in Galapagar at the time. I went with my parents to feed the bulls out in the fields and my dad said: 'Sit on this fence and don't let any animals come into the corral until I fill all the feed troughs, because if the bigger animals get in first, they won't leave anything for the rest'. I remember sitting there, absolutely terrified, and looking at the animals straight in the eye, but they didn't come near me ... they just stared back."

Victorino *hijo* fought his first calf in public when he was 13 years old, and when he announced that he wanted to be a bullfighter his father insisted he complete his studies first: "No degree, no bulls". So he graduated as a veterinary surgeon from the Universidad Complutense of Madrid. "My dad wouldn't even let me participate in the *tentaderos* until I was finally accepted into college. The morning after graduation, I had two big cows waiting for me in the corrals as a 'present'. I got the beating of my life, in part because I'd been up all night celebrating with my friends and I hadn't slept, and also because my father wanted literally to 'shake' the idea of being a bullfighter right out of me the hard way. I understand him now because I have two daughters, but I was really angry with him at the time. He didn't help me at all; in fact, he did everything he could to make my career more difficult. He always asked for the largest and toughest animals for me, and I finally became discouraged. I was struggling for seven years in the small towns with big bulls, and it proved to be a wonderful but very ungratifying learning experience. I even killed four-year-old animals in *festejos* without picadors ... When I finally moved on to fighting with picadors, Papa looked for animals from the most dangerous ranches, such as Cebada Gago, Cortijoliva ... No favours for Victorino's son! And he got what he wanted in the end. I fought for the last time in September 1984 in Calahorra with *Gallito de Alfaro* and Jaime Malaver, killed my two *novillos* from Cortijoliva with dignity and never put on a suit of lights again."

Even though leading *apoderado* (manager) José Luis Marca wanted to manage his son's career, Victorino *padre* insisted on attending to it personally. Perhaps had this not been the case, his son could have been a leading matador, and the following story illustrates how his father did everything he could to dissuade him from becoming a professional. "I fought a *novillada* without horses in Galapagar, my home town, with another torero, Paco Villalta. I was going to kill two *novillos* and he one. The custom in a situation like this is that the torero who is going to kill two animals chooses the one he likes best and then they *sortear* or draw lots for the other two. The *novillos* were from El Tomillar that day, a truly tough strain from a ranch my father owned at the time. Those three-year-olds grew up on grazing land, with no artificial feed, so they were strong! My *cuadrilla* [team of toreros] asked the others how to arrange the lots and Villalta's *cuadrilla* said: 'We don't care! If the father brought these animals for his son, they must be fine!' My banderillero insisted that they take a close look at the bulls and when they came back, they stammered: 'If that man treats his son like this, what won't he do to the rest of us!'"

Victorino hijo as a novillero

It soon became clear that Victorino Martín *hijo* was a classical, elegant and intelligent *novillero*. "I wasn't a daddy's boy by any means. In fact, quite the contrary. And the bullfight reviews are there to prove it. I was unable to accomplish more, but in the end, I'm satisfied with what I've achieved, and the experience proved very useful to me because it enabled me to understand the animals that much better—and the toreros who face them. Many spectators forget to take the bull, its bravery and its conduct into account and concentrate only on what the torero does. That's a big mistake. It takes two to tango—or to *torear*."

Victorino *hijo* can now fight in the privacy of his own ranch, for the pure fun of it. "It's a whole different ball game from knowing you have to do it at 5 o'clock in the afternoon before a paying, demanding public. Being a bullfighter is a very tough profession; everyone has good days and bad, but the spectators think that because they have paid 30 € or more they have the right to insult you and your family. I understand that if it weren't for the aficionados, there would be no Fiesta, but sometimes they can be cruel and merciless, and they forget that the bull can kill the man at any time. That is a part of the Fiesta I'm glad I'm no longer exposed to. I am exposed as a *ganadero*, however, and I can accept that."

What did his father teach him? "More than sitting down and explaining things to me, as a man born and raised in the country, he taught me by setting an example and I learn from him every day. The first thing I learned was, 'El que algo quiere, algo le cuesta', in other words: 'Nothing comes free'. I think he's accomplished what he has because he had a dream and worked hard to make it come true."

It seems Victorino *padre* was as strict as a father as he is as a bull-breeder, despite the fact that one could see how proud he was of his son, in every way. However, Victorino *hijo* complains that he never said it in so many words. Nevertheless, the father found in his son his best partner and ally, and his direct experiences as a bullfighter and a veterinary surgeon are indeed invaluable to the ranch, not to mention the intelligence, courage, determination and industrious spirit he has inherited from his father. All you have to do is watch him working side by side with the ranch hands in the *herradero*, where the young animals are singled out from the herd, registered, branded, rid of parasites and vaccinated. Victorino *hijo* admits: "I got involved in this world out of love, respect and admiration for my father. We all need a hero in life, someone to look up to, and he is mine. Besides, everything I am and everything I have, I owe to the bulls. Nevertheless, I would still like to have received a word of praise or a pat on the back from my father every once and a while, instead of criticism—but that's how he was".

Victorino hijo prepares to vaccinate one of the cows

How do you explain the success and the essence of the victorinos? "I think it's really a philosophy of life. First of all, we have the Saltillo bulls, a unique *encaste*, and that has been an advantage from the very beginning. My father had the foresight to see its possibilities and he bought the first calves from Juliana Calvo when no one else would have spent a penny on them. Saltillo has represented a clearly defined bloodline throughout its long history and genetically it is important. All of the Mexican ranches descend from the original sixteen Saltillo cows and two bulls brought over by the conquistador Hernán Cortés. The fact that they even survived the trip gives us an idea of the mettle of this breed. My father is a romantic and he bought the herd when it was practically on the way to the slaughterhouse. We were like the dark horse in the race, but now we're the ones who are paid the most for our bulls. Afterwards, there was a symbiosis and a correlation between the character of our family and the breed itself. I think from the very beginning my father identified with this *encaste* and knew deep down inside what its possibilities were. Maybe I'm not the right person to praise what Victorino Martín did for the brave fighting bull stock and for the Fiesta, because I am his son. I will leave that to others, but I am indeed very proud of him. The secret lies in plenty of determination, total dedication and *afición*, and God giving you a helping hand."

The Victorinos, padre e hijo

Victorino *hijo* continued: "The *ganadero* must begin with a good initial selection and then he has to take special care of the animals, give them the right feed, pamper them and finally draw up the right six-bull lots to send to the different rings. Each ring has a different kind of public and different standards, with Madrid being, of course, the most demanding of all. One of the most difficult aspects in raising brave bulls is that you do not see the results of the decisions you make for several years. It takes a long time to discover your mistakes and a lot longer to correct them."

If you were not called Victorino Martín, what do you think you would be doing today? "I think the circumstances mark the man ... or woman, and if I'd been born into a family of astronauts, with the love and respect I feel for my father, I probably would have tried to be an astronaut, too, but not just any astronaut; I would have tried to be the best, because that's what my father taught me. Nevertheless, I really love the countryside and am basic and earthy at heart, and even though I have learned to live with machines, like computers, because I have no choice, I prefer animals to mechanical apparatus any day."

For Victorino *padre e hijo*, paradise is their ranch and each animal is a unique experience. "Every time a bull is fought and dies in the ring, it is as though you lose a part of yourself. Two of our seed bulls, *Buenacara*, number 107, and *Matador*, number 95, from the herd of 1989, were fought in the Feria de Bayonne in France, one by Portuguese matador Víctor Mendes and the other by Javier Vázquez. I had grown so close to them over the years, that in the end I had their heads stuffed and mounted and they are hanging on the wall in my home. I felt we had shared a lot of experiences together."

The public is shown the name, number and birth-month of the next bull, together with its weight and the breeder's brand and the colours of the divisa

The up-and-coming: Pablo Mayoral
El Escorial, 1963. Divisa: green and white. Antiquity: 24 March 1974.
Ranch: Chinilla, Sotillo de las Palomas (Toledo)

Not all *ganaderos* come from legendary or historic ranches, although Pablo Mayoral Figueroa is actually third-generation, following his grandfather Pablo Mayoral Herranz and his father Pablo Mayoral Benito, who died aged 63 in 1998. "My grandfather was from Santa María de la Alameda, close to El Escorial in the centre of Spain. El Escorial was a region where there were many noteworthy ranches and so it was not surprising that he was drawn to the bulls. "When my father was 13, he learned from the local ranchers how to move the herds with the tame steers or *cabestros* along the cattle and stock paths, and he lent a helping hand in the *herradero* or branding, which was done at that time without the use of a crate to restrain the animal. They had to lasso the calf, and literally grab it by the horns to wrestle it to the ground as in the American rodeos, while someone applied the hot irons. In order to get the job done, they needed a lot of help and it took a long time to separate and brand each animal and everybody involved was pretty shattered and exhausted by the end of the day. Nowadays, with the holding crate and the gas furnace for heating up the branding irons, you need fewer workers and it takes less time. You don't need someone to keep the fire going, which was a pretty miserable job, and the only real disadvantage is the roaring sound of the propane torch, but it makes it possible to brand a hundred calves easily in one day."

Although Pablo's grandfather preferred to raise sheep and beef cattle, as it was more profitable, his son begged him to buy some brave animals too. "He agreed, but as he didn't understand anything about brave bull-breeding, he opted for the biggest and 'meatiest' animals he could find and didn't bother about the bloodlines. However, it didn't take him long to become hooked on the bullfights and he ended up buying the brave stock of the La Laguna ranch from José Moreno Yagüe."

As things were going well for the Mayoral family, the grandfather also founded a very lucrative dairy product company, in the northern province of Asturias. He produced high-quality milk, butter and cheese, which he marketed under the French-sounding name Remy Picot, because he thought it would sell better.

Pablo was very clear about his family's entrepreneurial skills, which overshadowed any romantic motivations. "My father sold our brave cattle for *novilladas* instead of *corridas de toros*, because he reasoned: 'if they pay the same price for my two-year-old animals as they do for the four-year-olds of other ranchers, why do I have to spend more money on feeding and tending to the animals for two more years?' Money is money! If the Mayorales are anything we are hard-working, practical and realistic. You can afford to be romantic and sentimental if your income comes from other sources, but if you have to live from the earnings produced by the ranch, you have to sell all your animals and sell them at a good price."

"Aspiring torero" Tony Curtis—with sombrero—at the Mayoral ranch, between Pablo Mayoral and José Nelo Morenito de Maracay

He shares Eduardo Miura's view that the *herraderos* and *tentaderos* are not meant to be a party. "I think it is the most boring part of the business, when you have to brand a hundred animals a day. It is really a pain: the heat, the smoke, the noise and the animals resisting and butting at you all day long! I wish they could be born with the ranch brand and their individual numbers already marked on them! We organise five or six *herraderos* a year among the thirteen ranches we own and except for one which is reserved for public and commercial relations, the rest are carried out with just the *vaqueros* present. What I do enjoy the most are the *tentaderos*, the sorting of the bulls and shipping them in their individual crates. We also do this in private, behind closed doors, because the *tentadero* is serious business. I consider it the 'ranch laboratory'."

Pablo explained that the family—his mother and the nine children—possess a total of thirteen ranches among them, although he clarified that only three are really working ranches and the other ten are dormant. "My father had the dream of setting up a different brand for each one of his children, although not all of my siblings are actively involved in the business: Javier is a *rejoneador*, Mar is a veterinary surgeon, and Ana, Marta and Paloma are great aficionadas; Mónica and Natalia don't like it; and Merche is neutral. My father wanted to give each of his children their own brand when they got married, but the truth is we have too many right now."

Pablo's father became a small-town bullfight impresario, working hand-in-hand with the town halls in the organisation of the festivities and festivals in honour of their patron saints. "I don't enjoy the business aspect as much as he did, because it leads to too many headaches."

Pablo studied agricultural engineering at the university of Madrid, but it took him eight years to graduate. "I skipped a lot of classes to be with the animals. I literally '*hacía novillos*' [played truant], because I preferred to be with my dad on the ranch. He was a man of the country and he taught me a hell of a lot more than I was learning in the faculty. He kept track of everything, when the cows were going to give birth, what to do if they didn't suckle, and if a young calf died, he would put its hide over a motherless calf, to confuse the cow and make her think it was her own offspring. He'd attach a tail to bulls without a *rabo* [tail] because it was unthinkable for an animal to be presented in a bullring without a tail. I really don't know why. They don't charge with their *rabo*, but with the other end: the dangerous horns. Once my father sewed a tail on to one of our bulls using a fine wire, but the animal had to spend two days in the corrals and while it was being moved about on the morning of the corrida, the tail fell off. The impresarios rejected the animal, even though it was otherwise in perfect condition. Its horns were intact and it had just undergone a touch of 'plastic surgery' at its rear, that was all."

In addition to the brave bulls, the family raises beef cattle, pigs and sheep, because it is a Mayoral tradition, which began with his great-grandfather Lázaro. Despite his more practical side, 53-year-old Pablo has really fond memories of the "early days", and regrets that the old cattle drives have all but disappeared. One of the key rural routes was the Cañada Real Leonesa which extended from Soria and León in the north to Extremadura in the south. "That's how we moved the stock years ago from the ranch to the bullrings, even though it took five days. I remember as a student I used to ride along with the ranch hands from El Escorial to San Lorenzo, something totally unthinkable nowadays, because of all the modern urban developments. My father rented land in Talavera and Segovia, and we would drive the cattle along the *cañada* [cattle route] to Segovia, where it was cooler in the summer, and to Talavera in the winter, because it had a milder climate. We finally gave up driving the cattle in 1990, when the seasonal migrations became totally impossible because there was so much building development and not enough grazing land along the way. We would count the animals in the morning when we set out and again when we settled down for the night. Inevitably an animal or two would escape and we would send a couple of men on horseback to find them. I remember once a seed bull fell behind and a troop of soldiers out on manoeuvres had the misfortune of running into it. They got so frightened they shot it. I loved the cattle drives. In winter, we usually left at the beginning of December, because the winters in Segovia can be really bitter, but if for some reason we were not on the way by the 10th or 12th of the month the older cows would start down the path all by themselves, as if to say, 'We're feeling cold, so if you're not going to get the show on the road we'll head out on our own'."

According to Mayoral, "the drives took five days in winter and four in summer because there was more daylight. Each one cost 100,000 pesetas [£500], while transporting the stock by lorry cost 300,000 [£1,500]". Furthermore, the animals suffered the consequences of the journey. "The calves had to be shipped in separate trucks from their mothers, and when they were reunited the cows frequently didn't recognise the scent of their own offspring and refused to let them suckle. It was better to spend five days on the trail with five men, and the journey also served as training for the *vaqueros* and good exercise for the animals. The experience also produced a lot of good picadors over the years; that is how they learned their trade, something which is no longer feasible nowadays either, because at the beginning of the 20th century, a picador performing with a *figura* fought thirty or forty corridas during the season, but nowadays, he could easily fight a hundred. You can't have someone working for you and pay all his wages and social security if he's going to be off the job for one-third of the year. Now it is the ranch foreman or a ranch hand who usually pics the animals in the *tentaderos*." Mayoral complains that many picadors nowadays lack experience precisely for this reason and in the ring they tend to worry more about not falling off their horses than picing well.

The youngest of the Mayoral family, Javier, is the only professional in the family, an excellent *rejoneador*, although their father liked to *torear* on foot in *festivales*, as does Pablo hijo. "When I was young, I loved to *tentar* or test the animals, but once the matador Gregorio Sánchez told me that he did not like *ganaderos* who 'fooled around' with their own animals in the *tentaderos*, because it took valuable opportunities away from *novilleros* who really needed to practice. And then Gregorio blurted out: 'Besides, you could never be a torero, because your bum is too wide'."

What are the main problems facing the breeder today? "The inherent weakness of many animals. The bulls are losing a lot of their *casta* and *raza* [race] because breeders are trying to produce more 'manageable' animals for the *figuras*. It's funny, but most ranchers claim their bulls come from the highly valued Juan Pedro Domecq stock—as ours do—but I certainly doubt that there has been enough Domecq blood to go around for everybody, just as there are not enough hot peppers in the town of Lodosa to supply all the produce which bears that Denomination of Origin, or all the baby eels that supposedly come from Aguinaga. Before, the bulls would be raised on what was available in their natural habitat: oak leaves, acorns and grass, all of which assured the strength and stamina of the stock. However, they probably looked somewhat lean by the standards of *trapío* [build] being demanded by today's audiences. Nowadays, the animals are fattened up with artificial feed and you can just see the fat hanging off the sides of beef in the bullring slaughterhouses. These bulls are good for the butchers, but not for the toreros. I think many animals appear to be weak because of poor breeding criteria and deficient raising of the stock. Curiously enough, the bulls which run in *encierros* [bull-runnings] like those in Pamplona fall a lot less in the arena. What my father was looking for was a bull with *raza* and bravery, which lowers its head to charge, follows the cloth and has spirit and strength. The truly great *faenas* are performed with spirited animals. That is what we want, but we don't always get it, because as we are working with genetics, we are still poking around in the dark."

Pablo's father can also be credited with making a very important discovery: a boy from Madrid whom he launched to fame and fortune and who is now a leading *figura del toreo*, Julián López El Juli, for whom Pablo *hijo* offers endless praise. "It wasn't really a discovery. He was a natural phenomenon, a genius and a privileged being who was born with fantastic qualities and the ability and intelligence to develop his skills to the utmost. My father used to say, 'Pablo, this world is meant for intelligent people and that is true if you want to succeed in any walk of life'. When Juli was sixteen, I realized that the world is not for intelligent people, but for the extraordinarily intelligent."

The Mayorals have always maintained a close relationship with the Madrid bullfighting school and regularly invited the students to practice at their ranch. It was Gregorio Sánchez who brought ten youngsters, including El Juli, with him in 1994. "We were surprised to see him perform before the cows with such smoothness, ease and intuition. He showed so much *afición* and everything he did was perfect ... and he was just a kid! He could spend an hour *toreando* one calf and never get tired. My father called him the Extraterrestre [ET—the alien], because he thought he was not of this world."

Pablo is optimistic about the future of the Fiesta and I think he is right when he says, "The only ones who can put an end to the bullfighting world are those who are responsible for the Fiesta, that is, the '*picaresca taurina*', such as the *ganadero* who sells bulls knowing they are going to be bad, or the torero who is only in it for the money. Everybody has to chip in and do their share: town halls with their subsidies for the bullfights, impresarios, bullfighters, *ganaderos* and aficionados. The truth is that the impresarios often lose money because a bullfight is a very expensive spectacle to put on, but most of them are sufficiently romantic to be 'in the red one year and come back the next'."

Pupils training in the Madrid Escuela de Tauromaquia at Batán

The *Mayoral* or Ranch Foreman: Julio Presumido
Zarza la Mayor (Cáceres), 1926

Every seasoned aficionado knows Julio Presumido, the *mayoral* of the Victorino Martín ranch, perhaps in part because of the number of times he has been hoisted up on the shoulders of the spectators delighted with the bulls he has helped to raise. He comments jokingly: "I've been carried out *a hombros* [on shoulders] more times than many bullfighters and I love it! In 1998, I took a lap of the ring in many plazas alongside toreros like El Tato and Pepín Liria."

Julio, whose personality belies his surname—"presumido" means "proud and haughty" in Spanish—is really a simple, easy-going man of the country, something which nowadays can be considered a privilege. "My father was a rancher all his life, but he only raised beef cattle, goats and sheep, and I have spent my whole life in the country, too. In fact, I was born here and this is where I hope to die."

Julio Presumido in the burladero de mayorales at Las Ventas

Presumido began as a ranch hand with Victorino in 1974, on the Monteviejo ranch in Moraleja del Peral (Cáceres), where the bulls graze at present (they no longer have any animals in Galapagar). He prefers to be called *mayoral* rather than *conocedor*, a term more commonly used in Andalusia, although he makes the distinction between the latter, who is in charge of the cows and calves, and the former, the *mayoral*, who is responsible for supervising all the ranch operations.

The profession of *mayoral* is still passed on from father to son; Julio has two sons, Domingo, the mechanic in charge of the ranch machinery, and Juan, a *vaquero* and a professional picador. Julio offers his job description: "I have to oversee everything and follow the bulls from the time they are born until they die in the ring. I get up every day of the year, in summer and winter, Sundays and holidays, at seven in the morning. I feed all the animals, beginning with the seven horses, so that when the *vaqueros* arrive at nine, the horses are all saddled, the stables cleaned and they can ride out to check on the stock in the fields. I am on horseback until around 1 p.m., which is when I stop for lunch, and then I ride out again in the afternoon."

Julio looks after the bulls as if they were his offspring. "I have seen them being born and I make notes in my book on every detail of each bull's life: when the cow gave birth, the number on the *crotal*, when it is branded, inoculated and rid of parasites, the date on which it leaves the ranch and is shipped to the plaza, and finally all the details of its *lidia*."

The placing of the *crotal* on the two-month old calves is an exciting and dangerous operation, according to Julio. "You have to distract the cow because she is naturally very protective of her calf. I leave my horse tied to a tree and then sneak up from behind to grab the calf. I hide behind some brush and clip on the *crotal*, but I have to do it all very quickly because in the meantime the cow is desperately looking for her offspring and she is potentially very dangerous. A few years ago, I didn't do it fast enough and the cow came after me and gave me a nasty tossing. Fortunately, I wasn't seriously hurt."

Calves are born between November and April and Julio has to spend a lot of time on horseback then to make sure the cows do not encounter any serious problems in giving birth. He also has to look out for poachers who may want to steal a Victorino.

When there has been enough rain, the cows graze in the country, while the bulls are given extra nourishment with grain. "I know all the animals and they know me. When I approach them, either in the fields or in the corrals, I call out to them and the cows obey me. In fact, when I go from one corral to the next, they move to one side so I can fill the feed bins."

The herding of the bulls into their separate crates and on to the lorry which will take them to the plaza is also a difficult, complicated task. "In summer, we load the crates at five or six in the afternoon, so that the animals can travel at night, when the temperatures are lower, but also because they tend to calm down in the evening. The bulls are usually shipped two days in advance of the date of the corrida in Spain, in order to be examined by the veterinary surgeons, and if we are *lidiando* in one of the many important rings of France, such as Nîmes, Arles, Bayonne or Mont-de-Marsan, we like to ship them a week in advance so they have time to recover from their long journey." Julio travels in the lorry with the animals; in fact, they are never to leave his sight, for safety reasons, and the best part of his many duties is when the time comes to *lidiar* them in the ring. Then, even today, the *mayoral* is expected to put on his classic grey or black *traje corto* and his wide-brimmed Cordoban sombrero.

Julio Presumido on the ranch, cutting the "sign" on a calf's ears

Julio says that every rancher and *vaquero* suffers accidents in the country like those to both Victorinos, described above, but most live to tell about it. He does not like to fight with the cape but he does like to pic the bulls. "I was in charge of picing in the *tentaderos* when I was younger, but now my son has taken over the job. When the time comes for me to retire, I hope the 'boss' will let me stay on the ranch and continue to ride the range, because this is what I love to do."

The Veterinary Surgeon

It is the role of every veterinary surgeon attached to a bullring to verify that the animals to be fought comply with all the requisites established in the *Reglamento Taurino*, among them, Title V, Chapter I, Article 44, referring to the fact that the animals have to be duly recorded in the Genealogical Book of Fighting Bulls; Article 45, that the bulls must be at least four years and not more than six years old for *corridas de toros* and three to four years of age for *novilladas*; Article 46, that the requirements for the weight of the bulls are complied with: a minimum of 460 kg in first-category rings (Madrid, Barcelona, Valencia, Bilbao, Málaga, etc.), 435 kg in second-category rings (those of the capital cities of the other provinces) and those of third-category rings, 410 kg. In the first two categories, the bulls will be weighed while they are alive and suitable scales must be available at the ring for this purpose, while in the third category rings, the animals are weighed "*en canal*" after they have been dragged out of the arena following their death, and their carcasses should register at least 258 kg on the scale. *Novillos* should not exceed 460 kg or 435 kg in first- and second-category rings, respectively, and the carcass, 270 kg in the third-category or temporary rings. Article 47 states that the horns of the bulls fought in either *corridas de toros* or *novilladas* should be intact, and that is the *ganadero*'s responsibility to guarantee that. Finally, Article 48 requires that the animals meet the general and specific conditions—that their vision is not impaired, for example—in order to be fought in the plaza in question.

The veterinary surgeon has to conduct three separate physical examinations of the animals. The first one will be approximately 24 hours prior to the corrida, in the presence of the *ganadero* or his representative and the impresario, who must present the *Guía de Origen y Sanidad de las Reses*, the official registration and sanitary certificates issued in accordance with the Genealogical Book of Fighting Bulls. The animals are unloaded from their crates on the lorry which transported them to the ring, and they are weighed. Chapter III, Articles 53 to 57 of the *Reglamento Taurino* refer in detail to the pre-corrida examinations and, among many stipulations, state that three veterinary surgeons must be appointed to examine each *corrida de toros* or *novillada*, but only two will be required for the other types of fight. Their fees and expenses will be paid by the impresario. In the first examination, the veterinary surgeon should focus initially on the horns, the *trapío* or physical appearance of the bull, and the suitability of the animal for the *lidia*, and will draw up a written report containing his conclusions. The second examination is carried out on the morning of the corrida, to guarantee that the animals continue to be suitable for the *lidia* and that nothing untoward has occurred during their stay in the corrals of the plaza. A record will also be made of this examination. Article 58 refers to the third and final examination, which is post-mortem, carried out by the bullring veterinary surgeon to determine that the meat is suitable for human consumption and, if necessary, to resolve any suspicions about possible tampering with the horns.

José Pedro Gómez Ballesteros
Madrid, 1944. Veterinary surgeon of Madrid Las Ventas Bullring and civil servant in the Ministry of Agriculture. Former Director of the Centro de Asuntos Taurinos of the Comunidad de Madrid

José Pedro Gómez Ballesteros

When I first interviewed José Pedro Gómez Ballesteros he was "just" one of the nine official veterinary surgeons of Las Ventas (although he was later appointed to the prestigious post of director of the Centre for Bullfighting Matters for the entire Madrid Community). Even though he had always attended the *reconocimientos* or physical examinations of the corridas as a hobby when he was a student and simply an aficionado, in 1985 he was formally appointed as one of the Las Ventas ring's veterinary surgeons. In order to occupy such a post, according to Gómez Ballesteros, "It is necessary to be an aficionado, because the knowledge and experience you need is only obtained by directly observing the reactions and behaviour of the animals in situ. It's not something you learn in veterinary college. When I graduated from the Madrid Universidad Complutense in 1969, there was little talk about or interest in the brave bulls from the professional veterinary point of view, nor was it easy to visit the ranches. Fortunately, things have changed; there are more theoretical classes, although little attention is still given to the practical and on-site education of future veterinary surgeons."

We can assume that it is no easy job to be a veterinary surgeon in the bullring and least of all in Las Ventas, the most important arena in the world. "The team of veterinary surgeons are clearly subjected to a great deal of pressure. It's a thankless job because it is almost impossible to please everyone. You find yourself often between 'a rock and a hard place'; the ganadero has his interests to look after and the impresario his, and then of course there are the toreros, and you often feel you have reached an impasse. However, our basic concern is really to satisfy the aficionados, because they are the ones who pay to see the spectacle. The Madrid public demands a certain type of bull and it is our responsibility to make sure that is what comes out into the ring."

Of the different interest groups involved, which proves to be the hardest to please? "Obviously the public, which we recognise as being 'sovereign'. The bullfight is really one of the most democratic events, for it is the spectators who pronounce the final verdict. We all know that there are certain sectors of the audience which are more difficult to satisfy. I think we are not doing such a bad job, in view of the fact that Madrid is the number one bullring in the world, with a crowd which is very demanding—but not impossible."

Madrid requires a bull which is more highly developed than in provincial rings. "In general, we are referring to an impressive animal, with trapío, a prominent morrillo or neck muscle, strong hindquarters and intact horns. It does not have to weigh 600 kilos in fact, we are lidiando bulls of 500 and 490 kilos, which are perfectly acceptable. We can't just opt for the 'elephant' bull, because kilos are not synonymous with bravery and large bulls do not usually have sufficient physical stamina."

A veterinary surgeon is typically one who loves animals, so initially there might seem to be something of a contradiction, being at the service of a spectacle which some consider "cruel". "The fighting bull is born and raised specifically for the Fiesta. It is an animal which lives a life of splendour in the pastures for four years and receives all the care and attention which few animals on this earth are given. If bullfighting did not exist, this costly and close attention would not make any sense. Economically speaking, it is not profitable to pasture and raise an animal for four years or more in order to ensure that it reaches a weight of 500 kilos, because there are other feeding processes which are faster and cheaper. The brave bull is pampered until it reaches adult age, and then it takes part in a lidia lasting no more than twenty minutes, which brings out its instinctively aggressive nature. I love animals, and the toro bravo above all else, and I think the more noble death lies in the ring and not in the slaughterhouse."

The bullring veterinary surgeon's work begins when the bulls arrive at the corrals, a day or two before the corrida in first-category rings. "Our first task is to weigh the animals, make sure they are healthy, have not been injured in any way and possess the biological characteristics corresponding to their encaste and particular breed. The animal's vision is also checked as best we can, because a bull blind in one eye can raise serious problems for a bullfighter. We try to determine whether the eye is clean and the cornea shows no opacity, nor any pathological process, a 'pajazo' in taurine argot, which would prevent it from seeing well. Any animal with defective vision is immediately rejected, but it is not always easy to perceive these problems, especially by someone unfamiliar with the toro de lidia. Even though the Reglamento Taurino requires only one veterinary surgeon to be present, all three usually attend, because it is better to study the reactions of the bulls in the corrals together and then exchange opinions. During the corrida one of the three accompanies the president in his box as an advisor, rotating according to seniority."

On the day of a corrida in Madrid, the definitive reconocimiento is held between 10.30 and 11.30 in the morning, immediately before the sorteo or drawing of lots, which commences promptly at noon. An official record is drawn up in quadruplicate, which specifies the six bulls approved for the ordinary lidia and the sobreros or spare bulls, with copies for the president, the impresario and the veterinary surgeons. The sorteo, in which the matadors' representatives draw their lots out of a hat and also determine the order of lidia of their bulls, is followed by the apartado, or separating of the animals into their individual pens. Both operations require the presence of the veterinary surgeons in case a bull is injured in the process by a cornada (horn wound) inflicted by another animal, fractures, a horn splitting as it makes its way into the pen, etc.

The veterinary surgeons also examine the picadors' horses: in first-category rings like Madrid, there should be six, while in other plazas, four are considered sufficient. Las Ventas has its own stable of horses, which are weighed at the beginning of the season to ensure that they do not exceed the maximum limit of 650 kg without the *peto* (the protective "armour") and the details are recorded for each animal: its name, morphological characteristics, weight, hide colour, etc. Then, on the morning of the corrida, the horses to be used that afternoon will be examined to make sure they are well trained and supple-mouthed, meet the weight requirements, etc., and any which are not suitable are rejected. An official report of this inspection is also drawn up.

The competent government authorities inspect the *petos* and the president or his delegate must verify their weights and the condition of the other equipment: banderillas, *puyas*, etc. Gómez Ballesteros feels that the *peto* should undergo certain modifications, using a more flexible, lighter material, so that when the bull charges the picador, the horse is sufficiently protected but the bull does not feel as though it is butting its head against a brick wall.

The third examination, post-mortem, is carried out in the *desolladero* or butchers' patio, to make sure that the meat is in excellent condition, since it is intended for human consumption. The horns are also examined for any visible alterations in the external cuticle. If there is any doubt, a biometric analysis is made using a tape to measure the length of the horn and then a saw is used to cut it open to verify that the core measures one-seventh of its total length and that its white "medullary line" is correctly centred. If there is any suspicion of fraudulent manipulation, the horns are sent to the Ministry of the Interior's laboratory for further study. The veterinary surgeons do not impose fines, but simply request more technically precise studies. However, it is preferable to reject any suspicious-looking bull in the corrals in the course of the morning's examination and send it back to the ranch rather than allow it to come into the ring. The spectators expect to see a strong, intact animal and they cannot be reimbursed in the event of fraud. However, it is important to say that splintered horns do not necessarily mean that they have been shaved.

According to Article 66 of the *Reglamento Taurino*, the veterinary surgeon sits to the right of the president in the official box and offers advice if the president requests it. What is this experience like? "It's stressful, because there are 23,000 people waiting on the decision of one person, the President, who must maintain his composure. Our mission is to advise him as the *lidia* develops, particularly if an animal suddenly goes lame or exhibits strange behaviour, but we just give our opinion and the President is the one who decides whether to take our advice or not."

A compromising issue: what does Gómez Ballesteros think of the ambience in the Las Ventas *tendidos*? "I respect the public because they often pay a lot of money for their tickets with the hope of seeing an entertaining corrida, but this may not always prove to be the case."

The "million-dollar question": what is the matter with the *toros bravos* today? "Many things. The bulls are being selected to suit the trends of modern *toreo*, which is often in detriment to their natural instincts and *casta*. The torero wants a bull that will obey his *muleta* and let him do what he wants to do. The *ganaderos* are opting for this kind of animal, but are endangering the natural *casta*; if we lose that, it will be almost impossible to recover. The Fiesta must have bulls which inspire respect, excitement, emotion and awe ... I think the situation is improving, but we are not home safe yet, and we have to be sure not to lose the typical indigenous *encastes* such as the Miuras, of Cabrera blood; the pablorromeros, of Gallardo; Contreras; Santa Coloma ..."

The remuneration of a bullring veterinary surgeon is a notional sum but as an aficionado, Gómez Ballesteros says: "The reward is extraordinary. I am delighted to have the opportunity to study the bulls close at hand and attend the corridas for nothing. I see about 120 corridas a year: all those put on in Madrid and, when I go on holiday, instead of lying on the beach as others do, I go to see more bulls!"

Gómez Ballesteros professes the greatest respect for the toreros, although he does coincide with many experts in the fact that not all the picadors are true professionals. "They used to be *mayorales*, ranch foremen, or *vaqueros*, who spent the whole day on horseback. Nowadays, a picador may be a postman, who only gets up on a horse from one Sunday to the next. It would be hard to create a school for picadors, but it is necessary to train them in some way to be more familiar with the horse, the bull and their specific job. The *suerte de varas* can be beautiful and it should not be degraded. It is exciting to see how a bull charges the horse from a distance and how the man advances the pic forward to receive the animal's charge. The toreros give the impression at times that the bull is their enemy, when they should look upon it as a friend, an ally or at least a collaborator."

Gómez Ballesteros says every corrida holds a surprise, especially as far as the bulls and their behaviour go. "I make my predictions in the morning according to how I see them react in the corrals, but they all fall apart in the afternoon. I remember a particular bull of Alfonso Guardiola, which would not respond to any provocations in the *apartado* and we had a hard time getting it into the pen. Everybody said it would be a colossal *manso* and then in the afternoon it turned out to be *bravísimo*."

Chapter 2. The Bullfighters

The Matador de Toros

The matador is the great hero, who, together with the brave bull, makes this unique artistic manifestation possible. He is the only artist who must risk his life to create his work of art, something practically inconceivable in this day and age, and he is the personification of the romantic, legendary, noble and valiant gladiator in danger of extinction.

A distinction should perhaps be made between the words matador, he who kills the bulls, and torero, anyone who fights the bull. The *matador de toros* has taken the *alternativa*, regarded as a kind of doctorate, which entitles him to kill the more dangerous four- and five-year-old animals. The *matador de novillos* or *novillero* is a novice bullfighter who kills the three-year-old animals.

According to Article 4 of the current *Reglamento Taurino*, a *novillero* must perform in at least 25 *novilladas picadas* (with horses) in order to be able to take the *alternativa* and be included in Section I of the General Registry of Taurine Professionals, supervised until recently by the Spanish Ministry of the Interior, and now by the Ministry of Culture, which is where many aficionados feel it rightfully belongs. Section II corresponds to Matadores de Novillos con Picadores; Section III to Novilleros sin Picadores, a lower ranking; Section IV to Rejoneadores, or toreros on horseback; and Section V to the matadors' assistants, the Banderilleros and Picadores. According to official records there are at present about 230 active matadors, 400 *novilleros*, and 50 rejoneadors.

The veteran: Antonio Chenel Antoñete
Madrid, 1932-2011. *Matador de toros*

Antonio Chenel Antoñete was considered the "torero de Madrid" par excellence, not only because he was born in the capital and was raised in the Las Ventas bullring, but also because of his extraordinary and historic triumphs in this plaza, before the most demanding and difficult of audiences. On May 2, 1992, a plaque was put up in the Puerta Grande in his honour. (I am immensely but humbly proud that when Antonio Chenel was asked to furnish a photograph with which to illustrate this mosaic, he selected one of him performing a *media verónica* which I had taken in 1983). Years later, the Comunidad de Madrid wanted to leave record of what Antoñete had meant to Las Ventas, so they put up another plaque in the *patio de arrastre* where he had once lived, with the inscription "Ésta fue su casa, ésta es su plaza" (This was his home, this is his bullring). In order to respond to this gesture and express his gratitude, on 24 June 1998, his 66th birthday, Antoñete decided to throw a "special party"; he killed two bulls to celebrate the milestone and invited all the aficionados who could fit into the ring to attend. He did a brilliant job with the two fully-grown animals from the Las Ramblas ranch.

Antoñete's *spectacular* media verónica

Antonio Chenel was born on the top floor of an old apartment building at 18 calle Goya, near where his father worked in the Spanish Mint. When the Spanish Civil War broke out, the Mint was moved to Valencia and then to Castellón de la Plana, and the family moved together with it, but as his father ended up on the "losing" side, at the end of the war he was left with no job and no money. The Chenel family returned to Madrid and moved in with Antonio's older sister Carmen and her husband, Paco Parejo, who was the *mayoral* and caretaker of the Las Ventas ring at the time.

His childhood was not a particularly happy one and the first years after the war were bitter indeed. "My family was ostracised because they had fought with the Republicans. Two of my uncles were executed and I was not admitted to a state school because I was labelled the 'son of a commie'. War is a terrible thing and a civil war pits brother against brother, and leaves a wake of hatred and rancour which lasts for generations."

The fact that he lived in the bullring during his adolescence must have contributed to marking his destiny. "When I was growing up, all I saw were bulls and bullfighters. The local matadors would train every morning in the ring and I loved to sit on the sand and listen to them talk, for hours on end. When I finally got to see my first formal bullfight, I was mesmerised. I used an empty canvas sack to emulate how the toreros practised in the morning, until someone took pity on me and gave me an old cape and a *muleta* cut down to my size."

Antonio fought a bull for the first time when he was 12 years old in a *capea*, a kind of free-for-all mêlée, in which anyone daring or crazy enough can try to give a few passes to an old and already very "wise" animal. At that time, his family had no idea what he was up to and thought he was a hopeless loafer. "I didn't go to school and I could not keep a steady job, but I was afraid to tell them that I was going to the *capeas* and *tentaderos* because I was determined to be a bullfighter."

When Antonio, the fifth of six siblings, finally got up enough courage to announce his intentions, his father just shook his head in despair, and turned him over to his daughter's husband. Paco Parejo was wise and thought that if his young brother-in-law was going to risk his life and limb foolishly in the *capeas*, he might as well do it under his sage tutelage. So he put him on in an evening *becerrada*, a fight with two-year-old calves, in which he did very well, surprising even the most knowledgeable aficionados. Paco had Antonio contracted again for the following week, but this time he chose the worst cattle he could find and Antonio received a colossal beating from his animal. His brother-in-law had done this purposely in order to test his bravery. To triumph in the bullfighting world, one has to have art and courage; Antonio proved he had both!

"Paco always demanded so much of me and very rarely did he have a kind word to say. Not even on my best afternoons, like the one with the 'white Osborne bull', or when I cut a hoof in Barcelona, or with *Cantinero* in Madrid, did he congratulate me. The best he was able to mutter was: 'Not bad, not bad'. But most of the time he would say, 'There was a lot of silver, but very little gold,' because he felt my *toreo* was 24 carat. My parents just asked me to be careful, but my sister Carmen, Paco's wife, always supported me. When he would shout at me and say that I should go out and find an honest way of making a living, because I was such a lousy bullfighter, she would whisper in my ear: 'Don't worry. Paco says you are on again for next week'."

Antonio said he learned how to *torear* by "running the horns". "I would pretend to be the bull and charge the professionals when they trained, and that is a great way to learn what to do and what not to do. I soon saw for myself who cited correctly with the *muleta* and who did not. Then my brother-in-law would ask me whom I had worked out with that day and got me to analyse the virtues and defects of each one. You could say I learned the trade of matador from the animal's point of view. I also learned the importance of giving each bull the right distance, its own space. The bulls forty years ago had a stronger charge and the matadors would choose their position, adopt their stance and wait for the bull's galloping approach, which sadly is no longer true. I don't know if you needed more courage then or not, but you certainly had to have enough serenity, knowledge and confidence in what you were doing."

Antoñete fought just seven *novilladas* without picadors, not counting the evening *becerradas* his brother-in-law arranged for him, and then he moved on to the next stage: *novilladas* with picadors. His Achilles's heel soon became evident: his fragile bones, due to his deprived, undernourished childhood. In his first year as a *novillero* he suffered three broken bones and is probably worthy of an entry in the *Guinness Book of Records* for the number of bullring injuries: no less than 36 fractures. "I fought 13 *novilladas* in 1951, beginning on 8 February, but in March I broke my ankle. After two months in plaster, I fought twice in Valencia, then in Seville and back in Valencia, where I broke another bone in my ankle, and remained in dry dock until September. I did really well in Barcelona and when they repeated me on 24 September, I broke my collarbone. The following year—I suppose it was divine redemption—I fought a total of 60 *novilladas* and miraculously did not suffer a single major injury."

According to Antonio, in his day—the 1940s—being a *novillero* was a more gratifying experience than in later years because you earned some money—nowadays many *novilleros* have to pay to perform—and if you did well, you were invited back over and over again to the same plaza. "I began to support myself and although I was not tossed by the bulls often, every time I was *cogido* [caught], my bones paid the price."

Although Chenel said he respected every bullfighter, in view of how difficult the profession is, he especially venerated Manuel Rodríguez *Manolete*. "I saw many great toreros but *Manolete* impressed me because of his bearing, his elegance and the way he carried himself both in and outside the ring. He inspired so much respect that I think people were afraid to even approach him." Antonio was also deeply fond of his brother-in-law Paco, who died in 1995. "He taught me everything I know and was like a father to me."

After heading the ranking of *novilleros* in 1952, Antonio took the *alternativa* in Castellón de la Plana on 8 March 1953, with Julio Aparicio and Pedro Martínez Pedrés, and bulls of Francisco Chica, a doctorate he confirmed two months later in Madrid, on 13 May in the big Feria de San Isidro, with Rafael Ortega and Julio Aparicio. He remained active in the ring in a somewhat irregular manner until 30 September 1985, when he decided to cut his *coleta* (to retire, cutting the torero's symbolic pigtail), although he did continue performing in charity *festivales*.

He viewed his career as being long, but with more ups and downs than a roller coaster. "The irregularity was due in part to all my injuries, and a broken bone takes two months to heal, whereas a goring is always more desirable because you can be back in the ring in less than two weeks' time. For example, the year I took my *alternativa*, I had 90 contracts, but I fulfilled only 30 of them, because a pablorromero bull broke my arm in Málaga and it has never been the same since: my finger is permanently bent back and my wrist is stiff. I was almost left totally incapacitated but I was stubborn and determined to recover. Fifty years ago, medicine and physiotherapy were in no way as advanced as they are nowadays."

After cutting three ears in Madrid in 1953, and suffering that serious injury in Málaga, Antonio went off to Mexico with two pins securing his arm. "When the doctors removed the pins, and I managed to move my arm again, I appeared in San Isidro and the very first bull of the fair gave me a serious goring. It seemed that no matter how hard I tried, I could not complete a whole season. At that time, the Feria de San Isidro set the pace for the rest of the year. If you did well, you fought all over Spain, if you did poorly, or did not even appear, the impresarios ignored you as if you didn't exist. While everyone else was cutting ears and tails, I was in the infirmary or on my way to the *Sanatorio de Toreros* [Bullfighters' Hospital]."

Some critics labelled *Antoñete* "apathetic and lazy". "I wasn't apathetic, it was just that if I was convinced that the bull was no good and that I could not do anything worthwhile with it, I killed it right away, rather than waste my time and that of the public. I became easily discouraged when things did not go right, but I was incapable of 'deceiving' the spectators, putting on a pantomime, or belittling myself to perform what I considered 'cheap' *toreo*."

An artist has the right to be sensitive and bohemian, but the critics accused him of being a "good-for-nothing". "Bohemian, yes, a 'good-for-

Antoñete in a derechazo (right-handed pass)
and a "head-to-tail" chest pass with the left

nothing' no! I liked to be open and honest about what I did and felt I had nothing to hide. There was a famous flamenco club, Villa Rosa, in the Plaza Santa Ana, which was popular with all the toreros from Joselito and Belmonte to Manolete. They went to listen to the great flamenco singers such as Pepe Marchena and Manolo Caracol, but they made sure nobody saw them go in or out. I didn't care, so they would see me leave in the early hours of the morning. It wasn't considered appropriate for a bullfighter to be seen in public with a woman either, they had to be 'married only to the bulls'! Well, if I felt like having a drink in an outdoor café on the Gran Vía with a girlfriend, I did. So everyone claimed that I was a drunk and a womaniser. Nowadays, the toreros are seen all over, including on frivolous, gossipy television programmes or advertising watches and sports cars, and nobody criticises them, but then it was a different story."

Antonio also explained that he did not find the support he needed at home. He eventually married Pilar López-Quesada, the daughter of a wealthy banker, but his new wife begged him to retire and his father-in-law wanted to turn him into a businessman in a bespoke made-to-measure suit. "They didn't understand me and that I had bullfighting here," pointing to his heart, "and it was all I wanted to do. In all honesty, I must say as well that I was being injured a lot by the animals in the ring and that made my family suffer."

Antonio complained that the taurine impresarios had extremely short memories and that, when he was laid up for weeks at a time, they immediately forgot about him and contracted other toreros. But then the unexpected happened. In 1964, separated from his wife, he was planning to become a banderillero, when his brother-in-law Paco was able to put him on in Madrid, on 8 August, in a corrida which marked the presentation of a new ganadería, that of Félix Cameno. On that afternoon, Antoñete managed to cut two ears and his career was back in full swing, and the following year, on 15 May, he was performing his legendary faena with the impressive white bull Atrevido from the Osborne ranch. He was in high demand once again and fought 51 corridas in 1967. He finally decided to retire on 7 September 1975, killing six bulls all by himself in Las Ventas and cutting one ear.

It was an impromptu performance in a festival at Isla Margarita, Venezuela, in 1977 that brought him back to the ring, so that the newer generation of professionals and aficionados could enjoy his profound, artistic and classical style of fighting. Antoñete explained how it all came about. "My friend, the Venezuelan torero Curro Girón, was organising a feria with all the top figuras and he needed a substitute for José María Manzanares (padre). As I had done well in the festival he asked me to replace

Manzanares in the feria and I replied, 'Are you crazy? I can barely perform in *festivales!*' However, he plied me with a couple of whiskies and I suppose I finally agreed. I never thought of seriously returning to the ring, but all went well and I was offered an exclusive contract to fight in Spain in 1981."

On the days toreros fight, they usually have an early, light lunch, such as chicken soup and an omelette, in case they are injured and have to be operated upon later in the afternoon. *Antoñete* just drank black coffee and smoked. At that time, he was a terrible chain smoker, until he suffered a mild heart attack and his second wife, French-born Karina Bocos, made him give up the cigarettes. "I liked to start dressing two or three hours before the corrida! It helped me to relax. Friends have visited me in the hotel at noon or one in the afternoon and seen me huddled in bed, shivering from the cold, and they wondered how I would be able to perform in the corrida. But when I put on the suit of lights, I am transformed. I think I begin to feel better once I slip on the first pink stocking."

What was of great concern to him and to the majority of the toreros was not just their physical integrity but their professional dignity and reputation. "It is more a fear of failure than anything else. There were corridas that went so badly that I prayed for the bull to gore me! Nothing too serious, just enough to send me to the infirmary and put an end to the misery of not being able to triumph. You are obviously not going to throw yourself on the horns because you don't know what will happen, but if it is just a minor goring, it would be a relief."

Antoñete reminisced about how the bullfighting world had changed over the years. "I remember when the toreros would ride down the calle de Alcalá towards the bullring in open, horse-drawn carriages and the picadors would trot down to the ring on their horses, with their *monosabios* sitting behind them. It was a spectacle and the people would line up along the street to watch, whether they were going to the corrida or not. Of course, times change, there are many more corridas nowadays and there is no time to waste. We are always in a rush. Sometimes we barely have time return to his hotel, shower and change , before jumping into the van for next corrida.

Antonio spoke with nostalgia of the early 1900s, the epoch of *Joselito* and Belmonte, which his father had witnessed: a romantic era of *toreo*, when the top bullfighters would fight bulls of different breeds—from easy to difficult, including the Miuras—and appear in three corridas in each feria. Thus, they had time to linger around the cities, make friends, enjoy chatting in *tertulias* with the eminent local aficionados, and then take the train to their next feria.

"There was a quality of life which we do not enjoy nowadays. There was time to fraternise with writers, artists and intellectuals, and with other bull-

fighters, and although there was absolute rivalry in the ring, deep friendships were also forged, because everybody travelled together, stayed in the same hotels and appeared in the same corridas. The matador shared more time with his *cuadrilla* too and there was a priceless camaraderie which no longer exists nowadays. In fact, the banderilleros and picadors often drive to nearby corridas in their own cars and then drive back home for dinner. I would have liked to have lived in that era. The banderilleros were usually 'unsuccessful' matadors who had a great deal of experience and you learned a lot from talking to them and enjoyed their wealth of anecdotes. There were restaurants every 300 km or so which stayed open late for toreros travelling from Bilbao to Málaga or Almería, like *La Perdiz* in La Carolina, or *La Barga* near Burgos, and we would meet up with other cuadrillas at a midway point to share experiences and catch up on what was going on. There was no internet then! In fact, we were happy to go a few extra kilometres out of our way, because we knew we would be well-received and probably run into people we knew. Now, with the fast cars and vans, modern motorways that bypass the small towns, and the constant rush, all this camaraderie between the toreros has been lost."

Antoñete also regretted the loss of many traditions and although some may appear insignificant, they are not, for they all form a part of the ritual, the spectacle and the history. "Little things, like the three matadors marching across the sands in the opening *paseíllo* all together, not one rushing ahead and another lagging behind. The older generations would stride elegantly towards the *burladero* with their *monteras* on their heads and their *capotes de paseo* hanging from their left shoulders and then they would lean over the *barrera* for their *mozos de espadas* to remove the cape and spread it out in front of some friend or famous personality seated in the front row. The matadors would assume their places behind the *burladeros*, still wearing their *monteras* and with their fighting capes ready in case a colleague needed urgent assistance, instead of signing autographs or chatting to a friend in the *barrera*. In the ceremony of the *alternativa*, only the *padrino* or godfather would go out onto the sand. Now the other matador, the so-called *testigo* or witness, joins the ceremony so he can appear in the photograph."

Antonio lamented that the bullfighter no longer "lives" like a bullfighter, not only in the ring, but also outside it. Before, people used to say just from the style of dress and the stiff, elegant stride: "There goes a bullfighter!"

The *toro* also changed a lot, according to Antoñete: "The bull is more noble but it is also more sluggish, whereas before it had more strength and power and the end result was more exciting and effective for the public. It was just as dangerous for the torero, but nevertheless more fulfilling. The bulls are bigger now, but the *grandeza* [grandeur] and the majesty of the animals lie not in the kilos but in the bravery. If they charge and then stumble and fall, you can't execute any clean passes, so what is the point? The Fiesta has lost a lot of its respect for tradition and there are fewer knowledgeable aficionados and more casual and often 'ignorant' spectators."

What were Antoñete's "Ten Commandments" or "Rule Book" for pure, classic bullfighting? "Respect the bull and give it its 'space'; pamper the animal, fight with *temple* and smoothness, giving it the right distance and understanding the rules of the *lidia*. All of these things are important and I didn't invent them."

Popular journalist Manuel Molés wrote a wonderful book entitled *Antoñete, el Maestro*, from which I have drawn the following pearls of wisdom.

"Linking the passes is like the rhyme of bullfighting verse .... The bull shows its intentions and its feelings in its eyes. Some bulls have a murderous look, while others one of madness or fear, and still others have a generous, willing-to-collaborate expression ... Location is absolutely necessary, in bullfighting and in everyday life. Even if you just want a glass of beer at the bar of a busy restaurant ... Juan Belmonte said: '*Se torea como se es*' [You fight the way you are] and that is why a good bull unmasks the bad toreros and the impostors ... It is a pity to see a good bull fall into the hands of a torero who is incapable of understanding it. I often think that a brave bull deserves the right to choose its matador so that it too can display its full potential..." and finally "There is no surgeon who can cure the goring you receive from a woman you love ..."

Antonio Chenel's passion in retirement was his family: Karina Bocos and their son Marco Antonio, born in 1999 (Antonio's seventh child). Karina was an excellent aficionada, a former pianist and ballerina, who worked as hard or maybe harder than any ranch hand on their *ganadería*, *Antoñete's* other passion, in Navalagamella. She loaded the sacks of feed onto the Land Rover and filled the food troughs of the bulls with absolute tranquillity. He sorely missed his seed bull *Romerito*, which died of old age: it was an extremely brave animal, but nevertheless was a dear friend. "He ate out of my hand. I would go out into the country, sit down somewhere to smoke a cigarette and he would come over. We 'talked', and he would nudge me for acorns, which I always carried in my pocket. Sometimes I could not feed him fast enough and he would put his muzzle on my chest and 'cradle' me between his horns, so I would say *Romerito*, give me a little room' and he would back off."

The million-dollar question: Would you want your son to be a torero? "No way! I know what a difficult profession it is and he would have to convince me that he possessed extraordinary skill and *afición* before I would even allow him to talk about it. I would make him face the worst animals, which is what Paco Parejo did to me, and if he was still determined to be a bullfighter, then I might help him. What I do want is for him to be a good aficionado."

Recalling Belmonte's dictum that "You fight the way you are", how can we describe *Antoñete?* A highly sensitive person who reflects this profoundly in his everyday life and in the plaza: "When I am in the ring, I try to *torear* to please myself, and that is the only way one can transmit his feelings and art to the public. I think my greatest virtue was my courage. I don't mean to sound vain, but I think it was my courage and determination which enabled me to keep fighting and not give up. Everyone said I had just the minimum amount of bravery needed to get in front of the bull, but the truth is that I think I had enough courage to overcome all the injuries, the adversities, the frustrations, the ups and downs and the broken bones which left me laid up for months at a time." It also requires a great deal of courage to cite the bull from afar, remain immobile as it charges towards you, and fight with the profundity and art he displayed, continuing to do so at 50 and even 65 years of age. The bull charges so fast that if you don't execute the pass properly, you have no time to rectify and you will be up in the air before you know it.

Antoñete was superstitious, especially in regard to his aversion to the colour yellow. He was also a devotee of the Virgen de la Paloma, popularly regarded at the patron saint of Madrid, although La Almudena is the official holder of that title. "But I am not as religious as I should be. I only go to her church to pray when I want something, like when I am going to *torear*, and I ask for her protection." A dream unfulfilled? "To execute the perfect *faena*, but that is a utopian wish."

Las Ventas, the patio de arrastre: *the handsome plaque to Antoñete*

The current star: Enrique Ponce
Chiva (Valencia), 1971. Matador de toros

Although Enrique Ponce's paternal grandfather was the very valiant torero Rafael Ponce *Rafaelillo*, the person truly responsible for 'giving birth' to this extraordinary matador was his maternal grandfather, Leandro Martínez. "My *abuelo* Leandro showed me his old capes and *muletas* when I was six years old. I tried to pick them up but they were too big for me, but when he saw the excited look in my eye, he bought me a little cape and *muleta* cut down to my size and began to teach me to *torear*. In fact, the happiest memories of my childhood were precisely those when my grandfather would take me by the hand to go to the corridas."

Enrique never got around to finishing secondary school, because of the bulls. When he was not performing he was going to *tentaderos*, and on one occasion, after missing three days of school, he showed up only to find out that there was an examination, for which he had obviously not studied and so did not pass. He finally decided to devote his full attention to the bulls and felt that if his career did not go well, he could always go back to school. "Fortunately", he said, "my career started to take off and I had no time to study. Nevertheless, I think that life and the bulls have taught me a lot more than I could possibly have learned in the classroom. I travel a great deal and meet many people from all walks of life, and all of that, together with my dangerous profession, made me mature a lot faster than any other boy my age."

Did he think it is a good idea to mature so young? "I don't think it's all that bad because I had focus in my life and I didn't waste any valuable time. Besides, even though I was *toreando* at an early age, I also had a very normal childhood and continued to have fun like my peers." Enrique was fighting *becerritos* in the country when he was eight years old, at nine he made his formal presentation in public in the "Monte Picayo busca un torero" competition and at ten, he made history as the youngest child to kill a bull in public in a first-category ring, that of Valencia. "I was also the last, because after my success—I was carried out on the shoulders of the crowd—they passed a law prohibiting children under 16 years of age from performing in *becerradas*."

Where could he go from there? If he wanted to continue fighting, he had to do so in secret and "undercover", something that was impossible in his native Valencia. So he went to a small town in Jaén: Castellar, on the other side of the country, where he was discovered by his current *apoderado*, Juan Ruiz Palomares. He started attending a lot of *tentaderos* in the area and appeared again in public at age 12. What did his mother think about all this? "Initially she didn't take it too seriously, but then it became really hard for her. She tried without success to persuade me to forget about being a torero and I know she had some big arguments with her father, but Grandpa remained invincible."

If bullfighting did not exist, what other road would Enrique Ponce have taken? "I discovered *toreo* when I was five or six, so I never ever considered being anything other than being a *matador de toros*!" He does like soccer, but only as a pastime and in fact, the day I interviewed him, he was going to play with his favourite team, Real Madrid, in the largest Spanish stadium, the Santiago Bernabeu, in a charity football match organised to raise funds for an anti-drug campaign. Despite the fact that this was going to be a major event, televised live, he appeared totally relaxed and calm. "I am tranquil by nature and on the most important and decisive afternoons, I try not to show what I feel, but as we say in Spain: '*La procesión va por dentro siempre*' ('Still waters run deep')."

Ponce continued to appear in *becerradas*, with false papers, and then between 1986 and 1987, he was able to put on a *traje de luces* (suit of lights) and perform in 30 *novilladas* without picadors. He made his début with picadors on 9 March 1988, in Castellón de la Plana, and fought another 33 *novilladas* that year, and 65 in 1989. He took the *alternativa* at 18 years of age in Valencia, during the Feria de las Fallas on 16 March 1990, from José Miguel Arroyo *Joselito*, with Miguel Báez *Litri* as the witness, and bulls from Hermanos Puerta. He confirmed his doctorate in Madrid on 30 September, with *Rafael de Paula* as his *padrino*, Luis Francisco Esplá as witness, and bulls from Diego Garrido. His *confirmación* in the Plaza México, the largest bullring in the world, with a capacity of close to 50,000 spectators, and where he is still an idol today, took place on 13 December 1992, when he shared the bill with Mexican matadors Guillermo Capetillo and David Silveti, and bulls from the Venta del Refugio.

Another very popular matador and former child star is Madrid-born Julián López *El Juli*. Is there any comparison between the careers of Ponce and El Juli? "Of course, we both started very young and were very successful at an early age, him more than me, because he took his *alternativa* at 16! My situation was different because when I was that age I still looked as though I was 13; I was short, scrawny and 'baby-faced'. Mentally I was certainly mature enough but physically I was not, and no matter how many vitamins and tonics I took, I did not grow tall enough to face five-year-old animals. When I made my presentation in Madrid at the age of 16, I killed a *novillada* as big as a proper *corrida de toros*. I did really well, but because I was short, I could not progress immediately to *matador de toros*, as I would have liked, even though I was more than ready."

Enrique Ponce acknowledges the applause of the spectators

Enrique married Paloma Cuevas, the daughter of famous matador, impresario and *apoderado* Victoriano Roger Valencia, in 1996, and they are the proud parents of Paloma and Bianca, born in April 2008 and January 2012, respectively. With so much taurine blood running through the veins of their ancestors, it would not be at all surprising should one of their offspring decide to become a torero, though Enrique is not at all keen on such a future for his daughters. As regards a possible son, "the truth is that I think it is such a beautiful profession, I wouldn't mind, but I wouldn't plant the idea in his head. However, one thing is certain, if he wanted to be a torero, I would insist that he be better than me! If not, I wouldn't like it at all." Speaking as a father, he is convinced that the sooner a child begins the better. "If you grow up with the cape or *muleta* in your hand, you get used to holding it, you take in the technical aspects of the *lidia* more easily and you learn everything a lot faster. If you start young, perhaps not at 10, but at 14, you have a better chance of succeeding, rather than starting when you are older, although there are also matadors who did that and became successful.

I reminded him that in taurine history, some very promising child prodigies suffered an identity crisis and a loss of *afición* in their twenties. "That is indeed true. It's possible to lose that interest and enthusiasm when one grows older, but that's been true in many other professions, like child film stars or singers. There have been many *becerristas* who displayed extraordinary aptitude when young, but were later incapable of finding the courage to face full-grown bulls or of assuming the responsibility of fighting before a demanding public." The motto of the Madrid Escuela de Tauromaquia is, in fact: "*Llegar a ser figura de toreo es un milagro pero al que llegue, le podría quitarle la vida pero jamás la gloria*" ("It is a miracle to become a top bullfighter, but if you do so, the bull can take away your life, but never your glory!")

Enrique Ponce has been fighting close to a hundred corridas a year for more than 25 years, despite the fact that he is always declaring his intention to fight less often in the following season. And when he is not performing in a corrida, he is fighting in a *tentadero*, participating in a charity *festival* or football match, tending to his own bull and livestock ranch in Navas de San Juan (Jaén), or off hunting, which is another of his great passions. He has some extraordinary trophies from safaris in Africa. In fact, he never stops. "I am fighting almost every day in summer, and in winter, I travel all over Spain to pick up the prizes I have been awarded in the summer fairs, and then I also perform extensively in the Latin American bullrings. I also like to travel abroad with my wife. We love New York, Los Angeles and Las Vegas, and we go every year."

One would think that after a hundred bullfights per annum, you would end up being *atorado* [bored with the bulls] and would think: "Oh my God, not another fight today!" "Never! It is what I love to do most. Right now, I have not fought a corrida for three months"—it was the winter hiatus of inactivity—"and I sincerely miss it. I ended the Spanish season in October and I start all over again in Cali, Colombia, at the beginning of January. In all this time, I have not even appeared in a festival. This is the longest time I've gone without facing a bull and I feel uncomfortable and it is beginning to worry me. I'm used to fighting very regularly and when I stop doing it for some time, I'm afraid that I won't remember how to do it or that I will not be capable. I even feel fearful, something which does not happen to me when I am fighting every day. I like to *torear*, perhaps not so often, but I need to do it in order to feel secure and confident. A friend of mind, the late maestro José Mari Manzanares, told me he felt the same way and assured me that it was perfectly normal. Every afternoon is like starting all over again and, if you spend a long time without fighting, the animals seem bigger and fiercer than before. When I fight every day in August, I am more relaxed, except when there is a truly important corrida or a highly compromising occasion. Aficionados don't realize that the beginning of a new bullfight season is very difficult for a torero."

What is Enrique Ponce's secret or personal definition of *toreo*? "I don't have any secrets, because I think *toreo* is the most transparent, pure and honest thing there is. There's no room for mystery, tricks or deception. The bull charges into the ring and you have to have enough courage, knowledge and skill to dominate it and then transmit your art and sentiments to the public. My 'recipe' would be first of all to have a great deal of afición, so that you can look upon every day as a new challenge and never have your dreams, determination and desire to triumph diminish in any way. Then, you have to have a very pure, profound concept of toreo and be capable of adapting it to each and every bull that comes out into the ring. That's the way to become a *figura del toreo*; very few can permit themselves the luxury of waiting for a good bull, the right bull, with which to express their toreo, because it's impossible for such a bull to come out every afternoon. Skill and courage are not in conflict with purity and art."

Enrique makes it clear that he admires all bullfighters: "Because you can learn something from everyone, but perhaps I identify most with *Manzanares padre*, although I also liked, when I was growing up, Juan Antonio Ruíz Espartaco, Pedro Moya Niño de la Capea, Paco Ojeda and Roberto Domínguez, each with his own style and personality."

Perhaps Enrique Ponce's only defect—if you can call it that—is that, whatever he does, he makes it look easy, natural and effortless, and at times the public does not attribute to his work all the merit it deserves, something which has been true with great toreros of every epoch. "I'm happy if my colleagues and the knowledgeable aficionados appreciate what I do, even though the spectators do not always understand what I am trying to accomplish. Maybe I would have to let myself get tossed by the bull for the public to see that the animal is dangerous ... but I would prefer not to! Let them think 'it's a piece of cake!'"

Enrique Ponce with capote and muleta

Enrique's smooth, but nevertheless profound style is indeed a gift, because it is not easy to understand and dominate all of the bulls, as he manages to do. There is certainly a lot of merit in making a bad bull look good. Of his many great triumphs, what are his most memorable afternoons? He mentions the day he killed six bulls in Valencia. It wasn't supposed to be that way, but there was a last-minute change in the bulls and at 4.30 in the afternoon the other two matadors took up their legitimate option to refuse to perform. Enrique was 18 and had only fought four full corridas up to that time; this was going to be his fifth. He could have dropped out, like his colleagues had done, but he decided instead to face all six bulls alone, and he cut three ears in the process. He would have obtained six, if he had done better with the sword. He remembers another great corrida, in Bilbao in 1991, and the Corrida de la Beneficencia in Madrid, when he was carried out through the Puerta Grande for the first time; another afternoon with Valdefresno bulls during the Feria de San Isidro of 1996, and 26 September 1999, when he cut three ears and left La Maestranza through the privileged Puerta del Príncipe on the shoulders of an ecstatic crowd. He shared the bill that day with Miguel Báez Litri who was fighting for the last time, and Julián López El Juli, facing bulls of Victoriano del Río. More recently, he cites 19 June 2016 as one of the most memorable afternoons in his entire career when he killed six bulls in Istres, near Marseille. cutting eight ears and two tails and pardoning one of the Núñez de Cuvillo bulls. It was indeed a historic corrida, in which he put on a dinner jacket and black tie, symbolic of the profound elegance of his *toreo*, to fight the last two bulls.

Further proof of his knowledge and understanding of the bulls is that he has suffered relatively few serious injuries. "Thank God, I have been very fortunate. I have killed over 2,500 bulls and have had few serious injuries. I have been caught and tossed a lot, but I was lucky enough not to have been seriously injured most of the time; I attribute this to divine intervention." Nevertheless, toreros say it is very hard to avoid 'paying dues' in their profession, and Enrique did suffer five major gorings in Seville, Alicante, León (2002), El Puerto de Santa Maria (2005) and Valencia (2014); the worst was a chest wound in León on 23 June 2002, which nearly cost him his life.

Ponce admits to a profound belief in God. "I was brought up to be religious and when I was a child I would go to mass with my parents every Sunday. As an adult, I no longer have time to do that, especially on Sundays, for the obvious reasons, but I do pray a lot and I have my own little 'chapel'," which his wife jokingly refers to as a small 'cathedral', "and I take it with me wherever I travel. I always say a prayer before I leave the hotel room and ask that nothing happens and then I pray again in the bullring chapel."

He is not superstitious but says he respects the obsessions of others: "I never wear anything yellow"—considered bad luck in bullfighting and theatrical circles— "not because I am superstitious about it, but because maybe the person next to me is. I think it's silly to be superstitious and yet I'm beginning to dislike that colour, although I remember my grandfather had a small yellow car. We would go to the corrida in it, but he would never park near the ring. I don't care if the *montera* falls crown up or down in the *brindis* (the dedication to the crowd): Crown up is considered good luck; crown on the sand is considered unlucky because it could mean a fatal injury and that the torero's soul will go up to heaven. "I never put my *montera* on the bed because my previous sword-handler, Franklin Gutiérrez, was very superstitious about that. Sometimes I would forget and he grabbed it right away and got all bent out of shape: '*Maestro, maestro, eso no se hace, ¡Por Dios y todos los Santos!*'" For goodness sake, maestro, don't do that!"

Once again, "*se torea como se es*", and *toreo,* like every art, is born from within. "I suppose my style mirrors my most intimate self and my personality. I think I'm a very normal, down-to-earth, sincere person and I hope that my *toreo* reflects that naturalness. I try to be honest and transparent, without any tricks or deceptions, and my *toreo* is like that too. My goal is to fight in the most natural, classic way possible, but not all bulls allow you to do that. I feel obliged to do the best I can, no matter what the bull is like."

What is a typical corrida day like? "I get up late, because I have usually arrived from the previous day's fight at around three in the morning. I don't have breakfast but I have a light lunch at one. Then I go up to my room and set up my 'chapel', watch television or read a bit until my sword-handler comes to dress me. If I'm really tired, I take a siesta but I don't like to do that as a rule, because I wake up in a bad mood, especially if I have to torear It's not the same to wake up from a peaceful siesta and go out for a walk with your wife as it is to get dressed for a bullfight."

Talking about the wife of a torero, what special qualities would she need in order to face the difficult life that awaits her? Enrique knows he has found the perfect spouse. A bullfighter's wife has to be special, because she has to put up with a lot: the fear of what will happen in the ring, the nerves, spending a lot of time alone at the height of the season, the commotion and activity, knowing that her husband can't be with her as much as she would like, or even accompany her on important occasions like baptisms, weddings and funerals. "I am lucky that Paloma grew up in this ambience, as her father was a bullfighter, an impresario and an apoderado; his life, like mine, was and continues to be the bulls. If a woman is not familiar with this world, she might have a harder time getting used to it."

Enrique Ponce and Paloma Cuevas

Enrique is not totally convinced, however, about the presence of a woman in the bullring. "I respect everyone, male or female, who goes out in front of the bull, because of the great merit it entails. However, I don't think it is a place for a woman, and it is not a question of machismo. A woman is a woman, and a man is a man. Men have a physical strength and bulk and I think it has to be a lot more difficult for a girl, as they are physically at a disadvantage, although bullfighting is not about power and brawn. You have to have courage and mental control, which women definitely possess, but then you need sufficient stamina to overcome a serious tossing. I have always admired Cristina Sánchez, but I must say that my personal concept of a woman is different; I consider her a more fragile and feminine being."

Ponce feels that the Fiesta has reached a historical peak, despite its modern-day detractors. "There are a lot of extraordinary matadors and they are fighting with greater perfection than ever before. People consider bullfighting a popular social event and they go to be seen, but that is not all bad, because it helps the toreros and the Fiesta itself gain greater prestige and prominence. We cannot expect to fill the plaza with only consummate aficionados; there have to be ordinary spectators too. *Toreo* is not something you learn overnight, not even as a mere aficionado, and you have to follow and study the finer points over a long period of time in order to truly understand and be in a valid position to evaluate it. But as it is an art, all you really need is the sensitivity to be able to appreciate what you are watching."

What would Enrique change in the Fiesta? "Many things, beginning with the police commissioner who presides over the corrida. I think a seasoned aficionado would be much better. Perhaps a school for bullring presidents should be created and another for the veterinary surgeons, because the vet who takes care of your dog or cat may not be sufficiently knowledgeable about the morphology and encastes of the toros bravos. I hold the veterinary surgeons of the major bullrings responsible for the gradual loss of the Santa Coloma *encaste*, because they don't understand that it is a bull with a much smaller frame. It's necessary to respect the individual physical characteristics of each breed or caste. Bulls are being raised with 600 kilos and they cannot charge with that weight, even if they want to. A bull has to have a normal weight and *trapío* and be healthy. A 490-kilo bull can be just as dangerous as one of 600 kilos, or maybe more so, because it is faster and more agile than a lumbering, obese animal."

Ponce has great faith in his new ranch Cetrina, which he bought in 1992 with 150 cows from the Salvador Domecq *encaste*. He is pleased about how things are going but he knows that a long road still lies ahead.

Traditionally, the goal of the torero was to buy his first car—often a Mercedes Benz—and then a ranch of his own, but when taurine journalist José Luis Benlloch interviewed the young and triumphant Ponce for the magazine *Aplausos* in 1988, he suggested that he might have to invert the order. "That turned out to be the case", says Enrique. "I couldn't drive in Spain until I was 18, even though I was a full matador, so first I bought part of the ranch I own today. When I turned 18, I had to do my military service, so I still had to wait before I could get my licence and buy my very own car."

The struggling contender: Raúl Galindo
Madrid, 1964. Matador de toros and industrial engineer

Galindo in a pase ayudado, Las Ventas

Raúl Galindo is the son of banderillero Fernando Galindo and the younger brother of Fernando hijo, *matador de toros*, who took the *alternativa* in 1984 but is at present a banderillero. So Raúl grew up in a totally taurine ambience. "My father was born in Valencia and became a torero the hard way, participating in the local *capeas*. As a *novillero* he went from one extreme to the other: he cut a tail on his presentation in Valencia and an enthusiastic crowd carried him home on their shoulders, but he was repeated the following Sunday and was unable to kill the bull. He became a banderillero almost immediately, and that was something unusual at the time. One becomes a banderillero nowadays due to a natural calling, but then it was a means of survival."

Fernando Galindo *padre* fought with many famous matadors such as Antonio Bienvenida, Luis Segura, Dámaso Gómez, Gabriel de la Casa, Juan José, and with his own children. "He appeared with my brother and with me a lot, but it was a dreadful experience for all of us for many reasons: the complicated father-son relationship in itself—when children think they know it all—and of course he wanted to be a father both in and out of the ring. We all had our nerves on edge, the adrenalin flowing and everyone was worried about everyone else. This made for a very tense situation."

The *apoderados* want parents to interfere as little as possible and if the would-be toreros are orphans, all the better. "I am sure our father made decisions with our best interests in mind, but he made some mistakes. He let his heart rule his head and didn't adopt the best taurine strategy for our careers. He also recognised years later that every epoch is different and he did not fully comprehend ours."

Both Fernando and Raúl went to university, but only the latter finished. "My brother got all wrapped up in the bulls but I had a guidance counsellor at school, who was an aficionada, and she encouraged me to study Technical Industrial Engineering, which was a relatively short, three-year course that I could combine with my toreo. It wasn't easy but I am glad I did it."

Raul's initiation into the bullfighting world was not easy either, and like many youths without sufficient financial backing, he started by performing in the serious portion of a comic-taurine spectacle, in his case, *El Bombero Torero*, in 1981, which allowed him to acquire valuable experience with young animals. Raúl possessed the necessary courage and acquired the knowledge and skill he needed to triumph, but you need a lot more than that to make it in the bullfighting world. "You need *suerte*, luck, and the ability to make the right decisions. My *apoderado* at the time made a lot of crucial mistakes and I paid the consequences. In the end, I was finally able to take the *alternativa* in Azpeitia (Guipúzcoa) on 2 August 1988, with Miguel Báez Litri and Rafi Camino and bulls from Concha y Sierra. The following year I fought four corridas in Madrid, which might be considered 'over-exposure', and even though I did well, I was seriously gored in the stomach in the last one, in September, and they had to remove a metre and a half of my intestines. I reappeared in October, again in Madrid, and my whole career amounted to 'I have this one corrida on Sunday and I have to do well or else there will not be another.' You are continuously performing under a lot of pressure and with little prior 'on-the-job' experience. You can't acquire confidence and expertise by fighting one difficult corrida, like Miura or Pablo Romero, a month."

Galindo likens *toreo* to playing billiards: every millimetre counts. It is like a sixth sense and you acquire that when you play or fight every day. "When you've not seen 'a horn' in a month and you're standing in the *burladero* in Las Ventas watching this huge animal race around the ring, you ask yourself: 'I have to execute *pases naturales* with that monster? Have the bulls always been so humongous?' I've been in circumstances like that many times and I have been able to perform those *naturales*, but it's not easy! You're not on the same footing as the other toreros, *figuras*, who are accustomed to being in the arena, in front of a bull, with an imposing audience observing them, on a regular basis."

Raúl totalled approximately 90 *festejos* without picadors before making his début with horses in Vieux Bocaire, France, on 14 June 1983, and then fought another 50 *novilladas* with picadors. "I also placed my own banderillas, so that gave me an extra advantage for fighting in the *pueblos*. At that time—the eighties—we *novilleros* still earned some money when we fought. In other words, what they paid us covered all our expenses, the salaries of the *cuadrillas*, the travel, food, hotels, etc., and we still had some money left over to live on until the next corrida. Nowadays, the poor *novilleros* have to pay to fight: they have to give the small-town impresarios money to put them on and then they have to cover all of their expenses as well."

He believes that the situation is critical for the *novilleros* today, because the public wants to see only the top stars, in everything from bulls to the cinema to sports. "Before, we used to go to the local cinema and see whatever they were showing, now we look at the newspaper to see where the latest Tom Cruise or Julia Roberts film is playing. The *novilladas* are being relegated to the *pueblos*, but tickets are not cheap and sooner or later they will have to be subsidised if they are to survive."

Galindo confirmed his *alternativa* in Madrid on 19 April 1989, in the so-called Corrida de la Oportunidad which the impresario of Las Ventas at the time, Manuel Martínez *Chopera*, organised to help promote "*toreros modestos*". As he did well, he was put on again in June, when he suffered another serious goring from an impressive Hernández Plá bull. He says he does not mind the term *modesto*: "It's a word as good as any to describe a position on a ranking: modest or average. Perhaps it is belittling in the sense that an artist is an artist, he might be successful and wealthy, or not, but he is not necessarily 'modest'. I am still a torero, '*modesto*' or not, because I have faced very difficult corridas, like those of Miura, Tulio e Isaías Vázquez, Concha y Sierra … Perhaps I have not triumphed in the true sense of the word, but the bulls have furnished me with some wonderful experiences and I feel fulfilled with what I have been able to accomplish."

Raúl has not officially retired from the bullring but he no longer steps on to the sand as a torero. He is involved nevertheless in other facets of the taurine world. "I don't want to be bitter and frustrated, waiting for the odd opportunity to torear and so I am involved in organising corridas and promoting promising young bullfighters." He was particularly satisfied with being the representative in Spain of the firm Tauromex, which organised the Encuentro Mundial de Novilleros. He is enthused by the idea of "globalising" the Fiesta. "Through the 'World Gathering of Novilleros', you could say we are engaged in 'importing and exporting' *novilleros* all over the world. Obviously, when we are talking about the bulls, the most important country is Spain, followed by Mexico, as regards the numbers of *ganaderos*, toreros and corridas organised. But if Spain and Mexico are like the Premiership, we cannot ignore Venezuela, Colombia, Peru, Ecuador, Portugal, and, of course, France."

However, in many countries, people do not understand or accept the Fiesta. "I have to admit that it's a spectacle which is not without its bloodletting, but it also offers an extraordinary artistic and cultural content. It is ridiculous to compare it to fox-hunting, which is a sport, because as an art, it has inspired so many extraordinary artists, beginning with Francisco de Goya."

Valiant, intelligent and well-educated, Raúl Galindo is a born fighter, who could well find his niche in the world of politics. "I was once a candidate for a minor political party, devoted to defending hunting, fishing, bullfighting and Mother Nature, similar to what existed in France. Actually, it was more of a lobby than a party, but we were not very successful and politics is not my 'cup of tea'. What we do have to undertake is a major change in the system itself, which is still so deeply rooted in the nineteenth century. The role of the impresario has become practically hereditary and I can understand that to some extent, because many of the bullrings are privately owned, but there are many individuals running the bullfighting business who lack even minimal *afición*."

Raúl also attacked the taurine press with the same courage he displayed before the terrifying "Tulios". "I don't think this is a great moment for taurine journalists. There's a very important national newspaper, the only one I like to read for general information, but it is clearly antibullfighting. It has a taurine section because "Los Toros" are of undeniable interest to society in general, whether the editors like it or not. However, if they had their choice, they'd treat it as they do boxing: not publish a word about it. Several years ago, the leading critic of that paper and all of its correspondents in the provinces highlighted the most negative and catastrophic aspects of the Fiesta. One described it as a 'ballet of the absurd', between a weak bull with shaved horns and a totally superficial torero in a low-risk situation. This paper did a great disservice to the Fiesta, but it also worried me a lot, because it's the one I choose to buy each day. If they tell the rest of the more important news of world events with the same lack of honesty and clarity, I have to question everything I read in it."

The Novillero or Novice Bullfighter

According to Article 5 of the *Reglamento Taurino* and what is established in Section II of the General Register of Taurine Professionals, in order for a person to exercise the profession of *matador de novillos con picadores* he or she should have fought in at least 10 *novilladas* without picadors. An *aspirante a torero* or beginner should register with the Ministry of Culture under Section III, as a *Matador de novillos sin picadores*, but in order to do that he or she needs to be sponsored by a professional bullfighter or a bull-breeder, to ensure that the novice possesses some basic knowledge of the art. The aspiring torero can also register in Section III if he or she is able to present a diploma to show that they have studied in an officially recognised *escuela taurina* for at least one year.

The Bullfighting School—*La Escuela Taurina*

Article 92 of the *Reglamento Taurino* states that potential students at bullfighting schools should be 14 years old and must prove their parent's consent to their enrolling. In order to continue their taurine studies, they also have to present quarterly report cards from their schools to show that they are progressing adequately in their other subjects. When the bullfighting schools organise their practical sessions, the students can fight cows without any age limit and male calves up to two years of age.

The idea of creating a bullfighting school is not new, for a Royal Order dated 18 May 1830, issued by Fernando VII, created the Escuela de Tauromaquia de Sevilla. This was the very first such school of an official nature, and the king appointed the well-known *diestro* (matador) Jerónimo José Cándido as director. This appointment did not please Ronda-born Pedro Romero, the true "Father of Modern Tauromachy", who had reportedly killed 5,000 bulls, without suffering so much as a single serious injury, when he retired at 64 years of age. The king eventually rectified his error and named Romero as the official director of the school. Needless to say, bullfighting has changed since that time—almost 300 years—and rare is the torero who does not pay his "dues" in blood in this difficult profession. In Romero's time, the object was to kill the bull; today it is to create art, man against beast, and the price the matador pays for any error can be very high.

The true concept of the taurine school would take almost a century and a half to become firmly implanted in Spain, however, and so in the interim the young aficionado's only option for becoming a matador was to frequent the places where the professionals trained and hope that some veteran would take the time to share with him a few basic notions on the handling of the cape and the *muleta*. Once he had learned the fundamentals, the novice would need to put his limited knowledge into practice, and the only way he could do that was as a *maletilla* [an itinerant aspiring torero] in the picturesque village *capeas,* where he would get the "opportunity" to face some old cows who had probably been fought before. It was a rough and dangerous form of apprenticeship.

Retired matador, writer and poet Pepe Dominguín, brother of the world-renowned Luis Miguel Dominguín (famous for his extraordinary skill not only in the bullring, but also in the boudoir, and for his love affair with actress Ava Gardner, among other beauties), wrote in his family biography Mi *gente*: "Of every ten thousand boys who try to become bullfighters, only six hundred manage even to don a suit of lights, only one hundred will do so in *novilladas* with picadors of any great significance, and of those one hundred, only one will become a *matador de toros.*" This paints a very grim picture indeed, but things changed somewhat in 1976 when the first formal bullfighting school, the Escuela de Tauromaquia de Madrid, was founded, which set an example for another twelve schools to follow, sprouting up throughout Spain and abroad (in Nîmes, France, and Cali, Colombia, in particular). The founders of the Madrid School were Manuel Molinero, an intellectual always sporting a classic Cordoban sombrero, who was responsible for the theory and history classes, while the practical sessions were run by former *novillero*, Enrique Martín Arranz, who eventually became the *apoderado* of a taurine school graduate *cum laude,* matador José Miguel Arroyo Joselito. More recently, other retired bullfighters, some of whom were obliged to give up their active careers due to injuries suffered in their profession, have led the practical lessons: Agapito García *Serranito*, Joaquín Bernadó, Juan Antonio Alcoba *Macareno*, José Luis Bote *El Bote*, Faustino Inchausteguí *Tinín* and Pablo Saugar *Pirri,* with Gregorio Sánchez as technical director.

The school's basic programme includes subjects such as history of the taurine art, fundamental theory and principles of the *lidia,* gymnastics and physical preparation, and then, of course, *toreo de salón*—shadow bullfighting—handling the cape, *muleta*, banderillas and sword. Pen and paper are not required for the examinations; calves are used for the tests and grading. Gregorio Sánchez explained that it is not a matter of passing or failing, but that the student learns from his own mistakes.

When the school reached its maximum capacity (200 students), it was necessary to set up age restrictions for admission: between 12 and 18 years of age, although exceptions are made, as in the case of a precocious ten-year-old wonder-boy, known today as Julián López El Juli. There is no discrimination as to sex or nationality: California-born Honey Haskin was among the first students, followed by an English girl, Thisbe Burns, and the most noteworthy of the women thus far, without a doubt, was Madrid-born Cristina Sánchez, who became a *matador de alternativa*.

The Madrid school received subsidies which allowed it to function from the Town Hall, the Regional Community and the impresario of the Las Ventas ring, who is also obliged to organise *tentaderos* and *novilladas* for the more advanced students. Students pay only notional monthly fees, although the school secretary assured me that no student had ever been expelled due to defaulting on payment.

The previous general director of the school, Felipe Díaz Murillo, stated happily that the old axiom of "Más cornadas da el hambre que los toros" (Hunger inflicts more gorings than the bulls), is no longer true: "A torero does not have to be born into a situation of poverty, and bullfighting should now be considered a profession of dignity and glory, not desperation and tragedy."

The Madrid school is a member of the Federación de Escuelas Taurinas, which groups together the training centres of Valencia, Salamanca, Albacete, Jerez de la Frontera, Seville, Málaga, Algeciras, Castellón de la Plana, Benidorm, Nîmes (France) and Cali (Colombia).

Gregorio Sánchez claimed that the teachers never tell a student straight out that he has no future as a torero. "First, because a young boy or girl needs time to assimilate the basic rules and to progress, and they eventually see for themselves if they are not advancing at the same rate as their classmates. Furthermore, without a doubt, the calves show each student his or her relative worth. There are many students who discover that they do not cut the cloth as matadors, but they become very good banderilleros and make quite a name for themselves, while others decide that their place is on the other side of the fence, as sword-handlers."

On 8 March 1991, the Mayor of Madrid, José María Álvarez del Manzano, opened the new installations of the Escuela Taurina de Madrid—the classroom, a small bullring, offices, infirmary and chapel—in the Venta del Batán complex of the Casa de Campo. A large sign on the classroom wall reflects the institution's motto mentioned above: "It takes a miracle to become a top bullfighter", a quotation from Santiago Martin El Viti, a true *figura* of the 1960s and 70s. Below are added the words: "But if one makes it to the top, the bull can take his life, but never his glory".

The Madrid school can boast important alumni: José Cubero *Yiyo* (sadly remembered by aficionados because at 20 years of age this great torero was killed by a bull in Colmenar Viejo, on 30 August 1985), Lucio Sandín, José Miguel Arroyo *Joselito, El Bote,* José Pedro Prados El *Fundi*, Carlos Collado *Niño de la Taurina*, Miguel Rodríguez, Cristina Sánchez, Miguel Abellán, El *Juli* ... and the list promised to be endless, fortunately for the future of the Fiesta. Sadly, however, in 2016, the newly elected mayor, Manuela Carmena, of the "Ahora Madrid" political party, withdrew the financial city's assistance to the bullfighting school for purely political reasons, and has threatened to shut it down entirely.

Fernando Cantos
Seville, 1979. Novillero and university student

Fernando Cantos was a normal secondary school pupil, who planned to study philosophy, although his primary goal was to continue his training sessions at the Seville bullfighting school. "My parents are football fans and they can't explain where my *afición* comes from. I think my father is more frightened just watching me practice before the training horns than I am when I stand before the bull."

Fernando was first attracted to the bulls when he attended a series of lectures for secondary-school and university students in Seville's legendary La Maestranza bullring. Such was the enthusiasm of those attending that the Escuela de Tauromaquia de Sevilla was born, and Fernando became one of its first students. He had the chance to fight his first calf when he was 15 years old in a *tentadero* on the Soto de la Fuente ranch, in which Manuel Díaz El *Cordobés* also participated. It so happened that the other novice that same day was the Japanese *novillero* Atsuhiro Shimoyama *Niño del Sol Naciente* (The Boy of the Rising Sun), who later became the protégé of Philadelphia-born matador John Fulton. Atsuhiro suffered a tragic tossing just two years later, on 16 August 1995, in Pedro Bernardo (Ávila), which left him paraplegic. Determination and the desire to return to the bullrings enabled him to abandon his wheelchair and walk again; although he will never be able to *torear*, he devotes himself to participating in sports competitions for the handicapped.

Fernando's parents were indeed surprised by their son's sudden *afición* but he explained that "because I began in the bullfighting school, they saw it as a formal, serious programme, and little by little they got used to the idea, although they also hoped it was just a passing adolescent fancy". Nevertheless, Fernando did find great support at home, and his mother, Lola

Calero, was the first to go and see him perform in bullrings near Seville, where they live. His father, Serafín Cantos, accompanied him wherever he went and so did his elder brother, Serafín hijo, a Spanish language student. Fernando is also grateful for the help he received from the *matador de toros* Pepe Luis Vázquez hijo, who taught him a great deal, and from the late Mexican bull-breeder José Chafik, whom he met in 1996, when he was 17 years old, because Chafik's Spanish ranch was in the village of Azuaga, 17 km from his mother's home town, Malcocinado. Chafik was impressed by the style and skill Fernando displayed in a *tentadero* and suggested, after Fernando made his début in Cazalla de la Sierra on 14 July 1996, that he travel to Mexico, where he could acquire valuable experience. "It was meant to be a 'trial by fire', but at the same time the Mexican *toro bravo* is smaller and more manageable as a rule than here in Spain, and I gained a lot of confidence about being in the ring there."

Fernando had to repeat a whole school year, in part because of his prolonged stay in Mexico and also because "the bulls" in general take up a lot of time. "If I go to a *tentadero* 400 km away, I come home too tired to sit down and open a book to study, so I have to get up at four in the morning to prepare for an exam, but that's the price I have to pay. As most fights are in the summer, I can usually combine my bulls and my classes and, besides. I am convinced that where there is a will, there is a way."

The great scourge existing today in the Fiesta is the practice known as the 33-33-33, in which each *novillero* pays all his expenses and covers the financial risks involved in the organisation of the event and, on occasions, may even pay for the right to *torear*. "I'm totally against this because my family doesn't have the money and, besides, I would feel ashamed if I had to pay to perform. On the other hand, I do understand that the 'small-time' impresarios putting on the *novilladas* in the *pueblos* [small towns or villages] simply do not have enough money. The Ministry of Culture should subsidise these events for beginners, just as they do other cultural events, like Spanish film productions, theatre, concerts, art exhibitions, etc. You need at least an initial million and a half pesetas [£8,000] to begin to organise an event, and that does not come out of thin air. Also, the press should promote the *novilleros* in some way, because they represent the future of the Fiesta, and the general public only goes to see the toreros whose names sound familiar. It seems that nowadays to become a torero instead of giving passes with the *muleta* in the ring, you have to do it with your cheque-book!"

In view of all of these difficulties, is it true what they say about "the bull making sure that everyone occupies the place he truly deserves on the ranking"? "I don't think this is always the case and a lot of good toreros have been lost along the way because they were not afforded adequate opportunities. There are matadors who had to become banderilleros even though they showed great promise. Some say 'They missed the boat!', but I respond that: 'The boat of success' doesn't necessarily dock at every port!"

Fernando did not talk a lot in school about his bullfighting. "I didn't want to attract attention and some of my colleagues considered a torero as something weird, at least at first. Although they eventually got used to the idea, I could still hear a little sarcasm in their voices when they said: 'Look, there goes the bullfighter!' This is in part because young people are more interested in other activities like football, films or rock music, and also because they tend to look on the bullfight as archaic, folkloric, a thing of the past."

The bulls and school did not leave Fernando much time for anything else. "I don't go out a lot, especially to discotheques. I prefer to get together with Pepe Luis [Vázquez] and talk about bulls, listen to music, especially, flamenco, the purer and more classic, the better: *bulerías, soleares, seguiriyas* ... and I love to read novels by Delibes, García Márquez, Baroja ... and books on psychology and philosophy: Freud, Aristotle, Kant ..."

Fernando remembered a special afternoon in Tafalla when he dedicated his novillo to the public and tossed the *montera* over his shoulder. "I cited the bull from the centre of the ring, but it turned right around and made a beeline for my *montera*. It picked it up with its teeth and retreated to the *barrera* where it began to chomp on it! I suppose the bull was hungry, but I had to go out and buy another *montera* the next day!"

Fernando Cantos eventually had to abandon his taurine aspirations, due to lack of opportunities to *torear*, and he returned to school to complete his education.

The Rejoneador or Bullfighter on Horseback

Toreo on horseback—*rejoneo*—may be one of the oldest form of *lidia* of brave bulls. The Spanish nobility has engaged in fighting bulls from horseback since medieval times, including El Cid on his famous steed *Babieca*, and the conquistadores of America, such as Hernán Cortés and Francisco Pizarro. *Rejoneo* reached the height of its glory in the 17th century, but by the middle of the 18th, the spotlight was focused on the new bullfighting heroes, who faced the bulls on foot. In the mid-1920s, it recovered some of its ancient splendour with the daring exploits of the Cordoban horseman Antonio Cañero and, ever since, extraordinary rejoneadors have been prancing on Spanish rings, like those who appear here: the famous Domecq dynasty.

In Portugal, bullfighting on horseback combined with classic dressage, has always enjoyed a great deal of popularity. However, the bull is not killed in the arena, something that has been traditionally prohibited for those on foot as well, although the animal is despatched the next day in the corrals or in a nearby abattoir by a local butcher. Another difference is the wardrobe, for most of the Spanish horsemen wear the typical *traje campero* or country dress, while the Portuguese *cavalheiros* dress in the lavish Federica costume (corresponding to the epoch of Frederick II of Prussia), with an embroidered silk waistcoat, long white leggings, black boots and a plumed tricorne, instead of the broad-brimmed Cordoban sombrero.

Article 7 of the *Reglamento Taurino* establishes two categories of rejoneador. The novice must comply with the same conditions as the *novillero* on foot and, once he or she has appeared in 20 corridas, is entitled to take the *alternativa* and fight 4- and 5 year-old animals.

Article 88 stipulates that the rejoneador must provide one more horse than the number of toros he will *lidiar* and will be assisted by two *peones* on foot. Should the rejoneador wish to fight bulls with unshaved horns—not, at present, at all common—he or she would have to provide an additional mount. The *Reglamento Taurino* also establishes that no more than three *rejones de castigo* (punishing spears, the equivalent of the picing phase) can be placed, three or four *farpas* or pairs of banderillas, and special permission should be requested to place the *rosas*, small harpoons covered with paper flowers. This is a *suerte* or manoeuvre created by famous rejoneador Ángel Peralta, which proves particularly spectacular and daring, due to the very close, tight circles which the rejoneador must trace in order to place a trio of roses in the bull's back one after the other. Finally, when the *clarín* or bugle sounds, the rejoneador must take the *rejón de muerte* in hand; he or she will have five minutes in which to despatch the bull from horseback, at which point the first *aviso* or warning call is sounded on the *clarín* (bugle). Three minutes later, the second *aviso* is heard, signalling that the rejoneador should dismount and despatch the bull using the sword and the *muleta* or allow the *sobresaliente* [assistant matador or *novillero*, on foot] to do so. The rejoneador is not permitted to use the *muleta* and sword until he or she has attempted to place at least two *rejones de muerte*. The rejoneador or *sobresaliente* will have another two minutes in which to kill the bull before the third and final *aviso* is sounded and the bull is returned to the corrals.

Three Generations of Rejoneadors

Álvaro Domecq y Díez
Jerez de la Frontera, 1917–2005. Rejoneador

Despite his fame, his aristocratic origins, his distinction as a rejoneador, being an innovative breeder of both horses and brave bulls, a fine writer and poet, and a former mayor of his native Jerez de la Frontera, don Álvaro had a warm, sincere and down-to-earth personality. Perhaps I have forgotten something: a sense of modesty. "Life presents opportunities and if you are able to take advantage of them," Álvaro Domecq explained, "people think you are a 'great man', but I never believed that. I have had some wonderful opportunities in my life to accomplish certain things and at times, I was able to do them well and at others, badly; but in any event, everything I have undertaken in life I have tried to carry out with the maximum dedication."

Álvaro Domecq's name was synonymous first of all with horses. "Horses have been to me more than just a hobby or a sport, they have been the very heart of my existence. I have always felt that the horse was the best pedestal for man and that is why the statues of historic figures are always placed on horseback. I suppose that were they not on horseback, one would barely notice them."

What was more important in Álvaro Domecq's life, the horse or the bull? "I divide my life into two epochs, one devoted totally to the horse and the other to the bull, although of course they have always overlapped. I was first devoted to horses and then I became excited about founding my own bull ranch. It all worked out well because as I grew older, I could no longer ride, but I could at least enjoy my bulls."

The life of Álvaro Domecq *padre* could well have been made into a film. He studied in a prestigious school in Madrid, but with the growing political unrest in Spain in the early 1930s, his parents sent him to a college in Bordeaux, France. He was studying Law in Seville when the civil war broke out and he enlisted in the Requetés, a volunteer group which fought on the Nationalist side, to defend religious and monarchic values, and this aristocrat spent the next seven months sleeping in a foxhole, until he was recruited into the Air Force, an offer which he was delighted to accept. When the war ended, he returned to the family ranch and bodega [winery] business and, many years later, undertook to open the Casa Domecq in Mexico.

One of the many "opportunities" of which don Álvaro spoke and which marked his life was how he actually became a rejoneador. A priest approached him one day with the idea of building an orphanage and school for poor children in Jerez and don Álvaro suggested fighting a series of *festivales*, charitable fights, in order to raise money. When the priest's dream became a reality three years later, Álvaro decided to continue *rejoneando* because he loved doing it and he felt the time had come to "earn an honest living in one way or another". In recognition of his most generous, altruistic activities, he was eventually granted the distinguished Cruz de Beneficencia award by the Spanish Government on 11 October 1945. Totally unpretentious as he was, he dismissed the significance of this honour. "At that time, they gave you the 'Cross' if you just helped a little old lady across the street".

A *dashing young Álvaro Domecq in the* patio de cuadrillas

A fully professional rejoneador by 1942, he averaged about 70 corridas a year until 1950, the year of his retirement. He was considered a pioneer of the *Arte del Rejoneo*, for he created a whole new way of fighting from horseback, influenced by the Portuguese style. The most popular rejoneador in the 1930s was Antonio Cañero, but Álvaro was interested in a more artistic concept, in which the *doma* (dressage) predominated, rather than Cañero's *campero* or country style. Don Álvaro clarified the differences between Spanish and Portuguese *rejoneo*: "Portugal was and is more concerned with the classic *doma*, while Spain focuses on brusque, energetic control of the horse. My idea was to combine the two: that is, to include the *passage* [an elevated, contained trot, slow and cadenced, while advancing forward], the *piaffe* [as before, but marking the rhythm in place], the *posada* [the horse standing on its hind legs, its body at 45 degrees to the ground] and the *corbeta* [or 'curvet', when the horse stands on its hind legs and jumps into the air], which were not at all typical of country riding. I removed the bit from the horse's mouth so that he would not suffer, but I used a country saddle, and everyone thought I was crazy: a shocking combination, but I was convinced that the horse could gallop and perform without any need to use the bit."

What Álvaro Domecq y Díez represented in the history of bullfighting is clearly evidenced by the one of his stories. "I earned 25,000 pesetas [£100] per corrida when *Manolete*'s manager, José *Camará*, bargained for 50,000 [£200] for his torero, which was indeed a great deal of money at the time. When I told José that I wanted to retire, he encouraged me to continue and asked me what my price would be: I said something ridiculous like 150,000 pesetas [£600] per corrida and that I would accept no more than ten appearances. He called me the very next day and said: 'You're on!' I fought more than that, of course, and the last time I appeared was to place a pair of sticks in one bull during my son Álvaro's farewell corrida."

The fact that Álvaro Domecq *padre* appeared in 70 corridas in one season is still amazing, considering that in those years, there were no modern lorries, fast cars, motorways or aeroplanes, just the labouring gasogene cars. "Imagine how I felt after those long trips, without sleeping and then having to go out to fight. It was a major triumph when I finally managed to convince the train company to take my horses in a freight wagon."

Don Álvaro liked to fight on foot as well, but only in the country, and occasionally in the bullring he would dismount and give a few *muleta* passes before going into kill.

He was very proud of his son, Álvaro *hijo*, Alvarito, who not only followed in his footsteps with great success in the bullring, but also founded the *Real Escuela Andaluza de Arte Ecuestre* (Royal Andalucían School of Equestrian Art) in Jerez de la Frontera and organised the incomparable spectacle *Como bailan los caballos andaluces* (The dance of the Andalusian horses).

Don Álvaro was an excellent writer and in his last book, *Memorias de 80 años. Mi vereda a galope*, he explained his philosophy not only of life in general but also of his *rejoneo*. "*Rejoneo* is like *toreo*, but is performed on horseback.

What I tried to do is place the banderillas the way the banderilleros do on foot. To fight a bull, you have to get close, ride around it as often as necessary in order to be able to mould it and correct its defects. You have to teach it to charge, temper it with the horse's rump and tail, using it like a silk cape, and provoke the bull with as slow a rhythm and music in your horse's gallop as possible, because *temple* (finding the most appropriate speed and rhythm) is the supreme virtue of *toreo*! Attract the bull's attention slowly, carefully, and then gallop towards the animal head-on, face to face, breaking out of a straight line only when you are about to place the *rejón*. And once you have placed it, you must wait there for the bull to resume its charge, and that is when your horse can make a *quiebro* or feint to one side, as if it were executing a *media verónica* with the cape. The true beauty and essence of bullfighting lie in the *lidia* and the moulding of the bull, with smooth control and temple. In *toreo*, everything must be done slowly, just as in life: moving the herds across the fields, training a horse, eating and drinking, courting a woman ... and praying."

How important is the role of the horse in all of this? "Immensely important! I owe a lot to my mare *Espléndida*; my son had a 25-year-long career and he had many great horses. Pablo Hermoso de Mendoza has some wonderful animals, but *Cagancho* was something very special. A rejoneador without suitable horses cannot torear. The horse of the rejoneador has to be as much of a torero as its rider and you are either born a torero or not. This holds true for both the man and the animal. You either have the innate courage and the possibilities of understanding bullfighting or you don't. The *lidia* of *rejoneo* is exactly the same as that of *toreo* on foot, with one very important exception: you have to count on the vital collaboration of your horse."

Álvaro's father, Juan Pedro Domecq y Villavicencio, started the family bullfighting tradition when he bought the important Veragua ranch in 1930, which appeared on the *carteles* [posters] under the name of Marqués de Domecq. "My father was not a rejoneador but he rode well, like everyone in our family. I think we ride before we can walk; even the ants ride horses on our ranch. Now the only one who does not ride is me, sadly, because of my age! I might be able to get on the horse, but after a half hour, I don't know how on earth I would get off. And I'd be stuck in bed for a week! It's not worth it now, although it is what I miss most in life!" Álvaro Domecq bought his own ranch, Torrestrella, in 1953, and raised his own horses. Although he considered the Portuguese Lusitanians ideal for *rejoneo*, he always preferred to use Spanish thoroughbreds. "Perhaps I am wrong but I have to be true to my roots. The Spanish horse is more complicated and

*Three generations in the tentadero: don Álvaro taking notes,
Alvarito in the middle ground, and Antonio and Luis further away*

temperamental, so you have to work hard to control not only the bull but the horse, too. The Portuguese animals in general are more docile and manageable. Hermoso de Mendoza has a fantastic stable; they don't move, they don't even blink an eye in front of the bull. It is very difficult to do this with a Spanish horse, but each rejoneador has to choose the mount which best suits him. My favourite horse, Espléndida, for example, was an extraordinary mare. I used her to place the sticks and I always found the bull in the right spot! How did that happen? Did I position her correctly or did she understand where to position herself? I think it was a little bit of both. She had eleven offspring and they were all exceptional."

Álvaro Domecq y Díez was a truly impressive human being, not only because of the glorious, immortal place he occupies in the annals of bullfighting history, but for his own humanity. A very religious man, his faith was indeed put to the test on many occasions. He first considered retirement when travelling from a corrida in Málaga to another in Bayonne in the south of France in 1947, when the wagon transporting his horses skidded off a cliff in the Guadarrama mountains. The two *vaqueros* were killed almost instantly but most of the horses survived.

He was the father of three children: Álvaro hijo and two girls, one of whom died in a tragic riding accident on the ranch. In 1991, four of the youngest of his ten grandchildren were killed in a car accident and it was then that he gave the greatest display of courage and strength of character in his life in an open letter published in memory of the four little girls: "Temple and faith are the key factors to succeeding or just surviving in life. With faith, every difficulty or tragedy seems less terrible. I do not know how to live without faith!"

The bullfighting world lost a maestro, an icon and a hero when don Álvaro Domecq y Díez passed away on 5 October 2005, at 88 years of age.

Álvaro Domecq Romero
Jerez de la Frontera, 1940. Rejoneador

It was logical that *Alvarito*—a diminutive nickname used in the bullfighting world to distinguish the illustrious father from the equally extraordinary son—would follow in his parent's footsteps. "When I was a child I always saw my father on horseback and so, obviously, I was riding before I knew it. When I went away to school, my father had a horse stabled very near my dormitory so I could ride during breaks. It was not a luxury; it was a necessity for my happiness and lifestyle even when I was young. I always knew I wanted to be a rejoneador and I would practice with my wooden horse until I could do it with a real one."

Álvaro fought for the first time in public in a charity *festival* in Tarifa, in southwest Spain, on 26 February 1956, at the age of 16, although he made his formal début in Ronda on 13 September 1959. His career progressed brilliantly to his official presentation in Madrid in the Corrida de la Beneficencia on 7 June 1962, followed by his equally triumphant presentation in the largest bullring in the world, the Plaza México, on 28 December of the same year. He took part in 2,000 corridas throughout his exceptional, innovative professional career, including the magnificent afternoon when he became the first rejoneador to kill six bulls in one corrida, in Jerez de la Frontera, on 1 November 1971. This was the extraordinary culmination of a great season and he even made a gift of the *sobrero* or reserve bull.

Forever innovative, it was in 1971 that *Alvarito* created the spectacle *Los cuatro jinetes de la Apoteósis* (*The four horsemen of the Apotheosis*), with three other extraordinary rejoneadors: the Peralta brothers, Ángel and Rafael, and the Portuguese Samuel Lupi. The quartet immediately became a smash hit, to the point where they fought a total of 100 corridas together throughout all of

Spain the following year. "It wasn't easy in the beginning because bullfight impresarios are reticent to accept new ideas and the whole concept of *rejoneando en colleras* [in pairs] was totally new, but it made the corrida even more exciting and attractive to people uninitiated in *rejoneo*."

Four horsemen in the ring at Las Ventas

Álvaro Domecq Romero retired from the ring on 12 October 1985, in a moving event in which he killed six bulls and in which all the current and past *figuras* of *rejoneo* participated: the Peralta brothers Ángel and Rafael, Samuel Lupi, Fermín Bohórquez *padre*, Leonardo Hernández and Manuel Vidrié, along with a third generation of Domecq rejoneadors, his nephew Luis, making his début. Even his father, almost 70 years old, appeared in the ring to place two pairs of banderillas.

Aside from his concern for always seeking new ways to enhance the art of *rejoneo* for the general public, *Alvarito* also admits to enjoying fighting on foot. "I suppose I never thought of being a matador, because as the horse was always a permanent fixture in my life, I simply tried to combine both passions."

He is rightly proud of having created the *Real Escuela Andaluza de Arte Ecuestre* in Jerez and *Cómo bailan los caballos andaluces*. "I first came up with the idea because I couldn't believe that with Spain's long history of refined horsemanship, there was no riding school similar to the one in Vienna. The

Austrian school perpetuated the Spanish customs of how to equip the horse, put on the bridle, train the animals and put them through their paces, which date back over 500 years. I felt it was imperative for us to do the same in Spain. It wasn't easy but there it is: an extraordinary institution. I must personally say that I feel that the Spanish horse is the best breed in the world and we have to defend it. The fact that the king granted me the right to call it *Escuela Real* (Royal School) was another achievement of which I am indeed proud." Politics came into play several years ago and even though *Alvarito* is currently not its director, he was the guiding light behind the creation of the school and a statue in its garden pays tribute to his great love of and devotion to the *caballo español*.

Even in retirement, Alvarito practices rejoneo in the small ring at Los Alburejos

Alvarito was also pleased that horses trained at the school participated in the Olympic Games in Atlanta in 1996, and while he repeatedly covered the entire international taurine circuit as a rejoneador, he has travelled even more widely throughout the world with *Cómo bailan los caballos andaluces*, "all over Europe and America, from Buenos Aires to New York!"

His concept of *rejoneo* obviously does not differ much from that of his father. "*Rejoneo* is clearly bullfighting on horseback and your horse has to be a torero too; able to *torear* but at the same time to protect you. The beauty of the spectacle resides precisely in galloping straight towards the bull and the encounter with it; the union between both animals is what the art of *rejoneo* is all about. Even though the pure Spanish horse is not the best for *rejoneo*, and a mixture of breeds might produce a better result, we are more than satisfied with the horses we are raising."

He complains there are not enough hours in the day for him. "I have to go to the office, attend to the paperwork, supervise our business and oversee the ranch operations, and of course I don't want one day to go by without riding. I have to take advantage of the few years I have left to enjoy my stable to the full."

Álvaro *hijo* has inherited his father's graciousness and elegance, his art, courage and religious faith. "We are a very close-knit family and we live on a wonderful ranch, Los Alburejos, which my father built slowly, brick by brick, and it is our own personal paradise on earth."

Antonio Domecq y Domecq
Jerez de la Frontera, 1971. Rejoneador

Obviously, as grandson of the great Álvaro Domecq y Díez, Antonio's future was predestined for the world of the bulls, as was that of his brother Luis (Jerez de la Frontera, 1968). He corroborates this: "Everyone rides from the time they are infants, like my sister Isabel's two boys, Isaac, 5, and Pablo, 2, who likes to fight with the *muleta*, too. My son *Antoñito* is not standing up yet, but I am sure he will be on a horse very soon. This does not mean, however, that there will be another generation of *rejoneadores*!"

Nevertheless, there is a certain feeling of "noblesse oblige". "I really don't know exactly when I wanted to become a rejoneador. I think I woke up one day and said: 'Bring out the bulls! I want to fight!' In this family, we cannot consider life without bulls and horses and for me they, together with my family, represent my entire life."

We have seen that Luis, the elder brother, performed in public for the first time when his uncle *Alvarito* cut his *coleta* in October 1985, and he made his professional début on 12 September 1987 in Villacarrillo, when his younger brother Antonio also made a brief first public appearance. He received his *alternativa* from his uncle in Jerez (who was in activity once again) on 21 May 1992. A rejoneador works towards the *alternativa* just as a matador on foot does: by fighting *novillos* in small towns until he feels prepared enough, with sufficient understanding of terrains and *querencias* [the bull's preferred places in the arena] to fight older animals.

Not a single day goes by that does not see *Alvarito,* Luis and Antonio riding across the fields and working their horses in the training ring. "I have

The Domecq brothers Antonio (left) and Luis in a lap of honour after a successful performance in Madrid

seven ready for next season," said Antonio, "but I am always looking for more 'equine toreros'. We try to cross the studs that perform bravely in the ring with equally brave mares in the hope of obtaining new toreros. Riding them in the country to cut out and move the herds of bulls about is an important part of their training, to get them used to being around brave animals. A good *caballo de rejoneo* is priceless. We begin training them when they are three years old and when they are six or seven, we take them into the ring on the ranch, show them the *carretilla* [mock bull cart] and then a small cow. If it looks as if we have found a *caballo artista*, we might have it ready for the ring when it is eight or ten years old."

Which are his favourite horses? "A horseman might have a favourite horse, but a rejoneador, no. There is no one which is better or worse, simply those who perform certain *suertes* better than others: banderilleras, *rosas*, *rejón de muerte* ... You have to understand and love all of your animals in the same way, as if they were your children."

The two brothers do not resemble one another at all; Antonio is slim and fair, Luis is bulkier and dark, and there are certain differentiating nuances in their style. "I think I connect easier with the public because I am more outgoing in the ring, while Luis has a purer, more classical concept of *toreo*. The differences in our personalities come through in our performances." What about sibling rivalry? "Of course! We forget we are brothers and we both want to be the *triunfador*!"

Antonio remembers a rather special afternoon, but not because it marked a major triumph in an important ring. "I was going to perform in a small town where they ran the bulls through the streets in the morning. However, the bulls were still in the centre of the ring by late afternoon and there was no way to get them into the corrals! The arena was packed, the public was getting very impatient and these bulls which had run up and down the streets all day long were the ones we had to fight! They finally got them out of the ring and the corrida got under way. Amazingly enough, the animals turned out to be brave and we had a great afternoon, but I suffered like hell all day for the well-being of my horses!"

Luis Domecq in Madrid

The Banderillero

Title II, Chapter I, Article 8 of the *Reglamento Taurino* refers to the registration of the banderilleros in the official General Register of Taurine Professionals in two categories. The first grants the right to perform in any kind of spectacle, including *corridas de toros*, and in order to receive this authorisation, it is necessary to prove participation in 20 *novilladas picadas*, at least 10 of which must be in first- and second-category rings. Automatically included here are those banderilleros who had previously been inscribed in Sections I and II of the Register, corresponding respectively to *matadores de toros* and *novilleros con picadores*. In order to be admitted into the second category, both banderilleros and picadors must be vouched for by a registered torero, *ganadero* or a duly recognised taurino, who will corroborate the would-be professional's preparation and experience. The *Reglamento Taurino* establishes that banderilleros and picadors may receive their own *alternativa* in the first *corrida de toros* in which they participate, but this traditional ceremony is rarely seen nowadays.

The veteran: Julio Pérez El Vito
Camas (Seville), 1928-2016. Ex-matador de toros and banderillero

Julio Pérez's name appears written in gold in the annals of bullfighting history. He was born in the famous "cradle of toreros", Camas (Seville), the birthplace of such great matadors as Curro Romero and Paco Camino. The son of a *novillero* who became a banderillero, *El Vito* was recognised as one of the best and most elegant banderilleros of all times.

He fought for the first time in public in the town of Ubrique (Cádiz) on 9 April 1944, and made his début in Madrid two years later, on 14 April, with Manuel Perea *El Boni* and Luis Parra *Parrita,* facing bulls from Jordán de Urries. "I remember that it was the last *novillada* of the season and it was pouring with rain. The impresario Livinio Stuyck wanted to suspend the corrida but I persuaded my colleagues to torear. I knew if they cancelled our fight we would not get another chance. The furious impresario came over to me and whispered, 'Okay, you get your way this time but you will never come back here again!' I replied with a shrug, 'That's all right with me. I'll be back for my summer holidays, then.' As it turned out, I did well, and the impresario and his family became good friends of mine, to boot!"

Julio always followed his father's advice: "Life is difficult and it has to be filled with heroic deeds and valiant gestures, taking the good and the bad, the triumphs and the gorings. If you see monuments to famous men, whether they are politicians, intellectuals, generals or toreros, it means they did their duty and faced their destinies head on. The other poor devils will never find themselves on top of a pedestal, even if they use a ladder!"

El Vito had a noteworthy career as a *novillero*, which led to his taking the *alternativa*, "prematurely" in his own words, on 1 September 1947, in Valencia, with the Mexican matador Carlos Arruza as "godfather" and Jaime

Marco El Choni as witness, and bulls from Felipe Bartolomé. He confirmed his doctorate a month later in Madrid on 3 October, with Curro Caro and Carlos Arruza again and bulls from the same ranch, in what proved to be a very successful afternoon for all.

He suffered a serious goring in Seville on 20 April 1947, and little by little the number of corridas he fought each season declined, so he decided to try his luck in Mexico, where he captivated the local aficionados with his incredible charm, art and personality, both in the ring and outside it. In fact, he was so versatile that when not in the bullring he was able to earn extra money as a flamenco dancer. He also liked playing football, riding horses and zooming around the city on a motorcycle. "I could do everything except sit still".

El Vito *as a matador*

Julio did not triumph in Latin America as he had hoped, and when he returned to Spain he decided to become a banderillero. Nevertheless, he insists that he did perform his best *"faena"* in Mexico. "I met the most beautiful girl in the world and brought her back to Seville to be my wife. I saw her at a party and asked her to dance, and then we had another dance, and then another … Her family was from Canada and she spoke Spanish, English, French, German, Russian and Italian, and she was a virtuoso pianist. Even her name was beautiful: Gloria! We celebrated the wedding banquet in the Hotel Colón and I was so happy I invited all of Seville. When we arrived at the Hotel, my bride and I couldn't get through the door because of all the guests. A few years ago, we went back to Mexico on a visit, and she was already not feeling too well. She had left a note saying: 'God, let me die in Mexico where I was born and be buried in Seville where I lived so happily'. Her wish came true."

El Vito made the decision to become a banderillero because, as they say in Spanish, he preferred to be a "*cabeza de ratón que cola de león*" (a big fish in a small pond). His first matador was Juan Posada, whom he considered as family, and afterwards he worked with Manolo Vázquez, Miguel Báez Litri (*padre*), and Jaime Ostos.

El Vito, *banderillero*

Julio looked back with nostalgia, because he felt that in the past the toreros had more class, more style and a greater sense of *vergüenza* [pride or shame]. He also insisted that the matadors were more respectful of their *cuadrillas*. "I was with Litri for 8 or 9 years and with Ostos for about the same amount of time, and they always treated their *gente* [people] splendidly. We ate at nice restaurants—and, of course, they picked up the bill—and ordered fine wines and a bottle of cognac for after dinner. I suppose that the *subalternos* [banderilleros] earn more money nowadays because their union is stronger, but before, if the stipulated wage was 2,500 or 3,000 pesetas [£12.50-15.00], the top *figuras* such as Litri, Antonio Ordóñez and Luis Miguel Dominguín paid 5,000 pesetas [£25.00] to each of their *subalternos*. Today, if they can 'push you through the tunnel' they do. In other words, in exchange for your fighting with them a lot, they pay you less for each corrida: a sort of package deal. Also, the *figuras* used to take on an extra banderillero in the major *ferias*, so that when Luis Miguel fought in Málaga, he would tell an elderly banderillero: 'Put on your suit of lights tomorrow and you can keep the *botijo* [water-jug] company'. I remember one time Ordóñez told a friend in Seville: 'I'll pay you for the Miura corrida on Sunday,' and the *subalterno* complained: 'My God, does it have to be the Miuras?' He wasn't going to do anything, not even place a pair of banderillas!"

Julio Pérez was indignant about the so-called *túnel*. "Even the small-time impresarios paid us enough to cover our expenses, so I can't explain how the union lets the *túnel* exist. When I was a matador, I respected my *cuadrilla* and took them to dine at a good restaurant and never in a 'greasy spoon'. I wanted everyone to be happy, because I thought if the bull caught me, they would rush to save me a lot faster!"

Julio nurtured many wonderful memories of *compañerismo* [camaraderie]. "One time my matador Ostos and the *cuadrilla* met up at a roadside restaurant with Dominguín and his group and Jaime said: 'I'm tired of being with these guys all the time. Let's switch!' and he sat with Luis Miguel's *cuadrilla* while we ate with Dominguín. The truth of the matter is that there were some extraordinary and highly professional *cuadrillas* then: Chaves Flores, Manuel Carmona, Antonio Fernández Almensilla, Alfredo David, Antonio Labrador *Pinturas* ... We had all been *matadores de toros* in our own right and had fought in all the major ferias in Spain. It was a wonderful experience to be a bullfighter in that era!"

The matadors always used to travel together with their *cuadrillas*, first by train and then in those huge foreign cars, Cadillacs, Hispano-Suizas and Rolls Royces. "Even though we were really crowded, nine people one on top of another, it was a privilege to have one of those monster cars, because there weren't a lot of vehicles on the roads to begin with. The first matadors to travel by car with their *cuadrillas* were Manolete, Arruza, Pepe Luis Vázquez and Litri, and we would run into other *cuadrillas* and have a good time before we each continued on our separate ways. Nowadays, people are always in such a hurry that I don't think they have half as much fun! Toreros also dressed with a lot more style and class before. We would leave the hotel dressed in a suit and tie, even if we had a long trip ahead of us. We'd stop along the way in a service station to take off the tie and change into something more comfortable. It is such a pity that this *torería* has been lost."

Julio explained why many of the classic matadors of the past are rarely seen at the corridas nowadays. "They were so devoted to their profession that they are disgusted with a lot of the things they see in the ring nowadays, such as spectators throwing shoes and bras to the matadors who feature in the popular press. *Toreo* is something else entirely, something a lot more serious!"

El *Vito* complained that the public is on the whole less knowledgeable now; there are more simple spectators and fewer real aficionados and even the banderilleros seem to take their profession more lightly. "I took off my *montera* only to acknowledge an ovation when I really felt I had done well. Today the banderilleros salute if they manage to place both sticks on the bull's back. With that norm, I would have had to salute every afternoon. I was recognised as a very good banderillero, as were *Pinturas,* Alfredo David, El *Boni,* Almensilla, Luis González, Andrés Luque Gago and *Michelín*. I am not saying that they don't place banderillas well nowadays too, we were just more modest. It is not simply a matter of putting the sticks in the right place, but achieving a perfect union between the man and the bull, the torero cradled between the horns, bringing the sticks together and drawing them up from below in order to drive them into the right spot. It is important for the spectators to be impressed by the encounter."

El *Vito* distinguished the typical fighting bull of his time from what we see today in the ring. "Our bull was more complicated because it was fiercer and charged with greater violence. I am not saying it is necessarily easier today, because nothing is ever easy in bullfighting. However, the matador used to say to his banderillero, 'Go out and run it with the cape', in order to study the reactions of the animal first, but now the matador usually steps out and receives the bull himself. Do you think Curro Romero would have still been fighting at 64 years of age if this were not the case?"

Julio was not overly pleased with the press either, particularly in the televised corridas. "A lot of the commentators think they know more than the torero, they try to predict what he will do, and if they write off a bull as being 'bad' and then the matador performs a great *faena,* they exclaim: 'Look how the bull has changed!' They shouldn't try to be fortune-tellers, because the torero is the real professional and even he can make a mistake. It's like a maths class in school: you are given a problem and have just 15 minutes to solve it." Nor is he totally convinced by the bullfighting schools. "Each torero has to have his own style, personality and inspiration, but I wonder if an El Cordobés padre or a Diego Puerta can be produced in a taurine school. Look at that computer genius [Bill Gates] who didn't even graduate from college!"

El Vito retired in September 1966 at just 39 years of age. "The aficionados expected me to go all out every afternoon, regardless of the bull. My last corrida was in Barcelona in a special tercio de banderillas with Luis González. In the first pair, the bull tore the ruffles off my shirt, in the second he gored me in the armpit and although I was bleeding profusely, I asked for permission to place yet another pair. The ring went wild, and as I headed for the infirmary, I whispered to Luis: 'I've just retired!'"

Julio Pérez later put his knowledge and experience to good use as a veedor, a "scout" for livestock, for such bullfighting impresarios as Emilio Miranda (Granada), Ángel Bernal (Murcia), the late Antonio Ordóñez (Ronda), and those of Córdoba and Valencia. "I don't need much else, my children are married, and of my twelve grandchildren, seven boys and five girls, none of them, thank goodness, has wanted to become a bullfighter. It is such a difficult profession and you don't earn a lot of money; a plumber fixes a leak in your house in five minutes and asks for 10,000 pesetas [£50]. Besides, there are so many occupations which leave you Saturdays and Sundays free to spend with your family."

What was his advice to banderilleros beginning their career? "First and foremost, you have to take the bull through the motions with as few capotazos [cape passes] as possible. You should only cape a bad bull, because with the good one you run backwards in order to lead it to where you want it to go. They give too many cape passes nowadays; in my day with one pass it was positioned for the banderillas, but now, one this way, another that way, sometimes up to half a dozen passes, and I don't know how the matador doesn't choke on the water he's sipping, waiting for it all to come to an end!"

He remembered with particular fondness a corrida of Miura bulls, when he was performing at the orders of Jaime Ostos. One animal was very dangerous, and Julio had trouble putting in the first pair of banderillas on the right horn, Luis González had even more trouble with the second, going in on the left. Julio hated to leave just one stick. "If I didn't place the complete pair, I did not go out of my hotel room!" and as the public held its collective breath in fear, he suddenly switched horns, drove the third pair in perfectly and walked slowly towards the fence, as the band began to play, something rarely done in banderillas ... and even less frequently in Seville! Another unforgettable afternoon was when he fought as a matador in the

Paris Velodrome with Ángel Luis Bienvenida and the great rejoneadora Conchita Cintrón. "I dedicated the first bull to the Aga Khan who was seated in barrera with his then wife, the beautiful actress Rita Hayworth. He invited me to a lavish party afterwards and I didn't hesitate to ask 'Gilda' to dance and to swirl her around the ballroom. They were a charming couple. That is the way I am, fun-loving and outgoing, and I hope I never change."

The veteran: Antonio Chaves Flores
Triana (Seville), 1929-2000. Ex-matador de toros and retired banderillero

Antonio Chaves Flores was born not just in Seville, but in its legendary Triana neighbourhood, a circumstance he believed was the height of good fortune. His father, Antonio Chaves Moreno, was a picador, as was his grandfather, Antonio Chaves Ramos, who was well loved in his native Seville. "My grandfather died during the great flood in Triana, in February 1942. He took out a small boat to save some people who had been trapped in their homes, and he also saved a cow from drowning. As he was rowing to safety, the cow got nervous and overturned the boat. My grandfather managed to help his neighbours to safety, but when he went back into the river to untie the cow and save her too, a big wave swallowed him up. When the waters finally receded, they found his body, dressed in the typical traje corto or country outfit, and all Seville attended his funeral."

Instead of following the family tradition and becoming a picador, Antonio wanted to become a matador de toros, and he made his début in the small town of Cantillana (Seville) on 9 September 1945. It was an uphill battle for him until a key afternoon in his career, 20 May 1950, when he performed in Las Ventas together with the two leading novilleros of the time: Miguel Báez Litri and Julio Aparicio. "I was in the patio de cuadrillas, all excited because this was my great opportunity, but nobody paid any attention to me. They fawned all over the other two, with photos and the like. I cut two ears on the first bull, Litri one on the second, and Aparicio none on the third. I dedicated the fourth to Juan Belmonte and cut another two ears and the three of us were carried out on the shoulders of the crowd. The famous critic Ricardo García K-Hito entitled his review 'Apareció El Tercer Hombre', which was clever, because they were showing Orson Welles's big hit The Third Man, in the cinemas. This led to a whole string of performances for the three of us, but the other two got all the money and I made just enough to pay my cuadrilla."

Such was the success of the trio that Antonio was able to take the alternativa in his native Seville on 30 September of that same year, from the

Portuguese matador Manolo Dos Santos, with the Spaniard Manuel Calero *Calerito* as witness and the rejoneador Duque de Pinohermoso kick-starting the afternoon. He cut both ears from his first four-year-old bull. "I was carried out on the shoulders of the crowd across the river to my home in Triana. It was an incredible experience, although as we crossed the bridge, they started to shout 'One, two, three', and I was afraid they would throw me into the river ... but they didn't!"

Chaves Flores confirmed his *alternativa* in Madrid on 14 May 1951 and performed as a matador for five years, but he complained: "People didn't believe in me. If I cut the ears, they said: 'What a great bull that was!' If the bull was not that great and I didn't cut the ears, it was: 'He just doesn't have what it takes!' I couldn't win".

He insisted that luck is a major factor in a bullfighter's career. "You can have talent but if you don't get lucky, there's nothing to be done. I wasn't tossed a lot by the bulls, but when I was, it meant a serious goring. The same was true for Antonio *Bienvenida* and *Litri*, but on the other hand when El Juli was beginning, he could be tossed in the air five times on the same afternoon and nothing happened. He would bounce back into action like a rubber ball."

After fighting 18 corridas in 1954, Chaves Flores went off to Mexico that winter with the idea of becoming a banderillero on his return. He was supposed to double for Anthony Quinn in the shooting of the bullfight film *The Magnificent Matador*, directed by Budd Boetticher, because the famous director thought he looked a little like the star, but production was delayed and Antonio had to return to Spain. Back in Seville, he still hesitated about his future, and fought a few more corridas, the last on 10 July 1955, when a prestigious *figura* offered him a place in his *cuadrilla*. "We 'signed' that promise with a handshake, but the matador—whose name I will not reveal—wasn't true to his word. Nevertheless, Gregorio Sánchez's manager took me on 'for one day', even though the matador had fifteen consecutive corridas lined up. At the end of that first corrida, he said, 'Pack your clothes for the next two weeks, you are now an official member of the *cuadrilla*'."

Chaves Flores always went with leading *figuras*: Gregorio Sánchez, Miguel Báez *Litri*, Antonio Borrero *Chamaco*, Miguel Mateo *Miguelín*, Juan García *Mondeño*, Sebastián Palomo Linares, Rafael de Paula, Luis Miguel Domínguín, Ángel Teruel, and of course, Santiago Martín *El Viti*. At that time, good *subalternos* were highly valued and they were able to set their own conditions and demands: if the official wages were 7,000 pesetas (£35.00), a skilled *peón* could demand more, just like a matador. Chaves Flores felt very special affection for Santiago Martín El Viti, for whom he worked for 17 years until

Antonio Chaves Flores in illustrious company, seated between Juan Belmonte and Rafael Gómez Ortega El Gallo ...

his retirement. "I thought of him like a son, even though I was only eleven years his senior. Of course, we had our arguments, which I, incidentally, always won! As I was older, I advised him about things both inside and outside the ring, and he always respected my opinion. It is important, especially for a torero, to have someone at his side who will always tell him the truth, instead of a dozen who are lavishing false praise on him. What is particularly important in the ring is understanding one another, with just a look. Santiago used to whisper to me under his breath: 'I get your message, Antonio'."

For Chaves Flores, his word was sacred. "I have only one word and I have to stand by it. Honest men do not sign a paper, they commit with a handshake, but a lot of not-so-good things have happened to me by doing that, so I am going to sign with a pen from now on! When *El Viti* asked me to join his *cuadrilla*, I told him what I expected to earn. I didn't know what the others were being paid, but I lived in Seville and I had to go to Madrid whenever we fought, so I had additional expenses." His matador had no objections, quite unlike today, where the "tunnel" obliges banderilleros to take what they can get ... or not fight at all.

Antonio Chaves Flores remembered the very first time he performed in El Viti's *cuadrilla* and their first "confrontation". "We began on Palm Sunday in Zaragoza, and when the bull I had to *lidiar* [one banderillero capes— lidia one bull—while another places two pairs of banderillas, and the *tercero* or third banderillero acts as a back-up, placing one pair on each bull, and is also in charge of the *puntilla* (dagger), to finish off the bull, which is a very important job]. I said: 'I'll test him first'; Santiago protested and I insisted. After giving the animal three or four trial passes, I said: 'He's all yours'. When I returned to the fence, El Viti asked me if I had no intention of obeying his orders, since he was the boss! I responded that I insisted on going out first for a very simple reason: 'The bull comes out of a dark *chiquero* [cell] and we don't know if it can see well or not. I prefer to go first and. if someone has to be hurt, it is better for it to be me, because while I am in the hospital, you are still *toreando* and you can keep paying me, but if you are in the hospital, so is the entire *cuadrilla*!' He stared at me for a moment and said: 'I suppose you're right!' On Easter Sunday, we fought in Barcelona, and out came the bull and Santiago asked me politely: 'Do you want to go out Antonio, or should I?' 'I will always go first,' I responded, and from then on we were always on the same wavelength."

Antonio had his own views or guidelines for *toreo*. "The *cuadrilla* should call the bull to three *burladeros* before the matador comes out. Why? Because the animal doesn't know how to charge properly and you have to teach him and guide him with the cape."

As for the banderillas, he said: "Julio Pérez El Vito taught me on a training cart, equipped with bull's horns; you have to hold the banderillas at eye-level, look straight at the bull, cite it and then run towards it until the point of encounter, and leave the sticks nailed high on the *morrillo*. I remember one afternoon when we were both in Litri's *cuadrilla* and Julio had to draw the lots in the *sorteo*, and we were stuck with this awful-looking bull that nobody wanted. The manager, *Camará*, reproached him: 'You had to pick that one, didn't you!' and El Vito replied without missing a beat: 'It was on the ranch with all the rest and you were the one who brought it to the ring. If you hadn't accepted it, I couldn't have drawn it out of the hat!' As it turned out, Litri cut two ears and triumphed with that monstrous-looking animal."

Antonio was proud that El Viti was the godfather of his son Antonio, and he told the following story. "The *apoderado* never paid me the extra money I asked for in front of my colleagues, but every so often he gave me a cheque to cover the additional amount. I remember one time we fought some twenty corridas in one month and I still hadn't been paid. One day, Santiago asked me how his godson was and I replied: 'He's a bright boy! I bought him a piggy bank to hold all the extra money you pay me for each corrida, and when I spoke to him the other day, do you know what he said? "Dad, you owe me twenty corridas!"' 'Did he say that, or did you?' said Santiago, and I answered, 'I taught him well, maestro!'"

... and with fellow retired banderilleros de lujo Manuel Carmona and El Vito

Chaves Flores was appointed director of the Escuela de Tauromaquia de Sevilla and enjoyed it very much "It made me feel alive again because I can't live without the bulls. I never tired of talking to the kids about *toreo* and trying to pass on to them everything I had learned. I argued with a bullfight critic in Seville about the effectiveness of the bullfighting schools. The son of a banker has the same right to be a bullfighter as the son of a torero, or he can sign up for tennis school as well. I was just sorry that there were no schools in my time. I learned the hard way, in the *capeas*, though I had fun when I went to the bull ranches, with my uncle *Faíco*. The cows rejected in the *tentaderos* were sent directly to the slaughterhouse and if one escaped, my uncle would say, 'Antonio, grab that blanket and lead it back on to the truck'; those were my very first *capotazos*. I learned to *descabellar* [sever the spinal cord at the base of the skull using the *descabello*] in the slaughterhouse, too. One day I found myself there with the son of the famous matador

Cagancho, who teased me by saying: 'Look, the son of a picador wants to be a matador!' I got angry and said that some day we would meet in the *ruedo* [arena] and I would show him! A year later we did, in Zaragoza, and when *Cagancho hijo* greeted me, I replied: 'Hi. It looks as though today you get to fight with the son of a picador!' And then I decided to torture him, adding: 'Did you see the size of the *novillos*? And the horns they have?' He started to tremble there and then, and I got further satisfaction by teaching him a lesson or two in the ring afterwards. Me, the son of a picador!"

Antonio insisted that bullfighting is in the head and the heart and when he heard a noted matador shout to his son, who was in the ring: "*¡Echa cojones!*" (Use your balls!), he thought: "What a stupid thing to say. The bull has much bigger ones! You have to use your head ... in the ring and outside it." His philosophy was the following: "You have to approach the bull with the cloth advanced in front of you and say: 'Hello. How are you? I'm pleased to meet you. How is your family?' And then send it off with a '*Vaya con Dios*'. You have to talk to it tenderly and if it does not respond to that tenderness, you'd better despatch it right away or it will get you. If you 'speak' to it like any animal—a dog, a cat, a horse—with love and gentleness, it becomes your friend. I remember a bull from the Chiquichongo ranch that El Viti had to fight in Lima. I had never seen an animal that big in my life! I turned to Santiago and said: "We can't *pelear* [fight] with this animal. You can't provoke a man much bigger than you; it is better to greet him cordially, right? We have to be pleasant to it and indulge it'. The other matadors had a hell of time with their animals, and when it was our turn, I went out and spoke to it softly: 'Come on, baby. How's the family?' I told it to behave nicely, especially at the moment of truth, and Santiago placed an excellent sword and cut two ears. I imagine the bull must have thought to itself: 'What a *sinvergüenza* [shameless person] and liar you are, Antonio! You talked nicely to me and then you killed me!' Ever since, Santiago would say to me '*Dále mimo*' 'Be nice to him'. *Manolete* had the same idea of not coercing or 'mistreating' the bull, and today *Jesulín de Ubrique* is one of the few *toreros* who understand this concept. That is why he can perform a *faena* with 70 per cent of the bulls. Enrique Ponce as well. Most of the other matadors start off with a few punishing or doubling passes, but then the bulls are worn out and stop charging. I am convinced that the bulls respond to mimo (pampering) and also to the ovations and the *olés*, even though they are animals."

He highlights the importance of the *capote* over the *muleta*, because it is the tool for teaching the bull to charge and is indeed more difficult to handle. "It's even important to hold it the right way. The younger *toreros* grab it as if they were going to grind it up or it was the handlebar on a motorcycle. You have to *torear* with your palms, as if you are going to shake the hand of an old friend. The youngsters are also using too much starch in their capes. I never fought with a brand-new cape. I preferred to give it to the third banderillero to use and soften it up, and then he would return it to me after three or four corridas. It is still called a silk *capote* nowadays, but it is more like a washboard. It has to be flexible so that you can flick it subtly at the bull. It is more important to the matador what you do with the cape and how you *lidiar*, than how you place the sticks, which is a striking and colourful *suerte* for the public and allows the banderillero to 'show off' a bit."

Antonio felt that the *cuadrilla* is a team whose motto should be: "All for one and one for all". "If the bull heads towards the picador '*que hace puerta*' [the one positioned at the gate, the reserve picador], why can't he pic it? Why is the *lidiador* obliged to give a whole series of cape passes to bring it to the other side of the ring? Everybody has to do their part to make sure that the team captain, the matador, triumphs, because if he scores a 'goal', we all win". For this reason, Antonio never understood the term *robapalmas* [applause-stealer]. "If someone pics the bull well and another places a good pair of sticks, it helps to warm up the public. The only problem is those who are too much of a 'show off'. In my time, only El *Vito* took off his *montera* to acknowledge an ovation, because he was the best!"

In addition to *El Viti,* Chaves Flores also admired Manuel Rodríguez *Manolete*, about whom he had a story. "I went on my bike to a *tentadero* on the Clemente Tassara ranch in 1946. When I arrived, Rafael Vega *Gitanillo de Triana* introduced me to *Manolete,* but I was so intimidated that I couldn't say a word. When the calf came out, much to my surprise, *Manolete,* waved me over and handed me his *muleta*. When I finished with the calf, I returned it to him and he said: 'Stay here with me'. Little by little, I ended up fighting almost all the animals. I finally asked him: 'Maestro, aren't you going to fight?' and he whispered in my ear: 'Chaves, we were out on the town last night and I am too tired to do anything. I just didn't want to disappoint the *ganadero* by not showing up'. I am convinced that I've been very lucky, because I've lived the best era of bullfighting."

The contemporary: Arcadio Ferrón *Curro Cruz*
Osuna (Seville), 1957. Banderillero

Curro Cruz was born Arcadio Ferrón, the fifth of three brothers and six sisters, and although the family were aficionados, he was the first to become a professional, something for which Manuel Benítez *El Cordobés* was indirectly responsible. "One day *El Cordobés* was appearing in a televised bullfight. At that time, the average worker's family didn't have a television in their home and you couldn't go into the local Casino—more like a social club for the wealthier people in the town—unless you were a member, but there was a television in the main bar of the pueblo. When there was a televised corrida, one of the waiters would stand at the door and charge everybody a peseta to come in, as if it were a cinema. I remember when El Cordobés fought, it got so crowded you had to bring your own chair!"

Arcadio Ferrón Curro Cruz

Arcadio Ferrón did not sound like a great name for a bullfighter, but how did he choose Curro Cruz? "I went to the town of Baños de la Encina, in Linares, where a lot of maletillas would gather during the winter in the hope of participating in the nearby tentaderos. A local matador, Paco Bautista, saw me fight and thought I had potential. We went to see the film Currito de la Cruz, starring Pepín Martín Vázquez, and Paco liked it so much, that I said if he would help me, I'd adopt the artistic name of Curro Cruz." Ferrón fought formally as a *novillero* for the first time at age 17 on 1 May 1974, in Villanueva del Arzobispo (Jaén) and, after appearing in 50 more *novilladas*, he made his début with picadors in Alcalá de Guadaira on 19 March 1976, fighting in another 70 or 80 *novilladas* with horses over the next three years. After his presentation in Las Ventas with El *Víctor* and Pedro Mariscal on 25 June 1978, he took the *alternativa* in Linares on 2 September 1979, with local matadors Paco Bautista and Lázaro Carmona as the "godfather" and "witness", respectively. "I fought well and placed good sticks, but I lost the trophies with the sword. I was able to fight some 30 corridas as a matador, including my confirmation in Madrid on 15 August 1981, with Gregorio Tebar El *Inclusero* and Justo Benítez, but things didn't go as well as I'd hoped. I fought my last corrida as a matador in Barcelona on 27 September 1987 with the French matador Christian Montcouquiol *Nimeño II* and José Antonio Carretero (also now a respected banderillero), and, because I had family responsibilities by then, I decided to become a banderillero right after that corrida; I made my début as a *subalterno* the following Sunday in the same ring, Barcelona. It was not as traumatic a decision as many people imagined, because I knew I had no choice. It was inevitable and I'd seen it coming."

Today, due to the influence of the Escuelas de Tauromaquia, many young boys skip the aspiring matador stage and go directly to performing as banderilleros because they become aware of their possibilities and limitations very quickly, whereas in past epochs, almost all the banderilleros were former matadors, older, wiser and with valuable experience to offer. On the other hand, nowadays, all the youthful efforts, dreams and ambitions that were previously poured futilely into becoming a top matador are channelled towards being a noteworthy banderillero. Nevertheless, *Curro* complains that there are too many banderilleros looking for work. "It's as if they are being mass-produced in the bullfighting schools. I'm afraid they might be saying to young boys right off the bat: 'You are not good enough to become a matador, it's better that you should be a banderillero'. This doesn't benefit the Fiesta, and in particular the banderilleros' union. That's why the 'tunnel' exists: too much supply and not enough demand. There are young boys, 20-odd years old, who are good banderilleros, without having 'waged the war' of wanting to be a matador and it's not fair to push them through the 'tunnel' and make them blacklegs. The young miners—another difficult profession—respect the rules and rights achieved by their elders in their union."

Luck is obviously an important factor in the bullfighting profession. *Curro Cruz* was able to convince his *paisano* (fellow Andaluz) José Fuentes to include him in the all-important Miura corrida organised annually on the anniversary of the death of Manolete in the same Linares ring. Matadors Espartaco and Roberto Domínguez were scheduled to perform with Fuentes that day, and Curro thought it could be a good springboard to make his qualities and valour known. It worked. "Things went well for me that afternoon, Roberto Domínguez noticed me and contracted me for the following seasons, 1988 and 1989, when he retired. I went to South America with Manolo Sánchez and came back with a position in the cuadrilla of César Rincón, another exceptional figura and a great person. And finally, I fought with José Ortega Cano from 1993 until his retirement."

Curro views the role of banderillero in the same way as Antonio Chaves Flores. "You have to do your job well, so that everything is served on a silver salver for the captain of the ship, the one with the muleta and the sword. If necessary, you have to sacrifice your own brilliance or success on behalf of the matador, as long as you don't damage your personal interests or professional dignity."

With a complicated bull, is it better to place just one banderilla or start over and try again? "It depends. The banderillero is supposed to place two each time he approaches the bull, but if it's not a good bull, particularly for the faena afterwards, you're not going to triumph and show off with a pair of sticks, because the public doesn't always realise that a bull might cooperate for the banderillas but not serve for the muleta. In this case, it would be better to proceed in a low key and the fewer capotazos the better, because that will mean more muletazos [passes with the muleta]. A good banderillero is one who does his job effectively: he should be 'seen and not seen', that is, seen by the professionals and the knowledgeable aficionados, but invisible to the masses in general." In other words, the best banderillero is the one who is hardly noticeable, does not take off his montera to saludar unless truly obliged to by the spectators and invited to do so by his matador, and is not a robapalmas. "The truth of the matter is that many matadors are a little resentful if someone steals the spotlight. Although you have your professional dignity on one hand, you must respect your matador and his wishes. It makes no sense to risk your life unnecessarily on a bad bull, but you should not toss one stick at the animal in passing either, if you can avoid it."

Curro Cruz feels that nowadays the banderillero is paid fairly well, especially if he has the good fortune of working with a figura del toreo, but the profession also generates heavy expenses in terms of wardrobe, capes and other expenditure. "Some banderilleros can get by with two suits a season, which are very expensive, but a banderillero who fights with a figura must be well-dressed and needs at least a new suit for Seville and one for Madrid."

And then he adds with a touch of humour: "In Pamplona, rather than a new suit, what you need is a new carburettor, in order to deal with the monster bulls that are fought there".

Apropos Juan Belmonte's dictum that "You fight the way you are", what is *Curro Cruz* like? "I try to express as a torero what I feel inside: I am sentimental, sensitive, carefree, hopelessly bohemian and a spendthrift, and totally in love with my profession. I try to accept myself as I am, with my many defects and my few virtues." He laments some of the changes which have taken place in the Fiesta. "There used to be more romanticism and people really lived the corrida to the fullest. The *cuadrilla* should be like a close-knit family, because you spend eight months together, risking your lives on a daily basis. I knew a matador who would be dashing out of the hotel just as his banderilleros were returning from the plaza. On the other hand, Ortega Cano liked to dine with his *cuadrilla* and go over the details and events of the day."

An unforgettable afternoon? "My presentation as a matador in Barcelona on September 9, 1979. Had I killed the bull well that day, I might have cut the ears and tail ... and my destiny would have been different. You could have been interviewing me as a matador and not as a banderillero. Nevertheless, when I look back, it doesn't upset me, because I am still a torero!"

The Picador

Title VI, Chapter II of the current *Reglamento Taurino* lays down the obligations of the picador in the first of the three acts of the lidia. The professional who is going to pic the bull should place his horse opposite the *chiqueros* (the bullpens, whence the bull will enter the ring). The bull will be placed by a torero on the edge of the two concentric circles traced on the sand nearer the centre of the ring, while the picador's horse should not cross the outer circle, leaving a kind of "no man's land" in between, in which the bull is supposed to display its bravery by charging the horse. It is strictly prohibited to *barrenar* or "drill" or twist around the *puya* (the sharp point at the end of the lance), to perform the "*carioca*" by swivelling to block the animal's natural exit from the horse, or to continue picing the bull if the *puya* is poorly placed. Although traditionally the first *tercio* or act called for three pics—*puyazos*—nowadays in all but first-category rings, the matador can request a change of *tercio* after just the first *puyazo*, while in the first-category rings, at least two *puyazos* are obligatory. During the *suerte de varas*, all of the participants in the *lidia* must remain to the picador's left once the bull is in position.

The veteran: Domingo Rodríguez Rubio de Quismondo
Quismondo (Toledo), 1930-2016. Picador

Oddly enough, Domingo Rodríguez's only relationship to the bull world was initially that of having been born in the same town as legendary matador Luis Miguel *Dominguín,* and yet he has gone down in history as one of the greatest picadors of all times. "I became a picador, but I could just as well have decided to be a bishop! The early fifties were rough times in Spain and I supported my parents by setting out traps to catch rabbits. An epidemic of myxomatosis put an abrupt end to my little business, and the opportunity arose for me to become a picador, without my knowing what a horse, a *puya* or even a bull was. However, to be honest, I did want a little more excitement in my life; I never liked to go to bed at night knowing exactly what I was going to do the next day."

Although Domingo was a country boy at heart, he moved to Madrid in search of work and found it in a plant and seed store, where, after two months, he became the manager in charge of ten employees. He spent his Saturdays and Sundays in the Vista Alegre bullring—torn down in the 1980s and replaced with a modern, indoor structure and a major department store on ground level—which belonged to Luis Miguel *Dominguín* and his brothers. That is where Domingo began to learn about bullfighting, while cleaning the stables and taking care of the horses, putting on their *petos* and other trappings, and warming them up. It was also in the old Vista Alegre ring that he became a reserve picador. He made his formal début on 25 August 1957 in Valencia de Alcántara, in a *novillada* with Paquito Martín, Vicente Ortega and the Ecuadorian Manuel Cadenas Torres, who later became the impresario of the Quito bullring. "I did well that day and although my salary was 630 pesetas [£3.50], they paid me 700 [£4.00]!"

He began to fight much more often from 1959 onwards, mainly with Andrés Hernando, Ángel Teruel, *Dominguín* and finally Francisco Ruiz Miguel. While Hernando was very classic and brave, Teruel, for whom he worked between 1968 and 1971, was not only skilled but also highly artistic. Domingo signed on with Luis Miguel during the latter's comeback, from 1971 to 1974. "He was an exceptional, very straightforward man and a brilliant torero. He appeared rather haughty and I think that helped him to achieve his legendary status. He was an extraordinarily gifted matador." His last matador was Francisco "Paco" Ruiz Miguel, with whom he worked from 1974 until the matador's retirement in 1991. "Paco is extraordinary and very sensitive, but also extremely nervous and temperamental. In the ring, he might shout at you, but then come, give you a big hug and apologise."

Domingo fought his last corrida on 28 September 1991 in Seville, in the Feria de San Miguel. He was 61 years old but still in top form. Ruiz Miguel, had just retired, and Domingo was undecided about his future. "One day in December, at 7 o'clock in the afternoon, I was taken on as a member of the *cuadrilla* of Vicente Ruiz El Soro, from Valencia, and at 7.05 I was retired! I finally made up my mind when I was given an ultimatum: Retire or move out! I was at home in Quismondo when the phone rang. I picked it up and so did my daughter in another room. It was El Soro's brother calling to offer me a position in the *cuadrilla*. My daughter heard the conversation, ran to tell her mother and they both got so angry that I had to phone back and say 'No'. It wasn't easy to turn down an offer to fight 80 *corridas de toros* in the 'Special' Group, which would have meant 8 or 10 million pesetas [£40-50,000]! I fought one more *festival* with Ruiz Miguel in Barco de Ávila on 3 October and that was my last appearance ... and his," until Paco made one of his multiple returns to the ring!

He was in enviable physical form at 86 years old. "I've been very orderly and methodical, a sparse eater and an even sparser drinker. I've always led a healthy life and my only luxury was having a couple of sherries every day with my friends (the painter José Puente and taurine journalist Gonzalo Ángel Luque del Pino *Curro Fetén*, both deceased) and I don't even have a glass of wine with lunch. I am also lucky because I don't gain weight and the proof is that the *traje corto* that a tailor made for me in 1961, still fitted me for the last *festival* I fought in 1991. I don't have a lot of wrinkles on my face either. My secret? Just plain tap water. I suppose it's genetic."

There must be a big difference between going with a torero who faces the so-called *corridas duras* ("tough" corridas) or with a *figura* who fights the more "comfortable" animals. "Everybody wants to be with the top matador and there is no doubt that fighting with Enrique Ponce, José Tomás or Sebastián Castella is not the same as with El Fundi or Pepín Liria for many reasons. First of all, the bulls and the *carteles* [the combination of matadors] are different, although, needless to say, I respect everyone! Anyone who has sufficient valour and dignity to put on a suit of lights gets 'chapeau' from me!" But is it more difficult to pic a Victorino or a Miura than a Jandilla, a more "commercial" bull? "Unfortunately, the bulls have changed a lot in general. Before, you had to be able to pic a bull three or four times and the picador who couldn't do that was looking for a new job very soon. Regrettably, nowadays just about anybody who knows how to stay on a horse can be a picador, because the bulls are not as powerful and complicated as they used to be. In my time, there were days when the bull needed three pics ... and the animal would 'swallow up' half a metre of the pole. I remember a *festival* in

Valencia in 1959—not a corrida, just a *festival*—in which I fought with Roberto Antolín El Millonario and Rafael Atienza, another great picador, with Julio Aparicio *padre*. The *novillada* weighed an average of 230 kilos *en canal*—just the carcass! Rafael Atienza was thrown off his horse five or six times and the bull jumped into the *callejón* another four or five. I whispered to Aparicio that I thought the bull had not been piced enough so he told me to give it a try. The bull was so furious that it broke my pole and remained with the *puya* in its *morrillo*. Aparicio had a hell of a time with that animal and years later, when we met in Arnedo, he told me: 'Rubio, don't remind me about that nightmare *festival* ever again!'"

Rubio de Quismondo in *Las Ventas*

If Ruiz Miguel is well known for having fought almost the entire herds of Miura and Victorino, *Rubio de Quismondo* had obviously piced them all. "I calculate that I have piced about 2,000 bulls in my professional career and the percentage of Miuras and Victorinos and the like was very high. I'm counting not only my time with Paco, but also the five years I spent with Andrés Hernando, who also fought a lot of Victorinos, the strain called Albaserrada at the time." Did he sleep well the night before he had to face a corrida from Miura or Victorino? "I adapted to my profession very well and never lost any sleep over it. I wasn't concerned about what would happen to me but I was nervous about my responsibility to the public, for whom I had a great deal of respect. I worried much more about not doing a good job, before a paying public, than being thrown off my horse or being hurt." In fact, *Rubio de Quismondo* suffered only one serious injury in his entire career, aside from the typical bumps and bruises.

We have seen that today there is a custom of forcing *subalternos* to "go through the tunnel" and collect wages lower than those specified by the unions, but the opposite happened in Domingo's time, when the truly good professionals received a bonus. "The day I fought for the first time with Tinín, the official salary was 2,500 pesetas [£12.50] and I got paid 3,000 [£15.00]. It was always like that; the reason things have made a 180-degree turn is because just about anybody can pic or place banderillas on today's animals."

Domingo believed the picador to be absolutely necessary for the satisfactory evolution of the Fiesta. "The picador's work is vital for the matador as well as for the bull. An animal that has not been piced does not bleed and thus runs the risk of suffering a stroke. If not piced properly, it would charge helter-skelter and not follow the cloth, making it impossible for the matador to create an artistic *faena*. We see this all the time in the *novilladas* without picadors." He explained how the picing should be done. "You have to pic the bull high on the neck muscle, between the shoulder blades, and, in order to execute the *suerte* effectively and with its own inherent beauty, it is necessary to place the bull in front of the horse, not behind it, so that it charges the picador head on, as you spur the horse forward. When the bull initiates its charge, you have to turn the horse with your left hand to receive the bull at the right stirrup, because if he charges at the horse's chest, you will almost surely be knocked over. The bull must be made to bleed in order to avoid congestion, just as we used to slit the ears of the mules on the farm. We picadors are often unjustly blamed for the weakness of the bulls, but that is absurd, because we often see the animals fall down before the horses even enter the ring. So, in order to do things well, many factors must come into play: the bull has to charge straight on, the picador has to have sufficient courage to hold the pole in the air until the animal approaches and then toss the *puya* forward. If he holds the pole in a firm, fixed position, there is no beauty in the *suerte*. To be a good picador, you have to possess three fundamental attributes: to be brave, be thoroughly familiar with the fundamentals of the profession and know how to ride a horse!"

He complained that the majority of the public know little or nothing about the bullfight, especially in the major ferias, where many attend "just to show off and be seen". He particularly liked to perform in Seville, because they will applaud a good *suerte de varas*: "In fact, I have been lucky enough to have heard them play music in my honour, when I performed with Ruiz Miguel in a very dangerous Portuguese corrida of Palha bulls on 7 April 1989."

Picador Ramón Bejarano El Avispa and a monosabio assemble the lance

Rubio was very proud to have been a picador in his epoch because things were different. "Your work was appreciated because the bull was fierce and powerful. In my time, the matador would come over and whisper to you: 'Pic the bull well', while now they say: 'Be careful and don't punish it too much'. And that's why the *subalternos* are not as highly valued as they were in my time, a situation which led to the 'tunnel'."

Domingo also insisted that the life of a torero was different in the past. "Throughout my entire career, I belonged to only four *cuadrillas*, which shows that we all got along well with one another. We were like one big, happy family and the matadors took care to employ someone who was not only a good professional in the ring but a good person outside it."

Contrary to what many people may think, the picador is not usually a rough and tough individual, a rugged person with coarse manners. "It's not that we have more class and education, but we have a different concept of life. Perhaps we are not bitter or conceited, because many of the *subalternos* are frustrated matadors who never made it to the top, while we have only ever wanted to be picadors."

Something Domingo did not miss from his "picador days" was the long and uncomfortable trips in the car of the *cuadrilla*. "They were intolerable because, except for the top four *figuras* who had their own car, we all had to pile into the old Packards: the matador, the three banderilleros, the two picadors, the *apoderado* and the sword-handler. The roads were treacherous and a trip from Pontevedra [in the north] to Algeciras [in the south] was a nightmare. Your body was tense 24 hours a day: in the ring and during the trip, and when the corrida was over, if they said you had to do another 800 km back up to Santander, you just wanted to die! Today you can drive from Madrid to Barcelona in five and a half hours but then it took fourteen! All you wanted to do was get out of the car and find a decent chair to sit in and have a cup of coffee. Today's vans are comfortable, each passenger with his own reclining seat, but in those old cars, three of us squeezed into the front, three in the fold-down middle seats and three in the back as best we could."

Domingo was very active in the Asociación Benéfica de Toreros, founded by Ricardo Torres *Bombita* in 1909. One of its great accomplishments was the creation of the *Sanatorio de Toreros*. "It's a pity we lost the Bullfighters' Hospital. It was a luxury, and with only 17 rooms, it resembled a five-star hotel more than a hospital. The best specialists in general surgery, urology, traumatology, etc., attended the patients, who could certainly not complain about the food. They would be asked each day if they felt like eating meat or fish, and then they would get a sirloin steak or fresh hake. And, of course, the buoyant, positive taurine ambience was ideal for the toreros to recover quickly from their injuries and regain their morale."

Rubio de Quismondo led a much calmer life after retirement. "I get up when I feel like it, have a drink downtown with some friends, come home for lunch and after a siesta I go for a stroll with my wife. I want to take very good care of myself, because my motto is: 'The day I die, I will have lost my best friend!'"

Domingo Rodríguez finally lost his "best friend" in August 2016, at the age of 86.

The contemporary: Luis Antonio Vallejo Pimpi
Madrid, 1969-2010. Picador

It is not surprising that Luis Antonio Vallejo became involved in the bullfighting world, as he belonged to a family in which four generations had been related to the bullring in general and the raising and renting of the picadors' horses in particular. "Our taurine origins date back to Basilio Barajas, who was my great-grand-uncle, the brother of my father's grandfather, and my grandmother's father was a picador, who performed during the era when there was no *peto* [protective covering for the horse]."

Luis Antonio Vallejo Pimpi

Basilio Barajas Sánchez (1881-1964) had an interesting background, because he began as a carpenter in the old calle Felipe II bullring and progressed to working as a *monosabio* (horse-servant), who received a grateful hug from the great Joselito El Gallo, for having made an opportune, valiant *quite* to save a fallen picador. Then he himself became a picador and finally a rejoneador, one of a small number to graduate from picador to rejoneador, and according to José María de Cossío in his encyclopædic *Los Toros*, he displayed a capable, although not very elegant style. Basilio's brother, Fausto (1902-1934), also began as a *monosabio*, then went on to become a *becerrista* and *novillero*, taking the *alternativa* in Linares from the legendary Ignacio Sánchez Mejías, with Marcial and Pablo Lalanda as witnesses, on 30 August 1920. He died tragically, shortly after retirement, in 1934 when his car was hit by a train.

The youngest of the professionals of the *Pimpi* saga, Luis Antonio, was very proud of his family history. He inherited this curious sobriquet from his grandfather, Luis Vallejo Barajas, Basilio's nephew, a famous picador who performed with *Manolete*, Pedro Martínez *Pedrés* and Antonio Bienvenida. He was tall and handsome, known in his family as a "*príncipe*" [prince], a word his baby sister could not pronounce, so that it stuck as 'Pimpi', in a world with a great penchant for nicknames.

Luis Antonio could not wait for the school day to be over so that he could run down to the bullring stables to warm up the horses. In fact, he never finished secondary school and had been riding since the age of seven. He actually broke with family tradition in that his first ambition was to be a matador instead of a picador, and he signed up at the Escuela Taurina de Madrid, where he had the opportunity to *torear* for the first time aged 14. He continued struggling until the end of the 1992 season, when he decided to become a picador. "I was a little like the black sheep of the family in opting for fighting on foot instead of on horseback, but I was still 'in the business', so to speak. My mother had a hard
time for a while, with two of us in the ring: me, *toreando* as a novillero, and my father, as a picador. Fortunately, my brother and sister did not feel the same inclination for the bulls as I did. In the end, I realised that I was a torero with sufficient courage but not enough art or class, and the courage starts to dissipate with all the tossings and gorings and lack of a promising future." He finally made his début as a picador in Madrid with the Mexican matador Mariano Ramos in the Feria de San Isidro of 1993. "I prepared for the change in profession by going with my father to a lot of ranches and *tentaderos*. He helped me open some doors, but then I had the great responsibility of living up to the family name. It showed great

audacity on my part to appear in Madrid during my first year as a professional, but fortunately I performed well."

Before the *Reglamento Taurino* of 1996, every first-class bullring was required to have two reserve picadors in case one was hurt and taken to the infirmary, when the reserve would replace him, and that was how a novice picador learned the trade. In *Pimpi*'s grandfather's time—he fought with *Manolete*—the reserve picador always went out to give the first *puyazo*. Under the new *Reglamento*, which eliminated the reserves, the most junior of the other picadors presently fills in and the same occurs when a banderillero is injured.

Unfortunately, the *suerte de varas* is the aspect of the corrida which is least understood by the majority of the public. "I hate to be looked upon as the 'bad guy' in the show", said Vallejo, "especially since the *suerte de picar*, if done well, can be beautiful and exciting. Sadly, with today's bulls it's not always easy to execute the *suerte* properly; that is, the bull should be left at a distance for the first pic, and then further away for the second, so that you can *torear* with the horse. In the past, three and even four *puyazos* were necessary. However, today's bull will usually take only one or two *puyazos*, and so the picador has to try to *ahormar* or mould the bull in that first *puyazo* because he might not get another chance."

Pimpi laid out ground rules for the correct execution of the *suerte de varas*. "The bull must charge from beyond the inner circle, and if it is brave it will push strongly against the horse with both horns; if it uses just one horn, it is a sign of *mansedumbre* [cowardice], as it is looking to escape. Spectators often think that the picador is trying to block the bull's exit in order to continue picing it, but if the bull is pushing you to one side, you have to reaffirm your position in that direction. When the bull is charging with both horns, the matador should remove the bull and relocate it a few metres farther away, and if it gallops towards the horse again, it can be considered brave. You cite the bull from the horse's chest and then swing your mount to the left so that the bull charges the right stirrup. The pic should be placed between the shoulder blades because this is where the least damage is done and you cannot hit the spinal cord. If the animal doesn't lower its head or extend its neck, you have to pic it a bit forward of the *morrillo*. The picador should grasp the pole more or less in the middle and as the animal charges, toss it forward until the butt end is at his armpit and then, when the steel tip is in place on the *morrillo*, let the impetus of the bull's charge propel the pole through his grip to chest level.

He described the picador's role as follows. "We follow the matador's instructions, in order to temper the bull and have it lose some of its aggressiveness and violent charge. In other words, our job is to mould and accommodate the animal so that the matador can cut the ears."

When a bull charges the back-up picador, who is "*haciendo puerta*", the banderilleros insist on giving a whole series of cape passes to lead it back over to the original picador. "The true professionals don't like to do this, but the authorities and police delegates demand that the bull be piced opposite *toriles* [the gate through which it comes into the ring]. This is ridiculous, because if a bull is *manso* [cowardly or tame], the fewer the cape passes you give it, the better, as long as it is piced. We're all anxious to do our job well, and I for one would be annoyed if I didn't get to pic at least one bull in each corrida. I enjoy my work and it is my greatest passion in life."

Luis Antonio maintained that the *cuadrilla* must work as a tight, closely coordinated team. "We are a small group at the service of one person, the matador, and we have to respect his orders, because he is the one who really puts his life on the line. We must do everything we can to contribute to his success, because if he triumphs, we all triumph. Now, unfortunately, I get the feeling that it is the authorities who give the orders, and if they consider that you pic too much, or go beyond the bounds, or block the bull's exit, they report you and you have to pay a heavy fine. They don't know what it is like to try and manage a 500-kilo animal that is plugging into your horse."

He did not think it necessary to modify the *Reglamento Taurino* vis-à-vis the *suerte de varas*. "If the bulls came out of the *toriles* with more bravery, *casta* and mobility, there would not be any problems. I am not referring to bigger animals, or more kilos, or longer horns, merely more *casta* and bravery. In *Manolete*'s era, my father used a *puya* without a crossbar, which meant a good part of the pole penetrated into the *morrillo*, but the bulls didn't fall down. We're deceiving ourselves if we think we need less *puya*, a lightweight horse or a shorter *peto*; what we need is a stronger bull, with more bravery, *casta* and willingness to charge, so that the matador can give forty *muleta* passes instead of just twenty. If the main protagonist of the Fiesta, the bull, does not satisfy a series of basic conditions, then it is impossible for the professionals to do their job well; the picadors won't be able to pic properly, the banderilleros place the sticks, or the matador fight with art and success."

Vallejo loved horses and spent about five hours a day riding, but he never considered becoming a rejoneador, for the simple reason that he could not bear to expose his horses to any danger. He felt confident that the picador's horses are well protected, and explained that each picador prefers a certain type of horse. "I like one that I can move about easily and manipulate, rather than the common Percheron which was used some time ago, because it is like the bull butting a stone wall. It is easier to pic that way, but not better."

On the day of the corrida, three horses are offered to the picadors, who choose their mounts according to the order of seniority: the most experienced chooses a horse for himself and his colleague in the *cuadrilla*, then the next one does the same, and the third horse is left for the last *cuadrilla*. In some plazas, three bulls are piced with one horse and three with another. The same procedure is followed with the *puyas*, which are also selected according to seniority, out of respect.

The *monosabios* prepare and saddle the horses, put on the *petos*, and then warm them up. The picadors arrive half an hour before the beginning of the corrida in order to assemble their *puyas* and *garrochas* (metal points and wooden poles, which together form the *varas*), except in Las Ventas, where it is done in the morning after the *apartado* and the *varas* are then locked in a room set aside for this purpose.

According to *Pimpi*, a good picador knows a horse after mounting him for just a couple of minutes. "They're like people, with their good days and bad days, and their aches and pains, and so if they react strangely, you have to be able to resolve the problem in a matter of seconds, and that is why you need to be a good horseman."

Vallejo complained that the bullfighting schools do not worry about training picadors. "Picadors used to come from the ranches and were often the sons of *mayorales* or *vaqueros*, but now just anybody decides to become a picador. I hate the *domingueros* ["Sunday picadors"], who are plumbers or taxi-drivers during the week, and are just interested in making some extra money at the weekend. This is a serious profession and the fact that anybody can get away with being a picador is due to the lack of bravery, *casta* and strength of today's bulls. If the bulls were to charge with greater force, a lot of picadors and banderilleros would be applying for their retirement pension, and I say this with all due respect. If your horse is knocked to the ground, that is all part of the deal; that is why we became picadors."

Pimpi would have preferred to live in the epoch when his grandfather was about to retire and his father was just beginning his career. "There was more respect towards toreros in general, not just the matadors. It is terrible for a matador to be risking his life and focussing his five senses on a difficult bull and to hear someone shouting down from the stands. '¡Hijo de puta! ¡Arrímate! [Son of a bitch! Get closer!]' Just because someone purchases a ticket doesn't mean he has the right to insult the torero. In other spectacles, if you don't like what you see, you get up and leave."

What did he think about Pamplona? "I have good memories of the *sanfermines*, and I have earned a trophy there for the best *puyazo*. It's a strange fair in that half the public goes to the plaza to have a good time, while the other half is very attentive to what's going on in the ring. It used to be a lot worse, because before, we had to make a full lap of the ring to return to the *patio de caballos* and the rowdy crowd in the sunny section would throw everything imaginable at us: bread, food, cushions … In my grandfather's time, the picadors were like gods and in the 18th and 19th centuries, their names took top billing on the *carteles* [posters]."

Luis Antonio complained that bullfighters no longer have that panache and class which they had before. He remembered something the noted matador Agustín Parra *padre* told him when he managed his career as a *novillero*: "Whenever you are going to *torear*, think about your hand". "He said your hand has five fingers and if you cut just one of them it hurts. Those are the members of your *cuadrilla*, your *gente*: your two picadors and your three banderilleros. They are very important to you because they can help you to triumph and make you rich and famous, although they will always be 'at your service'. When I was a *novillero*, I always treated my *cuadrilla* with maximum respect, like the great professionals they were. This regrettably is not always the case. The important thing is to get together at the end of the corrida and discuss the details and if you have to tell someone he did something wrong, including the matador, you discuss it openly, like one big, close-knit family." Curiously enough, the matador and his banderilleros often make up one group and the picadors another. "We always have separate rooms in the hotel and go to the ring separately. The matador and the banderilleros can train together and go to the *sorteo*, but we picadors usually do not. I train like a matador, go jogging and play handball and tennis, and I like to go to the *apartado* to see the bull I have to pic, its size, its build, if it has a long or short neck, the *morrillo*, etc."

Pimpi was not superstitious, but he admitted to a small obsession. "When I come back from the *apartado*, I like to apply some fresh paint to my *pata* [metal leg protection] and cover any scratches or dents from the last corrida, because I want to look spiffy in the ring."

Many years ago, it was not unusual for a strong bull to toss a picador into the *callejón* [the passageway between the *barrera* and the public]. "That's when you can boast of being a true professional! One day I was *toreando* a corrida from Miura with Juan Carlos García, and a nasty *sobrero* [substitute bull] from Mercedes Pérez Tabernero lifted me and my horse up and was about to toss us both into the *callejón*! It's no joke, because you pay a high price in broken bones. I fell into the *callejón* and my horse remained rocking back and forth on the *barrera* for what seemed like an eternity. He finally fell back onto the sand and we were both all right. Had he fallen into the *callejón*, on top of me, I wouldn't be relating my experiences to you right now."

The bullfighting world was shocked when the corpse of Luis Antonio Vallejo *Pimpi* was found after an apparent suicide in Salamanca in September 2010, following a severe bout of depression.

The Comic Bullfighter: Manuel Pérez Luque El Chino Torero
Granada, 1934-2002. Comic bullfighter

No book on bullfighting would be complete without its chapter on comic bullfighting, which is also quite serious, just as no book on the history of cinema would be complete without a section on Charlie Chaplin or Buster Keaton. Manuel Pérez Luque had enough tales, stories and experiences to fill a book by himself. He was born in Granada, in the Plaza de San Nicolás, where, he stated proudly, "President Clinton was inspired to exclaim on his first official visit to Spain: 'Everyone should come here at some time in their life to contemplate a sunset in Granada'".

El Chino Torero *in a small-town bullring*

With no taurine ancestors, Pérez Luque decided to become a bullfighter at the early age of 11, beginning his difficult apprenticeship in the *capeas*. "I traipsed through all of Andalusia as a *maletilla* and managed to fight 13 *novilladas* without picadors, and then I thought it was time to head north to Barcelona in search of an opportunity. I threw myself into the Barcelona ring as an *espontáneo* [a member of the crowd who attempts to fight the bull] 13 times, and it got to the point where the police grabbed me as soon as I walked into the plaza and made me sit between them, just to make sure I didn't do it again."

As his career as a *novillero* did not progress, he decided to become a banderillero and fought with local beginners such as Mario Cabré, Antonio

Losada and Joaquín Bernadó. According to José María de Cossío, Manuel was a good banderillero. "In all modesty, I must say I wasn't bad, although I was only able to place the banderillas on one side."

His claim to fame, nevertheless, was as *El Chino Torero* (The Chinese Bullfighter) and it all came about quite by accident, as do so many things in life. "I went with Joaquín Bernadó to see a friend of ours perform in the serious part of the comic taurine spectacle, but it turned out that the comic torero did not show up, so they insisted on dressing me up as a woman. I had to dance in the middle of the ring and everybody roared with laughter. Word spread back to Barcelona and my colleagues called me a *torero cómico*, which made me furious because I still considered myself a 'serious' banderillero. The impresario José López Valle finally persuaded me that I could earn a lot of money as a comic, so I joined the troupe. I have been a *torero cómico* since 1955 ... and I'm proud of it!"

Pérez Luque claimed that you cannot learn to be a *torero cómico*, you have to be born one. "First of all you have to know how to *torear*, to fully understand the basic principles of *toreo*, and then be funny and have the ability to make people laugh." He explained the origin of his unusual name *El Chino Torero*. "I worked as a kid in the boiler room of a Barcelona theatre, and sometimes got to appear as an extra on stage, dressed up as a clown. There was a very funny Mexican comedian, *El Chino Herrera*, disguised as a Chinaman, who sang an Oriental-sounding song. I admired him so much, although I was too shy to speak to him, that I adopted a version of his nickname."

Manolo made a lot of friends in the bullfight and flamenco world in Barcelona. One of his closest friends was the famous flamenco singer Antonio Molina, and Manolo was the godfather of the *cantaor*'s daughter, the highly talented actress Ángela Molina. The godfather of Manolo's own daughter was the crooner Manolo Escobar. He was also a close friend of Granada-born poet Manuel Benítez Carrasco, exiled in Mexico after the Spanish civil war, and such noteworthy flamenco singers as Pepe Blanco, *El Príncipe Gitano*, Manolo El Malagueño, Emilio El Moro and Pepe Marchena. He created a *Toros y Flamenco* show with the last of these, which was a brief but highly successful venture until a bull broke Manolo's leg in several places, putting an abrupt end to their hitherto profitable season of contracts.

El Chino Torero filled all the bullrings where he fought because he paid close attention to every detail. "There were times when I had an exceptional band, a wagonload of horses and forty Disney characters, and I needed two buses to accommodate everyone. I dressed my people at the best bullfight and theatrical tailors, and we travelled not only throughout Spain and South

America, but also to non-taurine places such as Italy and Israel. We fought some 120 corridas a year. Nevertheless, putting on a quality production cost me a lot of money and my financial partner complained a lot, but we had the immense satisfaction of seeing how much the public of all ages enjoyed our show. I look at other spectacles now and I get angry. A little paint on the face doesn't make a taurine clown! And five lousy musicians don't make a band like the one I hired. I fail to understand why we do not progress with the passing of time, rather than degrade what is a potentially delightful spectacle."

The spectacle included the lidia and killing of four becerros [two-year-old calves] in big cities, and three in the smaller towns; the serious part, eagerly awaited by both children and adults, played a major role, because it was the "cradle" of future toreros. It provided valuable opportunities for aspiring young toreros to torear, without costing them any money. Such important toreros as Juan Antonio Ruiz Espartaco, José Ortega Cano, Dámaso González, Vicente Ruiz El Soro, Juan Cubero, his brother José Cubero Yiyo, Raúl Galindo, Javier Vázquez, José Nelo Morenito de Maracay and torera Maribel Atiénzar acquired their first professional experience with El Chino. "I am proud of having launched many successful future matadors, because I always hired two novilleros, one to fight the bull and the other as a sobresaliente, and they took turns performing. I even gave the famous rejoneador Manolo Vidrié his start. He would put on his traje corto at 12 noon and ride through the town with the big brass band marching behind him. It was a major investment for me because I had to have a special lorry for his horses, but even though Vidrié earned good money as a stuntman in the movies in winter, performing for me gave him the opportunity to practice rejoneo and train his horses for the season. I also discovered the Portuguese child star rejoneador João Moura when he was just 14 years old."

When he created his spectacle El Chino Torero y los Siete Enanitos (The Chinese Bullfighter and the Seven Dwarves), Manolo took on yet another challenge: finding seven dwarves who were capable of facing a brave novillo. "I taught them to torear with style and art and those who didn't have sufficient courage to face the becerros learned to dance sevillanas in their own inimitable, funny style. Imagine their merit: the calf must have seemed like a mammoth six-year-old Conde de la Corte bull to them, and I must say that some of my enanos really had the soul of a torero."

People thought Manolo had really gone crazy when he came up with the bright idea of teaching the dwarves to rejonear. "Well, not only did they not fall out of the saddles, but they proved to be great horsemen and placed the sticks fantastically well, particularly one especially 'short' rejoneador called

Fernando Martínez Cobo. Believe me, there are a lot of 'full-sized' rejoneadors who are a lot worse than he was!"

Pérez Luques's "enanitos", complete with Portuguese-style rejoneador, take a lap of the ring before a capacity crowd

El *Chino Torero* lamented the fact that the comic taurine spectacle is no longer what it once was. "It used to be extremely popular, and the rings were filled for such extraordinary comic bullfighters as Pablo Celís *El Bombero Torero* [The Bullfighter Fireman], Francisco Rodríguez Arévalo, Angel Villaverde Villasarte *Canuto* and Juan Losillo Micó *Laurelito*. But when we all retired, no young people appeared to take our place, perhaps because it's a lot more difficult than it may appear."

Could it be too that the tastes of children are changing with television, video games and the internet absorbing their free time? "There is no doubt that children are a lot brighter nowadays, but their parents enjoyed our nonsensical behaviour, too. Besides, it is not easy to fool a child, they know what they are seeing, they applaud only what is good and they laugh only at things that are funny. If a child sees a clown with a white face and a big red nose, and then that clown takes out a cigarette to smoke, they get angry and rightly so. I suffered a lot of injuries, but I always tried to make sure the kids never saw any blood so as not to frighten them."

Now, the *Reglamento Taurino* prohibits the killing of *becerros* in *charlotadas* (comic bullfights, named after Charlie Chaplin, *Charlot* in Spain), something that Manolo does not understand. "Sometimes I would use the trick of the *metisaca* [slipping the sword in and pulling it out again immediately] to kill the animals, and I did it in a funny way, so that the children were never upset. The biggest problem with not killing the animal is how to get it back to the corrals. We would receive a serious beating trying to grab a hold of it and lead it out of the ring."

Even though Pérez Luque enjoyed making children laugh and never regretted putting on a red nose and a funny hat to fight the bulls, he did not escape his serious injuries. "I have broken practically all the bones in my body and every rib several times."

Even after retirement, Manuel Pérez Luque continued to feel like a *payaso* (clown) inside, and was one of the founders of the Club de Payasos y Artistas de Cine. He was also the only *torero cómico* to appear in serious *festivales*, to be awarded Spain's *Medalla de Mérito de Trabajo*, a national distinction for meritorious work, and to have a special *festival* celebrated in his honour in the Leganés bullring in 1998, in which many of the toreros who got their start in his spectacle participated: *Antoñete*, Ortega Cano, Pepín Jiménez, Miguel Rodríguez, El Fundi, Javier Vázquez, Pepín Liria, etc. They all performed generously on behalf of this romantic torero who made fortunes and lost them; but one thing he never failed to possess was the affection and respect of everyone in the bullfighting world.

Manuel Pérez died in Madrid on August 6, 2002 of a heart attack.

Chapter 3. The Matador's "Inner Circle"

The *Apoderado* or Manager

Manuel Flores Camará
Córdoba, 1925-2006. Manager and impresario

Manuel "Manolo" Flores *Camará* was another whose life seemed predestined for the bullfighting world, as he grew up in a totally taurine family, the son of José Flores *Camará*, one of the most emblematic managers of all times. In fact, Manuel's father, before becoming the *apoderado* of the immortal *figura de toreo*, Manuel Rodríguez *Manolete*, was also a torero, who was in turn related to the popular matador Rafael González *Machaquito*. He made his formal presentation as a *novillero* in Madrid on 2 September 1917, and cut three ears that day. He received the *alternativa* on 21 March 1918, from the hands of the great matador José Gómez Ortega *Gallito* known more widely today, perhaps, as *Joselito*.

Nevertheless, author and historian José María de Cossío was not very kind to the first *Camará* in his great treatise *Los Toros*, and Manuel agreed. "I remember that my father invited Cossío to lunch in our home one day in 1945 and my mother jokingly reproached him: 'Don José María, you did not treat my Pepe very well in your book,' and he replied, 'Carmen, it was not my fault. The "*basto con la muleta, basto con el capote*" [extremely ordinary with both cape and *muleta*] was written by my one of collaborators and I didn't even have a chance to read it before it went to print.'" According to his son, Pepe Camará fought a considerable number of corridas, appearing on many occasions with *Joselito,* but when this outstanding torero was killed by a bull in Talavera de la Reina on 16 May 1920, he lost his 'benefactor'. His career went downhill, and he retired when his son was born.

Flores had a wonderful memory and recalled most vividly the day his father took him and his older brother, José, who also became an important *apoderado* and impresario, to see the great Juan Belmonte perform in Córdoba together with Vicente Barrera and Antonio Posada. "He wanted us to be able to tell our grandchildren that we had seen Belmonte *torear*. I remember he wore a gooseberry green and gold suit of lights and was truly extraordinary."

When the elder *Camará* retired from the rings, he became a small-town impresario, and one day a mutual friend asked him to lend a hand to a young boy called Manuel Rodríguez, nicknamed *Manolete*. When the Spanish civil war broke out, Córdoba was occupied by the Nationalist troops under Francisco Franco and *Camará* was asked—or forced—to organise several bullfights to enable people to forget, briefly, about so much tragedy. He not only organised the events but also fought in them, together with *Manolete* and one of *Camará*'s cousins, in 1936 and 1937. When a serious impresario appeared one day at *Manolete*'s house to hire him for a formal corrida, doña Angustias, *Manolete*'s mother, referred him to *Camará,* who agreed on the fee and signed the contract, and suddenly he found himself the official *apoderado* of someone who would become one of Spain's greatest matadors. Eventually, in 1946, a year before his death, *Manolete* did sign a formal contract with *Camará*, in which he simply "empowered him to do whatever he wanted to do", according to the latter's son. Manuel *Camará* keeps that curious document in his own private taurine museum, along with his father's characteristic dark glasses. "My father had very sensitive, light blue eyes and had to protect them, but at that time in Spain even prescription glasses were rare, let alone sunglasses, which made him appear very mysterious, someone of the elite class, which he wasn't at all."

Manolo Flores Camará

José *Camará* devoted his whole life to bullfighting and displayed an impressive, stern personality. He rarely signed a contract for a corrida, because he felt his word and a handshake were sufficient guarantee. "*Manolete* had a very close relationship with my father and, to prove it, I can say that his last coherent words were for my father: 'José, what a fool I have been!' He said it because during that last year my father had reproached him for many things and accused him of being distracted and not paying enough attention to the bulls."

There has been a great deal of speculation about the relationship between the famous torero from Córdoba and the actress Lupe Sino, but no one really knows the truth about their feelings, although Manuel said: "I think *Manolete* was happy with her but not with their relationship as such, and felt trapped. I believe he wanted to have a trial separation, because even though he took her to South America with him in the winter of 1946, he returned to Spain alone and she came back later."

Manolo's father, José Flores Camará, with his admired matador Manolete

Flores had the good fortune to spend a lot of time with *Manolete*. "He was an extraordinary person, very earnest and sincere, and he shared my father's profound sense of responsibility. In my opinion, he was the best torero that ever lived—and after him I would choose Antonio Ordóñez."

Manolo also knew doña Angustias, who was not from Córdoba, but from Albacete, and a very strong-willed woman. "She was tall and elegant and *Manolete* resembled her more than his father. As she had a great deal of personality, she exercised a lot of influence over her son. She had two husbands, both toreros: firstly, Rafael Molina Martínez *Lagartijo Chico*, and when he died she married Manuel Rodríguez, *Manolete*'s father. *Lagartijo Chico* was the great rival of *Machaquito*. One day a newspaper-seller walked along the street beneath her window, hawking a great triumph of *Machaquito*, and without a moment's hesitation, she grabbed a pail of water and dumped it on the poor boy. Character, indeed!"

As was to be expected, José *Camará* was greatly affected by the tragedy in Linares—the fatal goring of *Manolete*. "He was devastated, and didn't want to have anything more to do with the bullfighting world. Álvaro Domecq, who was still active as a rejoneador at the time, tried to snap my father out of his depression and begged him to accompany him. Then when Julio Aparicio, *Manolete*'s protégé, also asked him for help, he felt he couldn't refuse. Miguel Baez *Litri (padre)* followed, and before he knew it my father was 'back in business'. Everyone knows that *Manolete* was the best torero ever and my father, in his own profession of *apoderado*, was also the best!"

It is a pity that José *Camará*, who was witness to some of the greatest events in the history of bullfighting, did not write his memoirs, despite the fact that his sons wanted him to do so, but he explained: "Look, boys, if I were to write about my experiences, I would have to tell the truth, and as you are both still involved in the bullfighting world I could do you a lot of harm, so it's better that I do not".

Manuel tried his hand at bullfighting as a youth, but realised immediately that this was not to be his calling. His father sent him to Madrid, where he studied Political Science and Economics from 1943 to 1949. "I hated politics, but I had to study something in the Militia University or I would have been drafted into the army, and military service at that time was pretty brutal. When I graduated, my father asked me to manage our ranch in Carmona, but I preferred the bulls. As soon as my younger brother graduated with a degree in Agricultural Engineering he took over and I devoted myself fulltime to the bullfighting world. I made my début as an *apoderado*—or, rather, substitute *apoderado*—on 25 August 1956, in Almería with Miguel Báez Litri and Antonio Ordóñez, representing my father. My brother was managing *Chamaco*, who fought that day in Barcelona, and my father was in Seville attending to other affairs, because at one time or another he managed Parrita, Aparicio, Litri, Chamaco, Pedrés, Manolo González, Diego Puerta and finally Francisco Rivera Paquirri."

Paquirri was the first *torero* whose official *apoderado* was Manolo, a responsibility he assumed in 1969, while his brother, José, who died in 1990, managed another major *figura*, Dámaso González. "My brother was a very intelligent, educated person and was better at the theoretical aspects, while perhaps I was better with the practical side of the business. I am proud of our family history, because we discovered seven or eight *novilleros* and turned them into *figuras del toreo*. Anyone can manage a *figura*, but the true merit lies in seeing the inherent qualities of a 'rough diamond', and polishing that diamond until he shines with his true worth."

His father had discovered Francisco Rivera in 1966 and Manolo managed him until 1979. *Paquirri* died after being injured in the Pozoblanco bullring on 26 September 1984. If he was Manolo *Camará*'s first *torero*, *Paquirri*'s son Francisco Rivera Ordóñez, who adopted the name *Paquirri* in the later stages of his career, was his last. Did he manage the young Francisco because of his affection for his late father? "In part, yes, but also because his grandfather, Antonio Ordóñez, asked me to do it. Together with Emilio Miranda, I was then impresario of Algeciras and Córdoba, and I didn't think that at my age I was capable of handling all that responsibility, but I knew the boy needed someone reliable and experienced at his side, and Antonio persuaded me. I agreed, but without signing any binding contract."

Despite his age and the inconvenience and discomfort of the journeys, Manuel always accompanied Francisco. "As long as I could physically resist, I was there. That is one of the professional obligations an *apoderado* must always respect: to accompany his torero not only to the important plazas but also to the less important ones, because danger exists everywhere, and if one day there is a serious problem—God forbid—you have to be able to resolve it." In the back of his mind, perhaps, was the tragic death of *Paquirri* fighting in that small-town ring, where the torero suffered a very serious goring and where the medical and surgical facilities available in the rudimentary infirmary proved insufficient to operate adequately. He was rushed by ambulance to a major hospital in Córdoba 70 km away, but he died on the way.

The *apoderado* must enjoy the full confidence of his protégé, to be able to handle all kinds of matters without having to consult him every step of the way. "If there is any lack of confidence, it's better to terminate the relationship immediately, precisely because of the special circumstances surrounding the torero's life. The *apoderado* can't be just an employee or an administrator, and his job isn't limited to the bullring offices. In fact, the matador might progress to a point where he can handle his own affairs and may not even need an *apoderado* at his side all the time, but he should, nevertheless, be there. Their personalities must click and the manager has to anticipate the bullfighter's every need, so that he only has to worry about one thing: *torear*, which is quite enough!" In other words, the *apoderado-torero* relationship is almost like father and son. "The difference in age almost makes it necessary. Francisco respects me a lot, but I would say that it's not so much a paternal relationship as that of an 'older brother'. I find it amusing that he still calls me don Manuel, as did his wife, and I'm not going to protest, because it makes me laugh."

I wondered if it is more difficult to manage a *figura* or a beginner. "Nothing is easy, but perhaps it is more difficult to represent a *figura*, because when a torero is beginning you have your sights set on the future, and there is less responsibility; whereas, if you are making decisions regarding the career of a major *figura*, an error can prove very costly."

At present, there are only 20 to 25 professional *apoderados* registered with their official association, and there is talk of the figure of the *apoderado* disappearing, as that task is being usurped little by little by the leading impresarios. "I hope this won't happen, but it is indeed becoming increasingly difficult to organise a corrida, particularly from a commercial point of view. For example, contracts for corridas are being signed in the month of December to ensure the presence of the *figuras* in the major ferias of August and September, many of which clash with one another. If an impresario is not on the ball, he can find that the toreros who are the major box office attractions have already been signed up."

"Fortunately," don Manuel said, "nothing is ever written in stone." He explained that when Francisco Rivera Ordóñez took the *alternativa* on 23 April 1995, during the Feria de Sevilla, none of the major impresarios had included him in the season's big fairs. "*Chopera* was practically like a brother to me, but prior to the feria he pulled out his diary and told me that every corrida in the rings he managed was booked solid. Francisco had only two more corridas scheduled, in Córdoba and Algeciras—because I was the impresario there—and that was it, but then he triumphed, and *Chopera* and the rest of the impresarios had to make room for him in their ferias!"

He told us that the same thing occurred when his father was *Manolete*'s *apoderado*: "When *Manolete* took the *alternativa* in Seville, on July 2, 1939, he had just that corrida contracted, and another on August 31, in El Puerto de Santa María. The situation became more complicated in the era of Diego Puerta and Paco Camino, although when a new and important torero emerges, the impresarios can't afford not to put him on in their rings."

As he indicated, Manolo *Camará* was, together with his brother, also the impresario of several bullrings, and he did not feel that the two jobs were

Francisco Rivera Ordóñez in Ronda's Corrida Goyesca

incompatible. In addition to Córdoba, their home town, they managed Valencia, and he was proud of the fact that both rings were in a slump when they took them over and that they were able to improve their situations considerably both financially and in terms of ticket sales. "As an impresario you have a global view of everything and you can profit more directly from your work and a job well done. As an *apoderado*, you are somewhat limited in what you do, you experience the good and the bad, but in the end you are really working to benefit someone else, the torero. In other words, you plant the seeds, but the majority of the harvest—rightly so—goes to the torero."

Camará would have liked to manage the most important bullring in the world, Las Ventas, and he presented a tender for the management of the ring in 1997. "I thought that the group I represented should have won and I still can't explain why we didn't." He was not planning to repeat the disappointing experience because he felt he would be too old when the times for tendering came around again.

He was confident about the future of bullfighting, and hoped it will still be around in the year 2050. "It is like religion: there are many detractors, but somehow both the bulls and God manage to survive. I just hope that those who are involved in the Fiesta in coming years treat it with the responsibility and respect it deserves."

Camará was a man loyal to traditions and his roots and yet very much a man of his times, with a mobile phone and a pocket computer on which he recorded all the information he needed: telephone numbers, the dates of coming bullfights, details and results of past corridas, etc. He was a late-night internet surfer.

He wanted to be a torero when he was young and gave his first important public performance when he was 15 years old, in the small town of Guadalcázar, outside Córdoba. "I didn't do badly that day and I cut an ear. When I got home, *Manolete* was sitting in the garden, recovering from a goring he'd received in Albacete. I made a grand entrance so full of myself, striding around the room, and when he asked me how I'd done, I showed him my trophy. He roared with laughter and said, 'That's the ear of a cat, not of a Miura!"

Manuel Flores *Camará* died on 27 April 2006, at 81 years of age, while playing golf in Marbella. He was buried in his native Córdoba.

The *Mozo de Espadas* or Sword-handler

The *mozo de espadas*, as his name implies, has the responsibility of "serving" his matador during the entire *lidia*, furnishing him with the different tools of his trade: *capotes*, *muletas*, swords, water to rinse his mouth or moisten the *muleta*, and a towel to clean his hands and wipe the sweat off his brow. The sword-handler will be assisted by an *ayuda*, literally a "help", who among other duties must carry the *esportón,* the rectangular, hand-tooled leather case for capes and *muletas*, and the *fundón* or sword-case from the *cuadrilla* car to the *callejón*. The *ayuda* must also attend to the *subalternos*, handing them their *capotes*. However, the sword-handler has many responsibilities other than those we see in the ring. The writer Antonio Díaz-Cañabate described his role as follows: "I do not think that any magnate in the world, no matter how rich and powerful he may be, will find a valet or servant with the devotion and dedication of a sword-handler. A real *mozo de espadas* is the matador's most trusted confidant, and a whole lot more: his hands and his feet. A torero can do without many of the people who may surround him in the ring, but never his sword-handler."

Gonzalo Sánchez Conde *Gonzalito*
Huelva, 1931. Swordhandler

He is known in the bullfighting world as the ineffable *Gonzalito*, and most taurinos do not have even a vague idea of his full name, because he is one of those privileged few who enjoy such fame and affection that they do not need to be identified by their surnames. Gonzalito owes a great deal of his celebrity to the fact that he was the exceptional sword-handler of an exceptional matador, Curro Romero.

Born on a farm in a small town outside Huelva, Gonzalo wanted to be a torero from as early as he could remember. He did his best but soon realized that he had no future "down there on the sand", and so in 1956 he decided to become a *mozo de espadas*. "I also worked part time as a waiter in the bar my brother owned in Barcelona's famous La Bouquería market on Las Ramblas. In fact, at the moment the matador Manolo Carra asked me to go to Madrid to be his sword-handler, I was carrying a tray of sausages and beer. I jumped at the opportunity, and with the very taurine Hotel Victoria as my headquarters, I worked for a lot of toreros, such as Curro Montes, Paco Moreno, Aurelio Núñez, Manolo Escudero and Agapito Sánchez Bejarano." As he could not survive on his meagre salary as a sword-handler, he accepted all kinds of odd jobs, as a clothing salesman, a representative for a company selling Serrano hams, a house painter and a waiter. "I really enjoy any activity which involves dealing with people."

Gonzalito with Curro Romero in La Maestranza, all eyes on the bull

Gonzalo also sings flamenco very well and won several contests in his native Huelva. "When I was young, people paid me to perform, but as I wanted to be a bullfighter, I tried not to stay up late or drink alcohol. I have posters announcing me as both a torero and a *cantaor* in Barcelona in 1950." Now he reserves his singing for informal gatherings with friends, especially with his matador, now retired, Curro Romero, himself an accomplished singer, specialising in *fandangos de Huelva*.

Gonzalito was a "currista", a devoted follower of the artistic Curro Romero, from day one and so, when the opportunity arose to "serve" the Seville-born matador, he jumped at the chance. "I didn't want to 'fight' 80 or 100 corridas a season, so I refused offers from Miguel Márquez and Antonio José Galán." The Curro Romero-Gonzalito duo wrote 30 years of important taurine history together, much of which *Gonzalito* prefers to keep to himself. "He was a god to me before I even met him, and now we are like family. I must say that I'm very proud of how he treats me, because he is a good, honest, polite and shy man. He always asks for everything with a "*por favor*", something that's very hard to find nowadays. I'm talking not as his sword-handler but as a friend who worships him. I have never heard him say an unkind word about anybody, not even as a joke. Every time I have knocked on his door, he has been there to help me, which has not been the case with others."

Gonzalito explained that, contrary to what many people seem to think, the least important of the tasks of a sword-handler is the elaborate dressing ceremony of the torero. "Proof of this is that the young *becerristas* and the banderilleros dress themselves. The really hard part is organising the trips, reserving the hotels and meals at odd times for the entire *cuadrilla*, and the preparation of the matador's clothing and equipment. In fact, the sword-handler has a job which doesn't begin or end on the day of the corrida. You have to be loyal, honest, trustworthy and as wily as a fox. You're a combination manservant, butler, chauffeur, confidant, secretary and scribe. There are two hundred who can dress the matador but very few who can be a good *mozo de espadas*, because that's something else entirely."

It is obvious that the magnificent, hand-made suits of lights which are true works of art, valued at roughly 3,500 euros (£3,000) each, require a great deal of care, and *Gonzalito* sounds like an advertisement for a brand of detergent. "I hang the suit over the washbasin and try to remove the blood stains with a small brush. I never ever put it into the bathtub, although I know of some people who have even put it in the washing machine! Then, I remove the rest of the dirt and stains with liquid soap and water, trying to

Gonzalito's revered torero, Curro Romero, with capote and muleta
(under the unwavering eye of the mozo de espadas)

wet the suit as little as possible. I must have washed Curro's suits a hundred times, but they always looked like new. This is the part of my job I like least, and sometimes I let the laundry—shirts and suits—pile up and do it all at once. I have a hard time ironing the white frilly shirts and not all the hotels offer an immediate service, so I pack a small travel iron in my suitcase." Gonzalito points out that the fabrics of today's suits are much easier to take care of and he even uses a detergent to clean the *monteras*. "I let them dry right way up and they look perfect and smell nice. I take pride in my toreros looking impeccable."

Gonzalito adores his profession but complained that it is not well paid. "The wages are clearly specified and I've never seen a rich sword-handler, but what can I do? I like my job, I've had a wonderful life and I'm not bitter." He explained that if Curro had to fight on Sunday in, say, Santander, he would first have to find a hotel and reserve the rooms, then notify the entire *cuadrilla*, organise the trip and find a driver. "For me, the chauffeur is the most important member of the *cuadrilla*. I can remember having to sleep in the bath tub on more than one occasion, to give up my bed to the chauffeur and make sure that he at least got a good night's sleep. And finally, I have to get the suits ready and all the tools of the torero's trade. The matador's only concern should be to torear!"

Gonzalito was a *mozo de espadas* before the job was officially recognised with its own union card. Traditionally, to be a sword-handler one has to first undergo an apprenticeship as an *ayuda*, and *Gonzalito* argued that an *ayuda* deserves respect too, as it is his job to attend to the needs of the entire *cuadrilla*, while the sole responsibility of the *mozo de espadas* is the matador. He was with Curro Romero from 1968 to 2000. "People believe I'm rich, but that's not the case by any means! The year that Curro fought the most, he had only 46 corridas. I also buy and sell bullfight clothing and *trastos* [equipment] to make ends meet, because I don't have a monthly salary, but get paid only per corrida."

When Curro retired, *Gonzalito* managed the Portuguese matador Víctor Mendes, and then Manuel Jesús El Cid when he was a *novillero*, but he does not like the word *apoderado*. "Many people would die to have the word *apoderado* printed below their name, but I prefer 'artistic director'."

Gonzalito is not happy with the current situation of the Fiesta, and he worries greatly about the future. "Now you spend as much on promoting a *novillero* as you would on sending a child to university; it was never like this. The toreros used to come from a poor background and they were always paid something to fight, whereas nowadays they themselves have to pay! It costs a small fortune to become a torero and it's a great pity." He was honest and open. "I'm convinced that the toreros fight better than ever. I'm 85 years old and I have seen a lot of matadors, including *Manolete*; bulls today are bigger, the matadors risk more and they earn more money, but before it cost two million pesetas [[£10,000] to buy a ranch and now it costs two hundred million [£1,000,000]. Taxes are high, tickets are expensive, and there are no subsidies or tax benefits for the Fiesta as there are for theatre, films, football and other sports events. Taurinos and non-taurinos alike are only interested in making as much money as they can—for themselves."

The ayuda, entrusted with the paraphernalia of the whole cuadrilla

He was a direct witness to the "curse of the *sobre*", the envelope containing pay-off money and front-row bullfight tickets which matadors were obliged to give to each critic, major and minor, so that they would speak well of their performances. This form of bribery was highly prevalent in the sixties and seventies but there was a logical explanation for it. At that time, journalists did not receive a proper salary from their radio stations or newspapers; on the contrary, they had to pay to have their programme broadcast or their column published, and the only way they could do that and make some kind of a living was to get money from advertising and "sponsorship" from the toreros. This scourge disappeared to a great extent in the eighties, according to Gonzalito. "The *sobres* were detrimental to the truth and honesty of the Fiesta and I know of one bullfight journalist who bought a ranch with the money. I remember one day a critic insisted on seeing my matador right before the corrida, saying: 'I need your help because I have to pay for my radio programme!' But the matador replied: 'That's all very well, but the money I earn in the bullring is for my children!' I remember I had to distribute sixty envelopes to the press on one occasion, and in the end the novillero I was working for didn't get to perform because he had been gored the day before. Money straight down the drain!"

Gonzalito was delighted that the *sobre* no longer exists, but he expressed surprise that "everybody wants to be a journalist … they seem to come out of the woodwork, and I don't understand how a 20-year-old thinks he is qualified to write about bulls and criticise a matador's performance. They know only what they've read in books—that is, if they've bothered to read them—and when you look at their reports you wonder if you've been at the same corrida. Journalists have to report what they've seen: the good and the bad, and they should never forget the respect due to anyone who goes out in front of a bull."

Gonzalito is not a machista and has been the representative in Spain of the retired French matador and now major impresario Simón Casas, who was the former *apoderado* of *matadora* Cristina Sánchez, and also of rejoneador Marie Sara, recently proposed as a minister by Emmanuel Macron. "Cristina is a great torero. She was sitting in the *barrera* one day when Curro fought in Seville, and I brought her his dress cape as a special tribute, saying: 'Torero, here is the *capote* of your taurine godfather', and she was delighted. Curro gave Cristina the *alternativa* in Nîmes, making her the first woman to receive it in Europe, and during the auspicious ceremony, he said: 'First, it is a pleasure for me to bestow the *alternativa* on you and second, I am convinced that you deserve it: if I harboured any doubts about your ability, I would have refused the corrida'. And then he added: '*Torear* is like a caress, and who is better able to caress than a woman?'"

A matador's *esportón* is an Aladdin's cave, in which you can find just about anything, and Gonzalo is like a Boy Scout whose motto is "Be prepared!" He puts in everything except the proverbial kitchen sink: a pair of jeans, in case the matador is tossed and the *taleguilla* (the breeches of the suit of lights) is severely damaged, new slippers, braces, a very complete sewing kit—with all kinds of needles from thick to thin—four false pigtails, spare *machos* (tassels), black and gold braid for the suits, starch to stiffen the capes, tape to cover the hilts of the swords, etc. He also has stuffed his pockets with a shoe horn, a tin-opener, scissors, rubber bands, tourniquets, bandaging material ... He even has an extra set of ears and tail. "They came in handy on more than one occasion when the president granted the trophies at the last minute, and someone had to go running to the *desolladero* to try and retrieve them, but it was too late."

Among his many anecdotes, he remembers his particular "Bad Day at Black Rock": "I forgot the slippers, the sash and the shirt. Fortunately, the rejoneador Álvaro Domecq lent me a shirt and soft shoes which looked like bullfighting *zapatillas*. I found an old ribbon in my *guayabera* [a Mexican-style light cotton shirt with several pockets, popular among taurinos], which could serve as a sash, but I felt terrible because I hadn't checked everything carefully enough. I know it could happen to anybody, like the time my matador Víctor Mendes left his house and forgot to take his swords. I had to catch up with him on the road, get his house keys, and then go back home to pick them up. You can't kill a bull without a sword!"

The Bullfight Tailor

The corrida would not have the same dazzling beauty and grandeur were it not for the colour and lavish splendour of the bullfighter's attire, the traditional *traje de luces*, called the "suit of lights" precisely because of the sparkle of its sequins, embroidered tassels and gilded braiding which glitter and shine in the bullring on a glorious, sunny Sunday afternoon. Despite the fact that the suit has evolved and developed over the centuries until it has become an article of laborious, delicate and extravagant confection, haute couture, a true work of art, its elaboration has not varied all that much, because it still undergoes a slow, arduous and totally handcrafted process. The evolution of the suit of lights is as long and significant as the history of bullfighting.

It seems probable that the explanation for the rich elegance of the suit of lights lies in the aristocratic origins of the Fiesta. In the 17th century, the brave Spanish bull was fought by nobles mounted on horseback, with the help of their servants on foot. Their lackeys used their capes in a rudimentary manner to draw the bull away from a horse in danger or a fallen rider.

Obviously, they did not have an extensive wardrobe and would wear their everyday clothes into the makeshift bullrings, and only on rare, special occasions would the corresponding aristocrat decide to "dress up" his assistants, in order to impress royalty or members of the Court who attended this equestrian exhibition.

The situation changed considerably at the beginning of the 18th century, when Felipe V, the first Bourbon king, ascended to the Spanish throne. As this monarch, of French origin, displayed evident disdain for the "Fiesta Nacional", the nobles gradually ceased participating in the corridas, which by then had acquired great popularity among the common people, and the humble peasants decided to continue running and *lidiando* the bulls. As they lacked their own mounts, they had no choice but to discover how to do it on foot. It would stand to reason that the outfits worn by these early fathers of Modern Tauromachy were very simple—resembling peasant dress—and essentially practical. The trousers and jackets were plain and fitted, but sufficiently flexible so as not to restrict their movements in any way. These first professional matadors began to acquire fame and popularity, and the spectacle on foot became firmly rooted in Spanish life and culture, as it slowly evolved into something based on a much purer, more profound, aesthetic concept. A new profession had come into being, and the protagonists gained fortune and notoriety. In the 18th century they still dressed quite simply in red jackets with bulging epaulettes, tassels and silver buttons, and beige knee-length suede or leather trousers, red stockings, and black shoes adorned with silver buckles.

With the dawning of a new century, the bullfighters' attire underwent a major change. At that time, it was the bullring impresarios who were responsible for providing the wardrobe for the toreros and Seville's Maestranza decided to replace the worn leather outfits with lavish ones made of pure silk, in order to endow the spectacle with greater splendour. The Madrid bullring soon adopted the same custom. The *espada* (the matador; literally, the sword), who was going to kill the bull with the *estoque*, was distinguished by a suit with fancy gold braiding, while those of his assistants were embroidered with black, a tradition still respected today, although silver has come to be used in addition to black.

At present, a washable satin fabric, manufactured in Barcelona, is used to elaborate the highly ornate *chaquetilla* (jacket) and matching *chaleco* (waistcoat). The heavily embroidered silk cloth is attached to sturdy, resistant linen, which helps to maintain its almost frame-like form. The front of the *chaquetilla* is decorated with embroidered *alamares*, and on the shoulders are heavy epaulettes from which *machos* (tassels) hang, the same

Francisco Rivera Ordóñez prepares to enter the ring,
with a sumptuous capote de paseo ... and carefully adjusts his montera

tassels attached to the ties on the *taleguilla* (tight-fitting trousers). The back of the *chaquetilla* is also adorned with a hand-embroidered design, extending down along the sleeves, which are not sewn to the jacket below the armpits, so as to allow for greater freedom of movement. The *chaquetilla* is not supposed to be totally closed, so that the *alamar*-decorated *chaleco*—usually of the same colour and embroidered pattern—is visible over the fancy ruffles of the white cotton shirt. This has two fine ribbons at the waist, used to hold in place the narrow silk tie, the *corbatín*, which can be red, green or black, and matches the *faja*, the sash around the waist. The extremely snug *taleguilla*, held up with braces, extends from mid-chest to below the knee and is secured at mid-calf with four metal buttons and the tightly laced *machos*. The outer part of the *taleguilla* is made of heavily embroidered satin, and the inner part is a knitted fabric, which can easily be replaced if necessary.

The attire is completed with the silk tie, also called the *pañoleta*, and the sash, which has in fact undergone major modifications in size, for in the 19th century it was four metres long and one-and-a-half metres wide. It was wrapped tightly around the waist and was considered a means, albeit meagre, of protection in the event of a goring in the stomach. Finally come the pink stockings—originally white—the black ballet-type slippers, and the crowning glory: the black astrakhan *montera*, often likened by foreigners to old Mickey Mouse ears, which was adopted at the beginning of the 19th century to replace the black crocheted net used to hold the matador's long hair in place. The *coleta* (pigtail) was in vogue and became the symbol of the bullfighting profession until the second decade of the 20th century, when Juan Belmonte cut his own natural pigtail and replaced it with a false one, the *castañeta*, which all except the most romantically traditional clip on today.

The production of the *traje de luces* is difficult and complicated, in part because it must be cut and tailored to perfection to ensure that it is as comfortable as possible to wear. The enormous range of colours, with the most picturesque of names, such as *burdeos* (Bordeaux purple), *sangre de toro* (bull's red blood), *azul obispo* (bishop blue), *azul celeste* (heavenly blue), *verde esperanza* (hope green or turquoise)—makes the opening parade exceptionally colourful. *Grana* or red is considered the "colour of the brave" and a white suit, as traditionally worn for first communion, is customary when a torero takes the *alternativa* and fights fully grown bulls for the first time. Rarely will one see a yellow suit; the colour is associated with bad luck in the bullfighting and theatrical worlds (Molière died on stage while wearing a canary-yellow costume). Although gold braiding is traditional for the matadors and silver for the assistants, *azabache* (jet) or black has become popular; it makes for attractive contrast, is less expensive and wears better.

The *capote de paseo* or dress cape is the most lavish and extravagant article of all, particularly when the matador has his tailor embroider upon it the image of his patron saint or the virgin of his *pueblo*, whose particular blessing and protection he seeks.

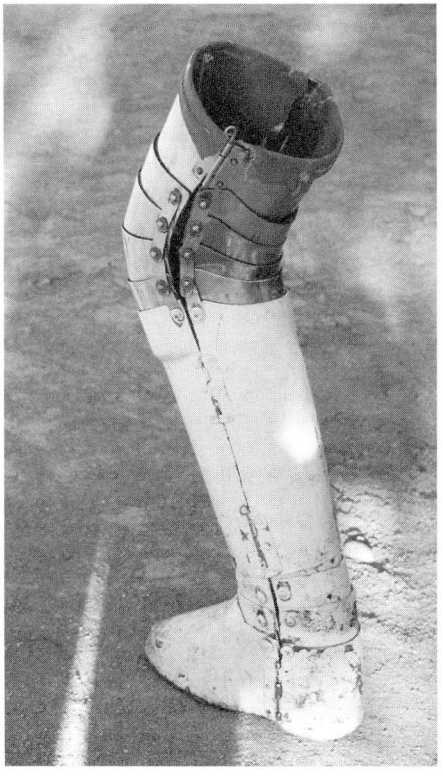

The *picador's* gregoriana

The picador's attire differs from that of the rest of his colleagues for the obvious reason that his job description is totally different. He does wear a profusely embroidered jacket and waistcoat, but because he appears in the ring on horseback he wears bone-coloured chamois-leather leggings, or *calzona*, and the *castoreño*, a wide-brimmed hat of a similar colour made from beaver skin, with a curious black pine cone-shaped adornment on the left side, the *cucarda*. His legs are well protected by steel boots, the right one (the *gregoriana*) more than the left, for that is exposed to the charging bull, so the boot extends from the tip of his toes most of the way up to his hip. The metal boot on the left, the *mona,* is shorter and is intended to prevent the picador's leg from being crushed against the boards of the fence or *barrera* when the bull charges the horse; it also has a spur.

Justo Algaba
Villa Palacio (Albacete), 1948. *Bullfight tailor*

When Manuel Benítez El Cordobés performed in Albacete, he impressed young Justo Algaba so much that the boy decided to become a torero. "I think all of us who have become involved in some way in the bullfighting world have always harboured within us the *gusanillo* or 'little worm' of being a torero, although most of us came to the conclusion very soon that this difficult profession was not meant for us. I remember that the day El Cordobés fought, a ticket which normally sold for 100 pesetas cost 700, equivalent nowadays to 300 euros." After appearing in a few minor bullfights in Albacete, Justo came to Madrid, aged 16, determined to open the doors to the plazas as a torero or as a bullfight tailor, which was his other passion. "I quickly gave up all hope of becoming a matador, when my hands began to sweat and my heart to race, and I would get tossed right away by the calves. However, I did feel a little sad when I picked up a cape or *muleta* in the tailor's, knowing full well that it was not intended for me; but in the end, I have learned to be happy being what I am: a *sastre de toreros*."

Moreover, Justo Algaba did become a *figura* among bullfight tailors, a success which he attributes to his hard work and determination. He was an apprentice to the late Fermín López, before setting up his own business in 1976. He poured all the artistic inspiration which he could not express in the bullrings into his workshop, and is convinced that the bullfight would in no way be as spectacular were it not for the suit of lights: "The corrida would lose a great deal of its beauty without the torero's lavish attire; just as it's not the same to dance sevillanas wearing jeans and a pullover, as it is in a flouncy flamenco dress. And of course, one does not get the same feeling from seeing a torero in a suit of lights, as a football player in a sweaty tee-shirt and a pair of shorts, however much one may adore the sport. I see the bullfighter as the participant in a special ceremony, in which his costume plays a major role, much the same as that of the priest saying mass."

Justo insists he could not have chosen a more complex profession and not just because the suit is so elaborate to make: "Every torero wants his clothes right now! They don't know how to plan ahead, and we go crazy in spring and summer trying to get the orders filled, orders which they have placed practically the night before! And we can't forget that this is a handcrafted job, which only a handful of trained, experienced specialists can perform."

Under normal circumstances it takes about 25 days to make a suit of lights, about thirty people being involved. "Imagine the calendar, multiplying 25 by 30, and the process is as follows. I prepare the designs and the patterns, cut the fabric and then give it to the *cordoneras* or braid embroiderers. When they return their work, it is sent to the sequin sewers; then, the embroiderers, who specialise in sewing on the flowers, putting on the epaulettes, adding the linings; those who mount the fringe, who make the *machos*, embroider the jackets ... Each group is made up of four to six people, depending upon the work, and when they've finished their individual tasks, the suit is assembled, the sleeves, the shoulders and the collar. After several fitting sessions, the next step is the quality control inspection, where the patterns, buttons, stitching, etc., are reviewed before the finished suit is ready to be turned over to its torero."

Justo learned this production-line system of working during the course of his many trips to America, and he feels it is the most functional, rapid and effective way to do the job. He has also studied the potential fabrics in detail and has opted for a mixture of silk, nylon and cotton, which is water-, dirt- and sweat-repellent.

Toreros are generally very demanding customers and perfectionists about their attire, except for a famous torero from Albacete in the seventies, who would come for measurements at the beginning of the season and then call Justo up and say: "Send me half a dozen suits in different colours". "I, as a tailor, prefer a more demanding client and I believe in the old proverbs: '*Como se ve al hábito, se ve al monje* [Clothes maketh the man]' or '*Para serlo, hay que parecerlo* [You have to look the part]'. I am convinced that a bullfighter does not worry as much about the street wear he buys in the El Corte Inglés department store as he does about his bullfighting wardrobe."

Justo is a restless, diligent, innovative man who has exceeded purely taurine limits in order to make new inroads in a wider-ranging fashion world. "I didn't do it for money, but to satisfy my own curiosity and enterprising nature. I enjoy designing clothing and accessories with a taurine theme for women as well. I sincerely believe that a woman is a perfect pedestal for my designs. Initially, out of respect for the bullfighters, I was somewhat reluctant to venture into the fashion world, but I felt it was a challenge and a very attractive one at that! I've designed wedding dresses and evening gowns and I must say that the women who wear my creations evince greater appreciation for my work than the toreros. I suppose it's because the bullfighter regards his suit as working clothes, but that shouldn't be the case. A knife you use to cut bread is a knife, but a fine silver carving knife has more value. It upsets me to see that the suit of lights may have lost some of its magical aura, although I notice that foreigners are still dazzled and overwhelmed when they see it for the first time."

Justo Algaba with a highly personalised chaquetilla for Said Kazak El Palestino, based on Arabic script and designs

Dressing the bullfighter from head to toe is a very expensive proposition, especially if he is about to take the *alternativa*; he can easily fork out 10,000 euros, beginning with the suit which starts at 4,000 euros (£3500), depending upon the design, the work involved, the fabric and the adornments (gold, silver or black braiding, etc.) and its overall lavishness. The torero's "trousseau" can be added up more or less as follows: the *traje*: 4,000 euros; two magenta and yellow capes: 300 euros (£270) each; two *muletas*: 150 euros (£130) each; a set of swords, with at least two killing swords and a *descabello*: 1,500 euros (£1300); a *fundón*: 400 euros (£350); a *montera*: 350 euros (£320); pink stockings: 100 euros (£90); slippers: 150 euros (£135); an embroidered dress cape: anything from 300 (£250) to 6,000 (£5500) euros; a white ruffled dress shirt: 80 euros (£70); plus the sash, tie, braces, pigtail, *esportón* ... Justo also has less expensive suits for the banderilleros with limited finances, for about 2,500 euros £2,300).

Among his most well-known clients have been Curro Romero, *Rafael de Paula, Antoñete,* Curro Vázquez, Julio Robles, José Ortega Cano, José Mari Manzanares, Juan Antonio Ruiz Espartaco, Luis Francisco Esplá and Emilio Muñoz, although he is somewhat hesitant to mention names. "I am sure to forget somebody, and besides we are only five bullfight tailors in the whole world and the toreros might prefer one *sastre* over another, but they tend to order suits from each one to see who does the best job."

Everybody has his own preferences as to colour and patterns, but Justo studies the torero with an experienced professional eye and makes the appropriate recommendations. "A torero might well like something which does not suit him. For example, I dressed Curro Romero in darker colours because of his corpulent figure, and he never considered wearing pink, pearl grey or light blue, because he looked much better in Nazarene purple, tobacco, lead grey, navy blue and deep 'Soraya' green. Younger, slimmer toreros like Finito de Córdoba or César Jiménez can wear whatever they like because their age, physical appearance and personalities allow it. On the other hand, Miguel Abellán tends to choose modern, daring lines, while El Juli prefers the more classic designs. I also appreciated the confidence a torero like Luis Francisco Esplá placed in me, for he is intelligent and a very skilled painter. I understood what he was looking for and I always tried to come up with ideas which I thought would please him."

Justo also had the good fortune to be a close friend of American matador de alternativa and painter John Fulton, who was born and brought up in Philadelphia, but lived in Seville from the late fifties until his death in 1998. "John did designs for me, and in return, I gave him all the bullfighting trastos—clothes and equipment—he needed, including the suit he wore for his farewell performance in San Miguel de Allende, Mexico, in April 1994. We never talked about money or felt any need to do so."

Rafael de Paula, dressed in a beige suit of lights with brown embroidery, designed by Justo Algaba (right)

Algaba remembers with particular fondness the day some years ago when he dressed *Rafael de Paula* all in brown for an important performance in Las Ventas. "I look back on it now and think what a bold statement it was for both of us to make, breaking with tradition in that way. He wore a light brown suit embroidered with dark brown braid, beige stockings and a brown *montera*, brown slippers and dark brown accoutrements. Only *Paula* could get away with such unorthodox attire. I have many wonderful stories about Rafael, but I remember one in particular, on the day he triumphed in Madrid in the Feria de San Isidro of 1987. I was putting the finishing touches to his suit in his hotel room, and I don't know what I was thinking but I managed to put the *montera* on the bed five times! And face up! Any aficionado knows that's bad luck, and for a superstitious gypsy it's even worse! Five times Rafael chided me: 'Justo, please don't put the *montera* on the bed!' And somehow, the *montera* would end up on the bed again ... and it even fell on the floor twice! Rafael got angry with me, but later gave a memorable performance, while I suffered all afternoon!"

The importance of the transformation which a torero undergoes when he dons his *traje de luces* was expressed very well by the aforementioned Alicante-born matador Luis Francisco Esplá. "The ritual of the corrida is incompatible with jeans and running shoes. The suit of lights is magical. I am short, thin and very shy, not the least bit seductive, but when I put on my suit, I seem to grow taller and more muscular, and women seem to find me irresistibly attractive!"

Chapter 4. The Bullring

The Impresario

The role of the impresario has changed a great deal since 27 January 1612, when, according to the historian José Sanchez de Neira, Felipe III granted the privilege, for "three lives", to Ascanio Machino for the sale of bulls in his home town of Valencia, a right inherited by his widow, although she sold it soon after her husband's death.

The impresario is responsible for organising the event, buying the bulls, signing the toreros, obtaining the official licences and permits, and announcing the corrida, with the hope that the *cartel* (the combination of bulls and toreros) offered will please the aficionados. If this is the case, the bullring will be filled, as will the impresario's pockets. If the weather is bad, or the star of the programme cannot appear due to illness or injury, or a championship football match is being televised at the same time, the results can be catastrophic.

Article 23 of the current *Reglamento Taurino* establishes that first-category bullrings include those of provincial capitals and cities in which more than 15 bullfights are held each year, ten of which should be corridas de toros, plus those which have traditionally been in the first category, even if they do not currently put on the required number of corridas. At present, first-category rings are: Madrid, Barcelona (La Monumental, which was shut down in 2012 for political reasons, and will hopefully be reopened someday soon; the other major ring, Las Arenas, was turned into a modern shopping centre), Seville, Córdoba, Valencia, San Sebastián and Bilbao; Málaga recently entered this category, while Zaragoza and Pamplona may be included on the list as regards the toreros' salary scales. The French rings of Nîmes, Arles and Bayonne are also considered first-category. The category of the plaza determines the weight of the bulls to be fought, the fees of the toreros and in particular those of their *cuadrillas*.

The provincial capital rings not classified as first category, and those of other important cities such as El Puerto de Santa María and Aranjuez in Spain, Dax and Mont-de-Marsan in France, and Lisbon and Santarém in Portugal, are considered second-category. The remaining plazas of permanent construction and the temporary "portable" plazas are classified as third-category. All the provincial capitals of the Spanish mainland have a bullring, except Cádiz, Lérida, Lugo and Orense, but that in Oviedo has been closed for some years.

The largest bullring in Spain is Las Ventas in Madrid, which holds 24,500 spectators, but the biggest in the world is the Plaza México, in Mexico City, with a capacity of more than 46,000, while that in Valencia, Venezuela, seats 25,000. The smallest could be a local *portátil* ring, which accommodates approximately 1,500 people, and one of the most original is in Santa Cruz de Mudela (Ciudad Real), with its rectangular shape, first used in 1722. Other very old rings are those of Béjar (Salamanca, 1707), La Maestranza of Seville (1763) and Ronda (1784).

Most of the major bullrings belong either to local government bodies, as is the case of Las Ventas, which is the property of the Comunidad de Madrid, and the "coso de Pignateli" of Zaragoza, which belongs to the Diputación Provincial or Regional Government, or to noteworthy institutions, such as to the Casa de la Misericordia in Pamplona and the historic Real Maestranza de Caballería in Seville; and finally others are privately owned, like the rings of Barcelona and Palma de Mallorca by the Balañá family (third-generation impresarios), who have done nothing to prevent both rings from being shut down by local politicians, although two corridas were held in Palma in 2017.

Seville: Diodoro Canorea
Cabezamesada (Toledo), 1922-2000. Impresario of Seville and other provincial rings

Diodoro Canorea devoted more than forty years of his life to running the legendary and incomparably beautiful bullring of Seville: La Maestranza. Consequently, many aficionados tend to forget that he was born not in the south, in Andalusia, but in the central region of La Mancha, in the small town of Cabezamesada. His entry into the bullfighting world occurred quite by accident. After working in his home-town branch of the Banco Central, he was transferred to the main office in Madrid and happened to move into the same apartment building as the wife and daughter of Eduardo Pagés, impresario of Seville. He smiled with nostalgia as he recalled: "I met my wife when she was nine years old; I was 12 years older than her. She was bubbly and adorable and I used to take her with me when I went out on dates with the girlfriend I had at the time. When Eduardo Pagés died at 50 years of age in 1945, I became like a second father or an older brother to her, and then five years later, I became her husband."

Canorea gradually left the banking world to take over the family business: the administration of the La Maestranza bullring. He became so devoted to his work that he has been called '*más sevillano que los propios sevillanos* (more Sevillian than the locals themselves)'. "I've lived here for so long that I feel a part of this city and I understand the public, the breeders, the toreros and the aficionados. I am also outgoing and friendly by nature and I think I fit in very well with the Andalusian character. Even though I inherited the business, I was also an aficionado ... to do a good job you have to like what you do, and with the Fiesta, the more involved you get, the more hooked you become ... it's like a drug."

Diodoro Canorea managed one of the most important bullrings in the world from 1957 until his death in 2000, when his son Eduardo took over, with Ramón Valencia as partner. Running this unique ring is not easy. "It's different from any other plaza on the planet in every way. It is certainly beautiful on the inside, but it's irregular on the outside." According to Diodoro it differs from other rings, such as Las Ventas, which was carefully designed in mudéjar style in 1929, in that the Maestranza was continually undergoing reconstruction: one ring on top of another, up to a total of four, and in fact if we were to dig beneath today's plaza, we would unearth the seats and steps of the former ring. This explains why the ring is far from being a perfect circle; the arches are uneven and asymmetrical and some have a larger span than others.

Diodoro Canorea

Seville's plaza also receives special care and maintenance from the Real Maestranza de Caballería, to which it belongs, and so it is always freshly painted at the end of every season and impeccable in appearance. Another exceptional aspect of this ring is its public. "The great advantage here," Canorea explained, "is that the majority of the spectators have stood before a brave animal at some point in their lives, whether they were professional toreros or not, or they are relatives of a matador or a *ganadero*. It is not like in Catalonia where unfortunately there is less and less *afición*, or in Las Ventas, where people attend a bullfight in the same way that they go to the theatre, a football match or a basketball game." Diodoro was annoyed by the aggressive nature of a section of the Madrid public. "They show little consideration and don't give the torero a margin of time to understand and accommodate himself to the bull. Fortunately, the situation is quite different in Seville, and the audience is very respectful because they are well aware of the danger the torero is facing. In fact, I recognise the faces of at least half the spectators myself and that familiarity imposes an element of appropriate behaviour."

Canorea made a brief attempt at running the Madrid bullring, with business partners, but he remembered it as a nightmare and said he almost came down with a serious illness, which Seville bullring surgeon Antonio Leal Castaños diagnosed as "*feriaítis*": the stress involved in having to organise a major bullfight "feria" in the capital.

Although he also managed other rings, such as those of El Puerto de Santa María, Toledo, Córdoba, Pozoblanco and Andújar, he felt more closely identified with the desires of the Seville public, for he ran the Maestranza ring for over forty years, relying on loyal staff, many of whom had been in his employ from the very beginning.

When one season draws to an end, it is necessary to begin organising the next one. "I never stop. In general, I start a round of business lunches with the *apoderados* of Enrique Ponce, José Tomás and El Juli to talk about dates. Then there are the meetings with the *ganaderos* and the television companies. I am on a merry-go-around, although I would like a couple of weeks in between to enjoy the marzipan at Christmas with my family."

A bullfight has to be prepared well in advance of the date of its Sunday celebration, for the posters have to be in the street by the Monday before. Prior to that, the impresario has to sign the bullfighters, purchase the bulls, obtain the necessary permits, arrange for the advertising, ticket printing, etc.

According to Canorea, the reason impresarios do not organise more *novilladas* is because they attract few spectators. "Unfortunately, people are only interested in seeing the big names—not even the 'second division' matadors—unless there is some noteworthy novillero, such as the son of a famous torero. The public considers the matadors to be the true professionals and the novilleros mere amateurs, and as the expenses of organising a novillada are high, it's not worth the effort."

It costs at least 15,000 euros just to open the doors of the bullring, in taxes, social security payments and wages for approximately 200 employees; preparation of the ring, the corrals and the stands; printing of posters and tickets, and advertising. Then the impresario must take into account the price he has to pay for the bulls and the fees of the toreros. Canorea also said that the worst part of the organisation is the physical examination of the animals by the veterinary surgeons. "You buy what you think are good animals, ones which will offer the best guarantees for success, and then the vets reject a bull for sometimes insignificant reasons. Then you have to rush out to find some last-minute substitutes, which frequently don't please the toreros."

Diodoro Canorea died on 28 January 2000, and was succeeded by his son Eduardo, who learned his responsibilities well, working side-by-side with his father, particularly as a veedor, who visits the ranches personally to select the most appropriate-looking bulls. In 2015, Eduardo Canorea retired and turned over full control to his partner, Ramón Valencia. Despite all the problems, one thing was certain, Diodoro Canorea was well loved in Seville and never once missed his initial vocation: banking.

Small towns: Víctor Aguirre
Rascafría (Madrid), 1923-2016. Impresario of small-town rings and bull-breeder

Víctor Aguirre was one of those classic, romantic, rugged and tenacious taurinos who have been responsible for the Fiesta surviving to the present day. His comments could not be more direct, honest, invaluable or true. Born in Rascafría, in the Madrid sierra, he inherited from his father a love of the country, although it was Víctor who broke into the bull world. "My father organised the Fiestas in our pueblo and I put on my first bullfights when I was only 17 years old. Obviously, it was much easier at that time, with less bureaucracy, fewer permits and paper work, and minimal interference from the veterinary surgeons. All you had to do was buy the livestock and pay the young would-be toreros."

Eventually Víctor took over the whole business, from raising the animals to organising the bullfights, setting up his own "portable" bullring and selling the meat, the carne de toro de lidia, afterwards. In the end, he even opened up his own butcher's shop on the Avenida de Donostiarra in Madrid some fifty years ago, to sell the meat from the nearby Las Ventas and Vista Alegre bullrings directly to the public. He added that the bull meat was truly delicious, since the animals are range-fed for the most part, resulting in a juicy, meaty flavour.

What aspect did he enjoy the most? "Just about everything. If the animals I raise prove to be brave, I am happy as a *ganadero*. The butcher's shop is a guaranteed source of income for my family, and the most difficult part is of course the organisation of the bullfights, but I enjoy the challenge. Hopefully I break even, although sometimes I end up losing a small fortune."

Víctor Aguirre, impresario

As an impresario, Víctor Aguirre organised about 70 corridas a year, and he joked: "The same number as Las Ventas!". However, his rings were not "monumental", but located in small towns, including Villa del Prado, Meco, Navalcarnero, Consuegra, Becerril, Azuqueca, Las Matas, Torrejón, Rascafría, Anchuelo, Villalba, Guadalix de la Sierra, Manzanares, Villanueva del Pardillo, Las Rozas … Doubtless he would have loved to have been the impresario of Las Ventas. "Who wouldn't? It is every taurine impresario's dream. It is like a blank cheque made out in your name. Anybody can manage Madrid, because there is a line of *ganaderos* and another of *apoderados* just waiting outside, anxious for you to say: 'Come in and let's talk'. It's a passport to becoming a millionaire, in part because you're obliged to televise the Feria de San Isidro in May, which is the most important in the world, and the television rights together with the *abonos* [season tickets] for the Feria alone represent an important financial cushion for anything you undertake."

You have to have a lot of *afición* to enter into this risky game of organising bullfights, which is a costly affair with few guarantees. "Sometimes you have a really bad time: the bulls don't charge, the toreros bomb, there are last minute substitutions, the public doesn't respond at the box office, it's a windy, rainy day, the veterinary surgeons reject the bulls ... An endless possibility of calamities."

Any taurine event involves a very large budget. "To organise a *novillada* with picadors you need at least 18,000 euros. The permits cost 9,000, the social security payments for the toreros another 3,000 euros. For a *corrida de toros*, although there's not a lot of difference in the cost of the 'raw materials'—the livestock—the budget skyrockets with the wages of the toreros and the social security, which amount to twice that."

Víctor Aguirre owned five "portable" rings, with a capacity of 1,500 to 5,200 seats. He saved a lot of money by using his own rings, which he could store in a warehouse on his ranch, La Luna de Samaná, in Soto de Real, just 30 km from Madrid, which also has a small ring, corrals and a big dining room, for the organisation of *fiestas camperas*, *tientas* and other taurine gatherings.

Aguirre complained that the Fiesta needs more institutional support, lower taxes and greater subsidies. "It's a pity that there are people who abuse the toreros, obliging them to pay to fight, the so-called 33-33-33 arrangement, where each one assumes one-third of the cost of organising the event. Many village fights could not be organised were it not for the subsidies received from the local town halls."

A recurrent controversy is whether the televising of corridas is proving detrimental to the Fiesta. "I don't know what the long-term results will be, but for the moment we're seeing fewer spectators at the rings. If you can see a *figura* on television in the comfort of your own home, you won't want to go to see three unknown *novilleros* in your *pueblo*. But I ask: where will the future *figuras* come from, if we don't organise these *novilladas* and enable the youngsters to acquire valuable experience? I think they are televising too many fights, and, in particular, *festejos* which don't offer much guarantee of success. Before they weren't allowed to televise a corrida on Saturday or

Sunday, because it clashed with fights being held in other towns, thus creating serious problems for the other impresarios, but now—anything goes."

One thing that has improved considerably in the *pueblos* is the medical care. "This is a matter which had to be taken very seriously. Now there is a totally equipped mobile ambulance and an experienced surgeon and anaesthetist on hand at all the *festejos*, but before, you had to rely on the services of the village doctor, who might never have seen a goring or operated in his life. He prescribed aspirins and issued death certificates and if this poor man encountered a serious accident, he had no idea what to do. I remember one unfortunate *novillero*, Livinio Yepes, in Canencia, many years ago. They had to sew up his penis, with no anaesthesia! Fortunately, it was not a life-threatening injury but that poor kid was biting the dirty towel in his mouth to avoid screaming because he was going through hell!"

Víctor Aguirre organised many bullfights in the towns outside Madrid and in the region known as the Valle del Tiétar, nicknamed in taurine argot the "Valle del Terror" (Valley of Terror), due to the fact that it is usually synonymous with "*toro grande y billete pequeño*"—big bulls and small fees. "What's a 600-kilo bull doing in a small town like Cenicientos", he asked, "where poor Mariano Jiménez suffered a tremendous goring, in his own home town?"

A tienta or testing of an animal in the small ring on Victor Aguirre's ranch

Almost all today's *matadores de toros* fought in Aguirre's rings when they first began their careers, but he was never interested in becoming an *apoderado*, one part of the bullfighting industry he avoided. "I never liked the idea of struggling and sacrificing for someone else, spending a lot of money on their initiation, and then if they make it big, they abandon you in order to sign an exclusive contract with a powerful impresario. I can understand their strategy and I am not calling them ungrateful, because they also have to sacrifice an awful lot in their careers."

Although Víctor Aguirre was an impresario, *ganadero*, butcher and cattle dealer, he also never wanted to be a torero. "I was too afraid. I would have had a heart attack just standing in front of a calf. I fought once, when I was young, way back in 1950, in a *venta*—a restaurant with a play area and a little bullring—called La Taurina. We organised the *becerrada* but the bullfighters didn't show up, so I had no choice but to go out and fight the calves. I was terrified, and resolved never to do it again."

Among the many *figuras* who got their start in Aguirre's rings was the child prodigy Julián López El Juli. "I gave him some 40 *novilladas* and paid him 500,000 pesetas [£2,500] to kill just one *becerro*, but it was worth it because he put on a great show and filled the ring! I remember one afternoon it was pouring with rain in Consuegra, but he helped me put up the 'No hay billetes' sign—a sell-out!"

Víctor was a widower and the father of three girls: Sagrario, Victoria and Nuria, each with their own *ganadería*. "They are better aficionadas than I am! For the moment, my grandsons, Gabriel and Víctor, are into football, like all boys their age."

Víctor Aguirre's first *ganadería* belonged to the Asociación de Ganaderías de Lidia, but in 1979 he founded another ranchers' association, Ganaderos de Lidia Unidos, of which he was the Honorary President and with which his daughters' ranches are registered. He explained why he created this fourth breeders' group. "I wasn't a *ganadero* to begin with, I just bought a lot of animals from the other ranchers for the corridas I organised. I was a good client of theirs and paid them well, but when I bought my own ranch, instead of buying 500 head of cattle a year from others, I raised my own 500 and another 500 more which I sold to other impresarios. This didn't make my original suppliers very happy, so I founded my own organisation, which has over 150 members now, between Spain and Portugal."

Víctor Aguirre was not so worried about the current state of the bulls, because he claimed that animals have always displayed occasional defective behaviour in the ring, particularly the brave ones. "I saw the confirmation of Litri's *alternativa* in Madrid in 1950, and his *subalternos* had to grab the animal by the tail to get it back on its feet. He continued his *faena* and in the end cut two ears! A good bull often falls because it is so eager to follow the cloth."

Sadly, Victor Aguirre passed away in Madrid in April 2016 and his daughter Victoria runs the ranch today.

The President of the Corrida

According to the *Reglamento Taurino*, the appointment of the presidents of taurine spectacles is the responsibility of the Ministry of Culture in Madrid and the government delegate or subdelegate in provincial capitals, who can—and usually do—delegate this responsibility to a police official. Local mayors can also preside over bullfights and the latest version of the *Reglamento* provided for the possibility that an experienced aficionado could take on the thankless job of sitting in the *palco*, the presidential box.

According to Article 37, the President's mission is to direct and guarantee the normal progress of the bullfight, for which he relies on two advisors: one from the taurine and artistic point of view—usually a former matador—who is seated to the president's left, and a veterinary surgeon, who sits to his right. These advisors are limited to expressing their opinions, which the president can choose to accept or not. They receive a small stipend for undertaking this responsibility. The president also has a government representative (a member of the police force in first- and second-category rings), who has the three-fold task of maintaining "law and order" in the plaza, supervising what goes on in the ring, and carrying out the presidential orders. These delegates acquire valuable on-the-job experience and often become presidents themselves later on.

José Manuel Sánchez
Villanofar (León), 1950-2011. Police Commissioner and President of the Las Ventas bullring

No one would ever think that being president of the Las Ventas bullring on a complicated afternoon would be an easy task, but it is obviously also not easy to be the Commissioner of Madrid's central police station, with all the many incidents taking place in the heart of any major metropolis. José Manuel Sánchez handles both jobs—one obviously more important than the other—with the same passion, devotion and *temple* (smooth control).

Commissioner Sánchez was born in the small town of Villanofar, in the province of León, and it was a relative who encouraged him to enter the police force. Nevertheless, while stationed in Tenerife, he studied law in the

La Laguna University and then political science and sociology in the Universidad Complutense de Madrid, although he admitted that "you learn a lot more psychology while on the streets". He was assigned to some troublesome districts in Madrid in 1982 and then spent three years in Barcelona during the preparations for the 1992 Olympic Games. "They needed people with experience in handling conflictive situations ... like having presided over a corrida of Victorinos ... and that is why they chose me," he joked.

Sánchez saw certain similarities between the world of cops and robbers and that of the bulls, especially in Las Ventas, because you have to be the proverbial "cool, calm and collected" to be able to deal with either jobs. "I have a rough time in the *apartados* in the morning because I wonder how in the world the impresarios can bring these animals in from the ranch. The bulls have to comply by law with specific biological characteristics, health, size, build, *trapío*, horn structure ... and it 's not easy. I remember a corrida featuring César Rincón, Enrique Ponce and the Mexican Miguel Espinosa Armillita, with two bulls from each of the following ranches: Juan Pedro Domecq, Samuel Flores and Victorino Martín. One of Victorino's animals looked great but had *abrochado* horns, that is they were turned-in half-moons, and I was afraid the public would protest. I told Victorino: 'That bull has *trapío* but he is not attractive,' to which he replied: 'I thought this was a *corrida de toros*, not a beauty contest!' And he was right! I had no choice but to approve the bulls and, as I expected, when the animal came into the ring, a sector of the public protested, but what could I do? I couldn't grab a microphone and say: 'This is not a beauty contest, folks!'"

José Manuel Sánchez explained how he ended up in the *palco* of Las Ventas. "I didn't volunteer, that's certain! You enjoy the bullfight a lot more from the *callejón* or the *tendido*. However, one day my superior, who knew I was an aficionado because I have an *abono* in the first row of Tendido 7, called me into his office and said: 'We're running out of presidents. I want you to be a substitute this year and acquire the necessary experience, so that I can officially appoint you next year.' I attended the course given for bullring presidents and found myself sitting in the *palco*. In my adolescent years, I ran in front of the cows in my hometown and even tried once to *torear* a calf in a celebration of the day of the patron saint of policemen, "Ángeles Custodios", but that's something I will never do again. That animal pummelled me so badly I couldn't sit down for a week. It takes a lot of courage to be a bullfighter. I'm brave enough to be a policeman, but not to go before a bull!"

According to Sánchez, these are the requirements for being a bullring president: "First and foremost, you have to be an aficionado, because it would be a disaster if you were not. You also have to be thoroughly familiar with the Reglamento Taurino and the relevant laws, and courageous enough to sit in the presidential box, face the public and make crucial, split-second decisions".

José Manuel Sánchez in the corrals at the Las Ventas bullring

He remembered the first time he presided over a corrida in Madrid, on 28 May 1994, during the Feria de San Isidro. "It was a Portuguese corrida from Murteira Grave and the matador Luis de Pauloba performed one of the best *faenas* of his life, according to my notes—we keep a record of everything—and if he had killed well, I would definitely have granted him two ears, but he had to make six attempts with the sword! He needed those ears desperately and I would have loved to have made my début granting them to that highly artistic torero, Luis de Pauloba."

Bullring presidents do not get paid for what they do. "You do it altruistically, out of *afición*. I am paid my salary at the end of the month to be a policeman, and this is just one of my many duties."

There is more than meets the eye to the president's job. "You have to be present at the weighing of the animals and the first physical examination carried out by the vets the day before the corrida. On the day of the fight, we don't just make an appearance in the *palco* at 7 in the afternoon. We have to attend the *sorteo* and *apartado* in the morning, beginning at 11 am, until the

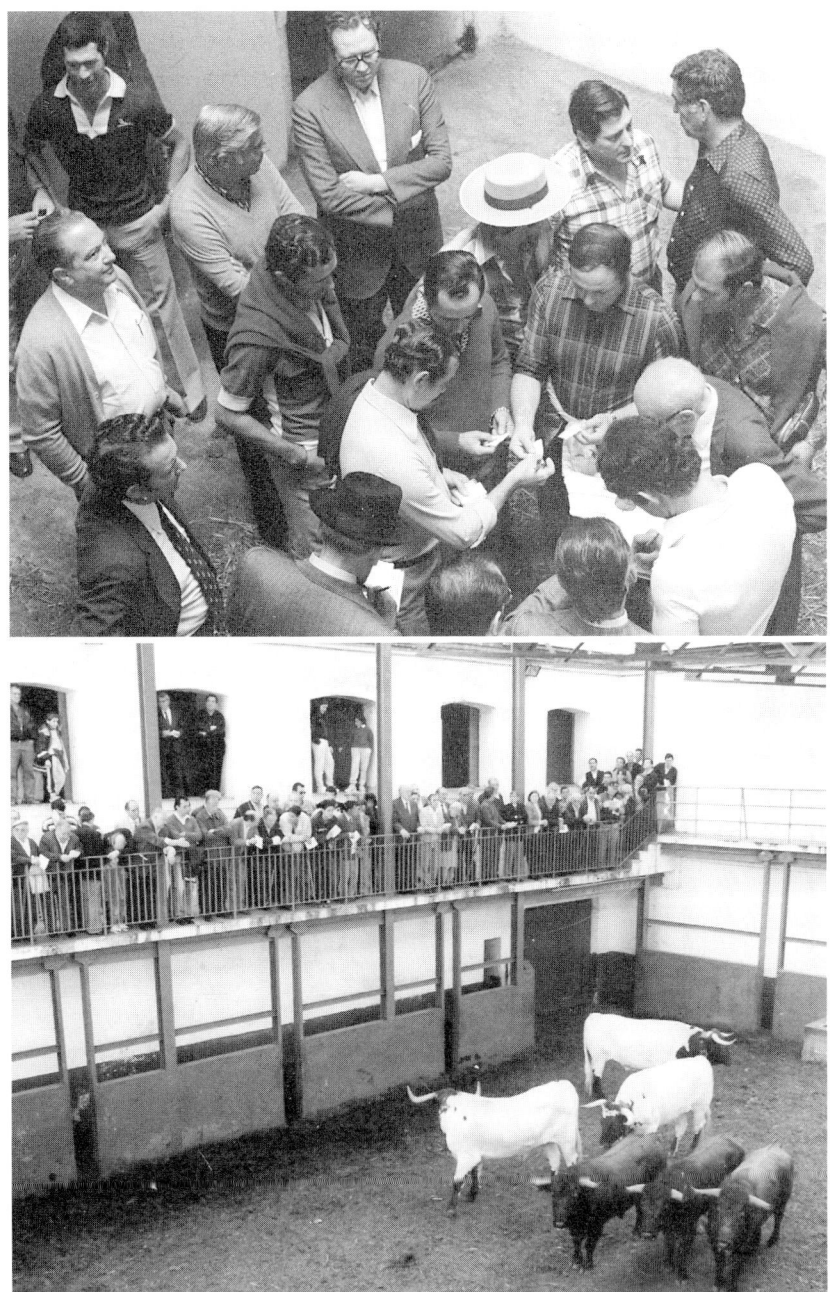

Top: the professionals at the sorteo, conducted in private;
bottom: the apartado, attended by the public

enchiqueramiento [separating the bulls into individual pens], making sure that the animals are not subject to any illegal manipulations and irregularities. Then we go for lunch and back to the plaza for the corrida. During the Feria de San Isidro, that is my schedule every fourth day. Very often, when I leave the plaza I go back to the police station to finish off my work, and then I must be at my desk again at 7 the next morning."

The president has to be objective, and capable of resisting all kinds of pressure from impresarios, toreros and aficionados. "You have to understand the public, too. I don't know if I could be a good president in Seville, because as one of my predecessors, Luis Espada, put it: 'In Seville, you preside with your heart and in Madrid you do it with your head,' and then he added: 'The bullfighting world is passion, and so is the presidency.' Luis was an excellent president and I remember sitting behind him in the *palco* one day, observing the impassive expression on his face while he applauded a fantastic series of *naturales* under the table."

José Manuel Sánchez did not reject the idea that an aficionado can preside over a corrida, as permitted by the *Reglamento Taurino*. "The only consideration is that we have to be aware of the fact that they may encounter serious problems. The president does not just wave a white handkerchief and decide on strictly taurine matters. Las Ventas holds almost 25,000 spectators and Plaza México 46,500, and passions run high, so I wonder if an aficionado is sufficiently qualified to make the right decisions. A wrong one could lead to public disorder and you have to know how to assume the consequences of your actions. It is part of my job to make major split-second decisions. If you take out the green handkerchief [to send an unsatisfactory bull back to the corrals] and then change your mind, you can't say: 'Oops, I made a mistake'. You have to consider the cost of the animal, the best interests of the torero and those of the *ganadero*, who puts a lot of time and money into raising it. Sometimes the bull can recover and it could prove better than the *sobrero* [substitute] that has been in the corrals for a couple of weeks. If you make a mistake the public and press attack you, but no one ever congratulates you for being right. I tape all the corridas and when I go on holiday I watch the videos to guard against making the same mistakes again in the future."

Sánchez admitted to having made a serious blunder the day José Tomás made his presentation in Madrid, by granting him only one ear. "If I had seen in the ring what I saw in the video, I would definitely have given him the two ears. He had been tossed twice, got up as if nothing had happened, performed a great *faena*, and placed what I thought at the time was a low sword. I saw afterwards on the tape that it was not!"

The green handkerchief: the bull will be returned to the corrals

Authority plays an important role in the success or failure of a corrida. "If it's predestined to be a disaster, there's little to be done, but if you as president make a wrong judgement, you can ruin everything, even though the true responsibility lies with the toreros and the *ganaderos*. The less the president intervenes in the corrida, the better. A bull with one *puyazo* too many may not behave well in the final *tercio*, but with one *puyazo* less you can put a lot of people in danger. I remember one time I didn't fully apply the *Reglamento* and changed the *tercio de banderillas* after only two pairs of sticks. I was convinced that that Cortijoliva bull would injure someone and unnecessary human risk is more important than any textbook regulations. The public protested and thought I'd gone mad, but afterwards, one of the banderilleros came over to me and said: 'We're very grateful. That animal was extremely dangerous and you saved our lives!'"

The Commissioner felt that the Fiesta should remain in the Ministry of the Interior, but that it should be linked to the Ministry of Culture, due to its extraordinary cultural content. He also believed that the laws and *Reglamento* needed to be updated and modified from time to time.

Despite his great responsibility as a police commissioner, Sánchez was of a warm, gregarious nature. "When you have to deal with a difficult situation, there is no reason to rant and rave; a lot more can be accomplished when you keep your temper. That way disagreeable situations appear a little less unpleasant. I am a happy, outgoing person as a rule, but I have a tough, intimidating side, too, when the situation calls for it."

José Manuel Sánchez, who used to see over 100 corridas a year, had an unusual custom which earned him the affectionate nickname *Pajarita*, referring to the bow tie he always wore when he presided over the corrida. "The president of the Madrid bullring has inherited the tradition of the old *comendadores* or constables, who officiated over the corridas and they obviously did not wear ties, but an old-fashioned *lazo* [bow]. At a dinner with colleagues, my superior dared me to wear a *sombrero cordobés* [broad-brimmed hat] and a bow, when it was my turn to preside. I carried the hat discreetly in my hand, but had no choice but to put on the bow tie. I've continued to wear it as a symbol and a tradition, but only in my role as president. I have fourteen *pajaritas* at home and my wife chooses the one I'll wear each day!"

The Bullfight Surgeon

In this spectacle, where the torero risks his life in the ring, the doctor's skills and the facilities of the infirmary play a vital role in the organisation and celebration of the Fiesta. The *Reglamento Taurino* of 15 March 1962, modified by Law No. 10 of 4 April 1991, and further developed by Royal Decree 176 of 28 February 1992, discussed this matter in detail and went so far as to stipulate the number of scissors, bandaging material, lights, and the physical size of the operating room and the other required installations. The current *Reglamento* is less precise on this point. The impresarios of first- and second- category rings are responsible for supplying and equipping the infirmaries, but there has always been concern as to the status of the medical facilities in the portable rings and the small-town plazas.

Dr Máximo García Padrós
Madrid, 1945. Chief surgeon of the Las Ventas bullring

Dr Máximo García Padrós, the son and successor of the previous chief surgeon, Dr Máximo García de la Torre, is confident that the Madrid infirmary has everything it needs to deal with any kind of emergency, although he personally prefers to bring his own more sophisticated instruments with him on Sunday afternoons. He feels that taurine surgery is a subspecialty of general surgery. "A bull can gore a torero anywhere, from head to toe, and so the doctor has to be thoroughly familiar with human anatomy, and skilled in chest, vascular and abdominal surgery, etc. Above all else, you have to know how to keep calm because the injured torero and the people who bring him to you are all highly agitated and nervous. Besides they have been through similar experiences before, and if they see that the doctor looks concerned, that's when they really begin to worry. That's an important lesson I learned from my father. We're still following the rules he laid down in the infirmary in his day."

Dr García Padrós in the Las Ventas burladero de médicos

Dr García also believes that the best way to learn is with practice, especially in view of the major advances continuously being made by modern medicine. "Previously taurine surgery was considered somewhat 'folkloric'. Nowadays toreros are admitted to normal hospitals for their treatment and recovery, and the resident doctors thus have the opportunity to study their cases closely and expand their knowledge. This also enables them to see the difference between gorings and knife or gunshot wounds. We organise special lectures, conferences and promotional campaigns, and publish books and the results of our research and experience with this type of injury and how to deal with it. Any surgeon is qualified to attend to a horn wound, but has to take into account the possible trajectories and this is the fruit of hands-on experience."

Despite the great responsibility being the chief surgeon of Spain's most important ring brings, the job is not well paid. The doctor receives roughly 1,000 euros less tax per *festejo*, a sum that is divided among the seven members of the team, who were, at the time of writing, Máximo, his three assistant surgeons: Máximo García Leirado—his own son—,José Antonio Pascual and Carmen Asenjo Sanz; anaesthetists Miguel López Vizcayno and Jorge Puertas; and nurses José Manuel Gutiérrez, José Manuel Manrique Moreno, Javier Sánchez García and Antonio Pajarín Lopera. Dr García confirmed that they sacrifice their Sundays, holidays and the entire month of May for the Feria de San Isidro, with the added nuisance of having to reorganise their other professional activities. The medical staff are also obliged to attend any event held in the arena of Las Ventas, including rock concerts, which don Máximo does not particularly enjoy.

Máximo García Padrós and his younger brother Miguel, also a surgeon, attended bullfights with their mother from the time they were young, as their father joined the Las Ventas medical staff in 1941. Máximo's own wife did the same with their three children, one of whom is now a member of his team and an accomplished trauma specialist in his own right. "As we always talked about bulls and bullfighters and their injuries, my children could not help but become aficionados," he states matter-of-factly.

Having studied in the faculty of medicine of the Universidad Complutense, he began to assist his father in the infirmary back in 1960, and also took slides of all the injuries they operated upon, while his younger brother, Miguel, filmed the operations on video. "These photos and tapes serve as a record of the seriousness of the injuries and help us to illustrate the classes we give to students, for now many medical faculties have included this in their curriculum. Furthermore, most doctors, particularly in small towns, end up treating more than one horn wound during the local fiestas, and so it is important that they know what to do and, most importantly, what *not* to do!"

After a dramatic *cogida*, the medical staff goes into action immediately, while the ring assistants bring in the injured torero and set him on the trolley in the examination room. He is undressed and a rapid but exhaustive study is made of all of his possible injuries, as such *percances* [accidents] are usually polytraumatic and even though the torero has received a goring, a neck injury could have more serious consequences. If there is a *cornada* and it is necessary to operate, the decision must be made as to the type of anaesthesia required—local, regional, general or epidural—and then the patient is moved to the operating room. The more experienced toreros tend to be a lot calmer than the younger ones, who are often terrified. Only authorised personnel are allowed in the infirmary.

If two toreros are injured, priority is determined by the seriousness of the injuries. "A minor injury can be stitched up anywhere in the infirmary. The order of precedence is clear: to save the life, then the function, and then the organ. I had as many as seven patients at one time in the infirmary when the Portuguese *forcados* performed in 1984. The bull caught them all: two with very serious gorings, one with a neck injury, another with a banderilla jabbed in his face and the rest with assorted bumps and bruises; we attended all of them perfectly. There is just one operating room as such, but we can also operate in the examination room and in the corridor, which is equipped with special lighting."

After the operation, the doctor must draw up an official report detailing all of the injuries, with an additional copy for the interested party and the impresario, who will distribute the information to the press. The patient is then transferred by ambulance to a hospital, and as it is considered an occupational injury, the torero receives full attention in a clinic associated with the plaza's medical insurance policy. Don Máximo follows up on their treatment—and then, it's back to the bullring!

Dr. García Padrós misses the old Sanatorio de Toreros on calle Sancho Dávila, just two blocks from the bullring, which was shut down in 1980. "It was a special place with excellent staff, who knew all the toreros well. The top specialists in their fields attended the professionals and they could continue their rehabilitation on the premises. The psychological factor was fundamental because they were surrounded by other toreros, who were all more than eager to get back to 'work'. It may have become somewhat antiquated and costly to run, but some formula could have been sought which would have made it more profitable, by using it as a general hospital during the other six months of the year."

It is obvious that the torero is a special patient, like no other, because after a serious injury, they are anxious to "get back to the job". The doctor explains this. "Toreros are athletes and in top physical condition. A goring represents an important hiatus in their professional activity and they can't wait to get back in front of the bulls, because they have a lot to lose. Not just the money, but what they call their *'sitio'*, their confidence and sense of control of the situation in the arena."

Matador Fernando Lozano gratefully dedicates a bull to the medical team led by Dr García Padrós

Dr. Garcia and his team usually operate on ten serious gorings under general anaesthesia per season, although an average of 75 toreros with different types of injury pass through the infirmary doors. They also have to attend to the general public. "On any one day, there could be 23,000 spectators with their 23,000 problems: heart ailments, high blood pressure, fainting spells and even going into labour. During the Feria de San Isidro, with all the people and excitement, many incidents occur. In one year, we have had to attend to approximately 250 people, some just for an aspirin, others because they were burned with a cigar or cut their hand opening a beer can, or the elderly who fall down the steps. Thank goodness, they have installed an extra lift!"

Don Máximo observes the corrida from the *burladero de médicos*, beside the tunnel that connects the *callejón* to the door of the infirmary and at other times on the closed-circuit television in his office. It is an obligation more than a devotion. "It's important to see how the *cogida* has been produced because it helps to understand the possible extent of the injuries. They can be very deceptive, because, despite the fact that the torero has a goring in his thigh, he could also have suffered serious neck injuries."

Among the most serious *percances*, he recalls the following. "Before I was a qualified doctor, I witnessed the fatal goring of El Coli (1964), Emilio Oliva's life-threatening injury (1963), and also that of El Cordobés (1968). When I finished my studies, I worked as an assistant and I particularly remember the *cogidas* of Vicente Punzón, Curro Vázquez, José Luis Ramos and also Antonio González El *Campeño*, who was clinically dead when he was brought into the infirmary. We managed to revive him, but he died seven days later. There were many, many more, but thanks to our well trained, efficient staff, we have been able to save almost everyone."

However, not everything is tragedy, for in thirty years of experience as a surgeon and fifty as a spectator, don Máximo has accumulated a lot of stories. "Silly things happen all the time, like when a lit cigar fell from the upper tier of seats, the *gradas*, and had the misfortune of falling into the plunging neckline of a famous actress's dress. The woman became hysterical while the rest of the *tendido* roared with laughter. Another time an injured *novillero* was brought in, accompanied by a man who said he was his father. Five minutes later another man claiming to be his father appeared, and finally a third. They were told to reach an agreement so that the 'real' father could come in. More than once, a torero was rushed to the Sanatorio amidst great urgency and it turned out that the tourniquet had been placed on the healthy leg instead of the injured one. I remember we received a phone call at home once, when Dad was still the chief surgeon, and they told us a seriously injured torero was being rushed to Madrid in an ambulance. We both got dressed and ran down to the Sanatorio and waited and waited: 11 pm, midnight, 1 am, 2 am ... and still no sign of the torero. It was impossible that the ambulance could take so long. Finally, a car drove up and a man got out and strolled calmly towards us. The torero explained that he got very hungry along the way and decided to stop in Aranda de Duero to eat some roast lamb. My father replied: 'As you do not have an empty stomach, I cannot anaesthetise you and so you can spend the night and I will operate in the morning'. It seems that the *mozo de espadas* had been really nervous, but the torero had not been gored at all!

The Bullring Chaplain

The chapel represents the last refuge of peace and tranquillity for the torero before he goes out into the ring filled with commotion, confusion, noise and danger. Permanent bullrings must have both an infirmary and a chapel.

Bulls and religion have been intertwined throughout the history of Humanity and bulls have been linked to mythological gods and ancient legends, particularly through the sacrifices offered by the Greeks and Romans, and even by Islamic cults. When the bullfights became very popular, the Catholic church grew concerned and questioned the morality and relevance of the *festejos* celebrated in the towns where they let loose brave animals in improvised bullrings, formed with wagons, carts and boarded fences. People jumped into the ring to face the animals with no protection whatsoever, not even an improvised cape, and many of them ended up hurt or even killed. This was one of the reasons that led Pope Pius V to publish his famous bull *De salutis gregis dominicis* in 1567, which prohibited the Fiesta under penalty of excommunication for all those who organised, participated in, or attended a *corrida de toros*. That decision did not please Felipe II, for, even though he was not an aficionado, he was aware of the great popularity of the spectacle among his subjects. The prohibition lasted eight years until Gregory XIII attenuated it and exonerated the spectators who did not participate directly and the expert *lidiadores,* as long as the organisers adopted the appropriate safety measures. The ban did continue in force, however, for archbishops, bishops, priests and monks.

In 1583, Sixtus V restored Pius V's ban and harshly reprimanded the religious orders and professors of the University of Salamanca, who defended the spectacle. The confrontations between the Church and the bulls would last until 1598, the year in which Clement VIII finally lifted the prohibition against attending a bullfight for the entire community except monks and priests, a situation which persisted until the middle of the 20th century, when the *a divines* ruling was suspended, which had prevented the priests from saying mass or hearing confessions if they attended a bullfight, until they received a special dispensation from the bishop.

One of the reasons clergy were always present at the bullfights was because the Episcopal Palace was usually situated on the main square of the *pueblo*, where the bullfights were held and it was often the bishops themselves who organised the corridas for the benefit of the church. After more than five centuries, there are relatively few *pueblo* fesitivities celebrated today in honour of the virgin or patron saint of any Spanish town, which do not include some kind of bullfighting event.

Father Mariano Frías
Cantalejo (Segovia), 1934. Parish priest, teacher and chaplain of the Las Ventas bullring

Father Mariano had his first contact with the bulls in his home town of Cantalejo, in the province of Segovia, where torero Victoriano de la Serna had his ranch and was a close friend of his family. His *afición* progressed to such a point that when he was studying at the seminary, he organised a *festival taurino* for the local youth club. He began to read about bullfighting and prepared his thesis for the theology faculty of the Universidad Pontificia de Comillas, near Santander, on the subject: "A study of thirty aspects of morality in the bullfights", which covered the moral obligations of the *apoderado*, the public, the torero and the government, the very real danger of death, the injuries suffered in the village fiestas, etc. Father Mariano did a great deal of research on the subject and came to the conclusion that there were just as many theological publications in favour of bullfighting as against it, and that is where he found his major arguments. "The Bible says that God created animals to serve Man. So, the question could revolve around whether the Fiesta constitutes 'service' or not. At first, the church argued that people should not find enjoyment in the death of a bull, a horse or a man, and so the spectacle could be considered 'sinful'. Others argued that the *toro bravo* is a special species which is born to attack and is well cared for, and has survived to this day only because of the existence of the spectacle." All of the arguments raised in the 16th century have been overcome, except for the matter of certain *festejos* and traditions in the *pueblos*, such as the Toro de la Vega, the Toro de Tordesillas, the Toro Ensogado and the Toros de Fuego (Bulls of Fire). These are 500-year-old traditions which have nothing to do with a proper corrida, for they entail a brave bull being pursued through the streets of the town and finally killed by the local residents. Most mainstream aficionados do not appreciate these *festejos* either, and their continued practice is today a matter of debate, although they still form a part of the festivities of certain *pueblos*.

According to Father Mariano, the church is no longer concerned with the question of the morality of the Fiesta. Even in the past, the village priest used to sit in the president's box, given that the celebration of the corrida was usually linked to some religious event, a custom which still persists today.

When he graduated from university, don Mariano was sent to Colombia to do missionary work, and his ties to the bull world deepened. As his bishop knew he liked bullfighting and happened to see photos of him *toreando* on the local ranches, he did not hesitate to appoint him chaplain of the Santamaría ring in Bogotá, a city in which he spent twelve years of his life, with another three in Cartagena de Indias, reinforcing his friendships with and support of all the toreros he met. In fact, he earned the nickname of El Apóstol de los Maletillas, because he helped the young, aspiring bullfighters to torear and even bought suits of lights, capes, muletas and swords for those who could not afford them. At the same time, he was able to forge close bonds with all the major visiting matadors, who would dine and stay at his home, such as Paco Camino, El Viti, El Cordobés, Palomo Linares, Diego Puerta, Andrés Hernando, Ortega Cano and the Girón brothers from Venezuela, along with Spanish impresarios, including the Camarás, Choperas and Lozanos, who were managing the most important rings in South America at the time. He even had his own radio program, not on religion, but on bullfighting, called "Taurine talks with Padre Mariano".

When the priest returned to Spain in 1985, Chopera, the impresario of Las Ventas, asked him to become the chaplain of the plaza, a job he was delighted to accept, although he had to combine it with the classes he gave on religion in Madrid's Virgen de la Paloma secondary school, talks to the students at the bullfighting school and his parochial responsibilities in the church of Nuestra Señora de Henar, about half a mile from the bullring, about which he explained: "Nuestra Señora de Henar is the patron saint of Cuéllar (Segovia), a town famous for its encierros at the end of August, which are the oldest in Spain, predating those of Pamplona. In fact, it is said that the first encierros in Navarra were celebrated when the farm labourers from Segovia went to work in the fertile fields of Navarra, harvesting the corn, wheat and grain, but when the time came for the celebration of the local festivities in Cuéllar, they wanted to return home. A clever Navarra landowner wanted to prevent them from leaving, so he decided to organise the traditional encierros using the local Navarra stock. Hence, the origin of the world-famous Pamplona encierros really lies in Cuéllar, as a sign at the entrance to the pueblo proclaims: 'Los encierros más antiguos de España'."

In addition to celebrating weddings, baptisms, communions and spreading the Gospel, the chaplain's mission is to administer the Holy Oil to whosoever may require it during the corrida. "I have to be there to comfort anyone who needs my services in the infirmary, a torero, a spectator or a bullring employee. I can watch the corrida from the doctors' burladero, but I prefer to sit in Tendido 8 with my friends. I don't usually carry the Holy Oil with me, because I have a lot of faith in God and in don Máximo [the Las Ventas surgeon] that nothing serious will happen. Besides, my church is close by, and if necessary I can send for it."

According to Padre Mariano, since the opening of the Las Ventas ring in 1931, when they killed 14 bulls in one day, because fights were scheduled in both morning and evening sessions, only five professionals have required a priest's services for last rites, the last of whom was Antonio González El Campeño, banderillero of José Miguel Arroyo Joselito, who received what proved to be a fatal goring on 22 May 1988. "It was a horrendous wound which affected the blood vessels in his neck. I gave him the last rites and he died, sadly, seven days later, in the Hospital Doce de Octubre. Fortunately, tragedies are not frequent in the more than 2,500 spectacles celebrated in Spain each year, thanks to the modern, very efficient medical care afforded the toreros."

Bullfighters, generally speaking, are profound believers, although they may not be highly observant: "Most of them travel with a briefcase containing a small 'chapel', with photos of their favourite virgins, rosaries, medals, candles, etc., in part due to devotion, in part to mysticism, and also because they are gifts from friends and family. They leave a candle burning before these small altars in their hotel rooms until they return. When they reach the bullring, they enter the chapel, with mixed feelings of fear, anxiety and piety and may say a quick *Ave María* or Lord's Prayer—if they know it. The most classic symbols of worship of the toreros are the Virgen de la Macarena and Jesús del Gran Poder, and above all, the virgin of their home towns, because she symbolises love and maternal protection, whereas Jesus represents an angelic life of more profound Christian commitment. Most toreros cross themselves before beginning the *paseíllo*, some up to three times, and they have even invented a new custom: tracing the sign of the cross on the sand with their right foot."

Father Mariano estimates that four-fifths of the toreros visit the chapel in provincial bullrings and 95% of those in Madrid, either for prayer or because it offers a quiet retreat from the people and chaos of the arena. "Anyone who risks his life often feels closer to God, even though toreros are usually not frequent churchgoers otherwise."

The Las Ventas ring was first used in 1931 without a chapel, but one was added afterwards, for its official opening in 1933. "That's why it appears like a last-minute appendage 'stuck' in a corner of the *patio de caballos* with a Mexican baroque style that has nothing to do with the rest of the neomudéjar monument." A painting of the Virgen de la Paloma, which many people believe to be the patron saint of Madrid, presides over the altar and there is also an image of the Virgen de Guadalupe, a gift from Mexican torero Carlos Arruza; one of the Virgen de Coromoto from Ecuador, donated by Vázquez II; the Cristo de los Milagros of Lima; and a large carving of Cristo de Medinaceli, which was kept in the home of the *Bienvenida* family until Antonio's tragic death in 1975. "The chapel's not meant to be a 'cathedral'", according to the priest, "and so even though many, many people have wanted to donate images and even valuable objects, we haven't wanted to overload its contents. There used to be a passageway connecting the infirmary with the chapel until Manuel Leyton *El Coli* died in this ring in 1964 and they moved his body directly from the infirmary to the chapel to keep vigil over his cadaver. After that tragedy they walled up the corridor so that you could not see the chapel from the infirmary, or vice versa."

Mariano has celebrated two multitudinous outdoor masses in the Las Ventas ring, one after the tragic death of Francisco Rivera *Paquirri* on 26 September 1984 in Pozoblanco and the other when José Cubero *Yiyo* was killed by a bull in Colmenar Viejo, almost a year later, on 30 August 1985. "We put up an altar in the centre of the ring, which was filled with people, as were the *tendidos*. *Paquirri*'s death especially affected me, as he had often been a guest in my home in Colombia."

José Cubero *Yiyo*

The official patron saint of toreros is San Pedro Regalado, a Franciscan monk from Valladolid, who, according to legend, was walking down the street one day when he encountered a brave bull which had escaped from a nearby ranch. The village folk were terrified, but when San Pedro approached it and raised his hand, the animal stopped dead in its tracks and became docile and tame; thus, he is considered the "protector of the toreros".

Mention should be made of don Mariano's special hobby. "I fought for the very first time when I was 12 years old and had a lot of opportunities to repeat the experience when I was in Bogotá, in charity *festivales* organised to raise money for worthy causes. I even performed with the late Spanish Olympic ski champion Paquito Fernández Ochoa and as the years passed, I became his *peon de confianza* [head banderillero]. I don't think the bishops were very pleased with my hands-on *afición*, but I know for a fact that Cardinal Suquía did not miss a televised bullfight."

Padre Frías exercising his afición

The Bullring Mayoral

Florencio Fernández Castillo Florito
Talavera de la Reina (Toledo), 1960. Mayoral of Las Ventas

The *mayoral* of the bullring assumes responsibility for taking care of the bulls when they arrive at the plaza. In Las Ventas, Florencio Fernández lives with his family on the premises during the entire season. He must prepare the corrals for the arrival of the animals, supervise their disembarking from the crates, manoeuvre them around with the utmost care for the veterinary surgeons during the first examination, as they are naturally highly-strung and nervous after their trip, and then give them food and water. He must also help in the *sorteo* and *apartado* and train and direct the *cabestros*, the tamed steers used to return a bull to the corrals for whatever reason. The bullring *mayoral* usually wears a *traje corto* for the corrida.

The success and popularity that eluded Florencio Fernández as a young torero came to him as the mayoral of Las Ventas. It is not surprising that *Florito*, as he is known throughout the taurine world, wanted to become a torero in his home town of Talavera de la Reina, for he was actually born in the *plaza de toros*, a ring famous for many reasons, including the fatal goring of the almost-omnipotent torero José Gómez Gallito (Joselito), on 16 May 1920. "My father worked for the impresario Manuel Martínez Chopera, and we lived in the patio of the plaza. I grew up in a taurine ambience and travelled a lot with my dad."

Florito's father wanted to be a matador and performed as a banderillero until he married, and took over the position of caretaker of the Talavera de la Reina ring. Florito fought his first calf in public at 9 years of age, together with José Pedro Prados, who became the famous matador El Fundi. "I wasn't allowed to kill at that age, so I had to simulate the *suerte* with a banderilla. I continued *toreando* even though I was under age, because my father signed a declaration before a notary public assuming full responsibility for any injuries I might suffer."

He made his début with picadors at 16, using the artistic name *Niño de la Plaza* (Boy from the Bullring) and appeared in about 60 *novilladas* without and another 30 with horses, but he did not manage to appear in Madrid. When his father died suddenly, *Florito* gave up his career in order to help support his family. "I realised two things, first that you have to be 100% focused on the bull and you cannot be thinking about anything else, and second, that if anything happened to me, my mother and my three younger siblings would be left helpless. So I decided to give up the bulls in 1978 and accept the job which Manuel Martínez *Chopera* offered me as *mayoral* of his bullrings. I never cut my *coleta* in public and if any impresarios phoned me, I simply said I was unavailable on the date they offered. I fought for the very last time in 1981 and I have not picked up a *muleta* since, not even in the country, although I'm often invited to do so."

When *Chopera* became the impresario of Las Ventas, *Florito* took over the job from the previous *mayoral*, who was retiring, and today he is one of the most popular, beloved personalities of the Madrid ring. "My father told me that although it is difficult to become a *figura del toreo*, the really hard part is to stay right there at the top, and I've applied that advice to everything I undertake in life. I want to improve all the time, and how do I do that? With a lot of hard work and *afición*. My father taught me his concept of the bull, the torero and *toreo* and it's like my personal encyclopaedia of life."

Florito has set very high standards, thanks to the efficient work of his highly trained and obedient *cabestros*, and to his own personal ability and courage. It is frightening at times to watch how he waits until the very last second before vaulting to the safety of the *callejón* with the bull hot on his heels, about to catch him. "I have sufficient confidence in myself, although anybody can have an accident. I can't jump the fence a second too soon because if I do, the bull will run off and I'll have accomplished nothing."

Despite the great confidence he displays before the *toros*, he feels most uncomfortable with the extensive praise and applause he receives. "I never wanted to be a protagonist. I go out into the ring to do my job and get the bull back into the corrals, one way or another, as quickly as possible, so that the corrida can continue. Sometimes, if it takes three seconds longer, the public gets impatient, but there are bulls you cannot rush, because they're fatigued. There are also bulls that refuse to follow the *cabestros* and take refuge in their *querencia*. I can spot this tendency quickly, and that's why I try to cite them with my body and get them to run behind me towards the corrals."

It is by no means an easy task to return a brave bull to the corrals. In other plazas, when the *mayorales* have problems, the public clamours for "*Florito de Madrid*", something which should make him feel proud. "Of course it does, but it's simply the result of many hours of hard work. I love what I do, I have a lot of *afición*, and I like to do everything as best I can, including the *enchiqueramiento* of the corridas. I try to get the oxen to do the job in such a way that the bull is not distracted or injured in the process."

How does he get the oxen to obey him so well? "I talk to them a lot and they have learned to respond to my spoken commands. I know they seem to just lumber in and out of the ring but I treat them well. They look at me and know immediately what they are supposed to do." This mutual understanding is the result of Florito running them into the ring every day so that they grow accustomed to the creaking of the doors and he has taught them how to go out into the centre of the arena, surround the bull and lead it back to the *toriles*. The *cabestro Cortijero*, who wears the largest bell, is the leader. He always keeps an eye on Florito and knows what to do from a mere wave of his master's hand. "Sometimes you have to tap them gently with the stick because animals have good days and bad ones, but if you train them well, it is not necessary. I use the stick as little as possible because they are intelligent, and if you punish them, they will think: 'Okay, smarty, let's see if you are so smug when we're standing beside the bull!' This is what happens in other rings." The *cabestros* have some fighting blood in them, but Florito tames them with affection and loving care. He insists that: "You cannot accomplish anything with a stick, not with animals or people".

Florito spends the winters with his family on a small ranch he owns in Talavera de la Reina, and it is like a holiday for his *cabestros*. When his children were young they were never afraid and used to feed the *cabestros* and bring them water. "I always wanted my youngsters to feel comfortable with bulls, horses, dogs and chickens, to love Mother Nature and all her creatures."

On the days of official *reconocimientos*, Florito waits for the wagon bringing the bulls in crates from the ranch to arrive, and he unloads the corrida very carefully in the presence of the Civil Guard and the authorities who must inspect the seals on the crates and make sure they have not been tampered with. The animals are unloaded one by one and the *cabestros* lead them from one corral to the next, for the veterinary surgeons to conduct the individual examinations. Once a bull is led into the smallest corral, the *cabestro* turns around rapidly and disappears, the door slamming shut behind it. When the inspections are completed, the bulls are reunited in the main corral and if the veterinary surgeons approve the corrida, Florito feeds the animals and lets them rest.

His many obligations include the maintenance of the corrals, the feed, the straw, and at the end of each corrida, returning the *sobreros*, which have been enclosed in the *chiqueros*, to the corrals until the celebration of the next event. He has ten trained *cabestros*, but usually brings six out into the arena at any one time. He buys them when they are a year and a half old and they live to 7 or 8 years of age. "They are like toreros and if they should be injured by a bull, they become afraid, but I do my best to help them overcome their fear as soon as possible. I cure any injuries they may suffer with the aid of a trained veterinary surgeon and I take very good care of them, because they are my 'hands and feet'. They don't disappoint me and I'll never fail them, leaving them to the mercy of a bull."

Everyone in the callejón follows Florito's attempts to persuade a reluctant, sharp-horned bull to go back to the corrals

There used to be a large number of ranches dedicated to raising these steers but there are fewer and fewer nowadays. "I'm very demanding and have to look for my *cabestros* in Andalusia and Portugal. I try to find a half-dozen similar looking animals with the same colour hide, so that they look like a team, although I can easily distinguish one from the other." The *cabestros* are semi-brave animals, which were castrated when they were a year old, and are used for moving livestock around. Some *ganaderos* prefer to use cows but Florito feels that a cow is not as good as a *cabestro*. "A cow has two disadvantages. One is she can become pregnant and if she has given birth recently, she can't run as fast as she should. The other is that if the bull gets cornered, a *cabestro* will be brave enough to confront him, but a cow may back away."

When the president signals for the removal of a bull from the arena, Florito rushes to bring his *cabestros* into the ring. They are usually resting in the corrals, but as soon as they hear the squeaking of the gate they are up on their feet and ready to go. When they enter the ring, they slowly surround the bull and lead it back through the *toriles* to the corrals, where it will be sacrificed by the butcher. The *cabestros* know that they have to go in through one door and out of the other, while the rejected bull is led into a crate and killed with a *puntilla*. The mules drag the carcass out to the *desolladero* patio while the corrida continues in the ring.

Florito takes good care of himself, does not drink or smoke and, even though he does not go jogging in Madrid's Retiro Park, he certainly gets his share of exercise in the plaza. He confesses to being very timid. "I get very embarrassed when the audience applauds me and I know I turn red as a beetroot, but I'm pleased inside. When the day is over and I'm relaxing in front of the television set at night, I am really watching another 'screen' in my mind, with its own video of how the corrida went and what mistakes I might have made."

The Bullring Caretaker

The *conserje* or caretaker of the bullring has responsibility for the maintenance and upkeep of the *plaza de toros*. He is in charge of the keys and is usually an employee of the impresario or the bullring owner, and his job can be likened to that of the superintendent or custodian of any municipal property.

Alfonso Alonso and Manuel Alonso
Madrid, 1926-2004 and 1962-, previous and current conserjes, respectively, of the Las Ventas bullring

The Alonso dynasty has been in charge of the maintenance of the Madrid bullrings for five generations, beginning with the old Fuente del Berro ring and up to the current Las Ventas arena, opened on 17 June 1931, although it did not begin full operation until 1935. When he retired, Alfonso Alonso, who died in 2004, passed on the position to his son Manuel, and he confessed to me that he hoped his grandson *Alfonsito*, would continue the family tradition. It was an easier job in Alfonso's time because he had fewer responsibilities and even though he was also in charge of the Bullfight Museum, very few cultural events, exhibitions and lectures were organised.

The Museo Taurino was created by the Marqués de Valdavia and opened on 15 May 1952. It was expanded considerably in 1968 and set up in its current position above the corrals, and further renovation work, completed in 2016, created a separate entrance to the museum from the car park. There are plans to enlarge it still further, in view of its popularity among aficionados, tourists, school and senior citizen group excursions. Just like the Prado Museum, the Taurino possesses many more valuable works than it has room to exhibit. "There was a time when the Diputación de Madrid was interested in displaying the pale pink suit of lights worn by Manolete on that fatal afternoon in Linares, in an entire showcase dedicated just to him", explained Alfonso. "It might have seemed more disorderly and old-fashioned then, but aficionados really appreciated it."

Alfonso recalled the "good old days" when the toreros arrived at the ring in their horse-drawn carriages and the picadors came on their horses with the monosabios mounted on the animal's hindquarters. "The people would line the streets to see the toreros arrive and it was quite a show! Now, the traffic along the calle Alcalá would make this impossible."

During the Spanish civil war, Alfonso lived in the bullring and he had many memories of that time. "Obviously, they didn't put on any bullfights, and one day the owner of the stable of picadors' horses said he was afraid his animals would be requisitioned, so he suggested we have a barbecue. We were really hungry because food was so scarce and we had not seen meat in a long time. They were delicious!" Without corridas, Las Ventas became a multi-purpose building. "First it was a car drop-off point, then there was a warehouse for potatoes in the patio de caballos, and the other patio, the desolladero, was turned into a butcher's shop. We were terrified when they used the gallery below Tendido 3 all the way to the Main Gate as a powder store, because we feared we might be blown to pieces at any time!"

It is a real treat to live in the bullring, if you are an aficionado, but when the season is over, it becomes quite lonely. "Over the past few years, a circus was set up during the Christmas holidays. We had to slip carefully past the lion's cage to get to our front door and there was a pestilent smell of wild animals all the time. Nevertheless, my little grandson was in heaven!"

One of their many responsibilities, according to Manolo, was to make the banderillas used in Las Ventas. "It was a family affair. I made my first banderillas when I was I child because my dad said we all had to do our share. We used broom handles and then sticks made of beech, which were more flexible and did not snap. We cut them to the proper measurements— 70 cm—and then sandpapered them down to remove the knots. Once they were smooth, we drilled a hole in one end to insert the steel barb and then my mother decorated them with strips of coloured crepe paper. The normal barbs measure 6 cm and those for the black banderillas a little more."

Alfonso even remembered the banderillas de fuego [firework banderillas], which were no longer used after 1949. "They had to be made by a firecracker expert. We prepared the sticks and the barb and he added the powder." Alfonso approved of the new collapsible sticks invented by the retired Valencia-born torero Manolo Sales, because they are much safer for the banderilleros, and particularly the matadors, as they snap at the base and they hang down the bull's side, so as not to be at the levele of the torero's face during the *faena*.

He complained that the current toreros lack the individual personality of those performing in his day, from Manolo *Bienvenida*, Marcial Lalanda, Domingo Ortega and *Cagancho*, to *Gitanillo de Triana*, Antonio Ordóñez and Santiago Martín *El Viti*. "I think the young toreros today resemble one another too much. As for the bulls: in my time, they didn't use the *cruceta* or crossbar and the pic penetrated a lot deeper, and you know what? The bulls didn't fall down like they do nowadays." And what about the third facet of the Fiesta, the public? "The crowd was a lot more knowledgeable in the past. Now people show up at San Isidro as if it were a great social event: not to see, but to be seen!"

Manuel Alonso at the old entrance to the Las Ventas Museo Taurino

One unforgettable afternoon for Alfonso was the first corrida in Las Ventas after the Civil War ended, on 24 May 1939. "It was like starting all over again for us. I also remember the fire, which broke out early on Monday morning, 8 July 1963, when the two upper wooden galleries, the *gradas* and *andanadas*, caught fire from a cigar butt. Despite the damage, we were able to resume the corridas ten days later." There are sadder memories, too, like when they gave the posthumous lap of the ring to the coffin of Antonio Bienvenida in October 1975 and to that of young José Cubero Yiyo in August 1985.

Manuel Alonso was born in Las Ventas, while his father had come into this world in the nearby Fuente del Berro ring. It must be an exceptional experience to grow up in the leading bullring in the world. "I'm used to it", says Manolo. "I think it's quite natural, because I know no other life. I grew up surrounded by animals: bulls, cats and dogs, and my favourite 'toys' as a child were the horses in the stables, and that was just what happened to my son when he was young. It's clearly a very different life from that of an office-worker's child, who grows up in an apartment."

Manuel loves to ride and he used to help the *monosabios* warm up the string of horses along the esplanade on the eastern side of the ring, which disappeared when the M-30 ring road was built to skirt the city. As an adolescent, he was an all-round handyman and even assisted the veterinary surgeons when they operated on injured horses. However, in the end, Manolo decided to study technical engineering rather than become a vet. "It's proved more useful in the long run, because I'm also the manager of the bullfight museum and so I have to tend to a lot of administrative work. Besides, as my father said, there are a lot more bullfights and cultural events going on in the plaza now, and also unrelated activities, such as political meetings, concerts, commercial trade fairs, circuses, sports events..."

Manolo Alonso is extremely busy during the Feria de San Isidro and Feria de Otoño (the Autumn Fair), when there are corridas every day and he must attend to the courtesy *burladeros* in the *callejón*, along with the endless series of lectures, presentations and exhibitions organised in the plaza. "I feel as though I'm the representative in Las Ventas of the Comunidad Autónoma de Madrid, and so I have to worry about the general condition of the ring, rubbish disposal, damage and graffiti. I not only have to make sure it gets fixed but also to file the bureaucratic paper work."

He also prepares for the visit of the members of the Royal Family when they come to the bullfight, especially if they choose to occupy the lavish *Palco Real*. "Ex-King Juan Carlos is an excellent aficionado and so is his daughter Princess Elena, but the best aficionada of all in the royal family was the king's mother, the Condesa de Barcelona. I would like to see Queen Sofía come back some time. She used to attend when she was a princess but has not returned since. It's a known fact that she adores animals and doesn't truly understand bullfighting, but I think it was her obligation to attend as the Queen of Spain and we are also waiting for King Felipe and Queen Leticia to return. There are parts of my job that I don't like, but I have to do them anyhow."

Alonso, who lives in an apartment over the *patio de cuadrillas*, considers the Museo Taurino an extension of his living room, for its care is one of his major responsibilities. "I'm used to giving explanations to foreigners about the Fiesta and the important pieces on display, such as the portraits of Juan Belmonte, painted by Daniel Vázquez Díaz, and that of *Joselito* by Roberto Domingo, as well as a painting of *Costillares* attributed to the school of Francisco de Goya. The museum was revamped recently and modernised, and it focuses more now on carrying out a didactic mission. Even though the so-called 'diamond' pieces are on display, there are a lot of 'rubies' and 'emeralds' in storage and hopefully one day the museum will be expanded to accommodate them, too."

Manuel Alonso is not in favour of the recent projects to cover the ring. "First because toreros have always had to deal with the elements, the wind and the rain and, second, because it is a valuable artistic and historical monument and it should be respected."

Manolo says he wanted to be a torero when he was young, like any avid aficionado. "I tried, despite my father's opposition, but it didn't take long for me to realise that I had no future as a bullfighter. Some friends of my father, popular matadors Rafael Llorente and Manolo Escudero, took me to a series of *tentaderos* and they laughed at my pathetic attempts at caping the animals."

He remembers many stories. "I must have been six years old and I knew every nook and cranny in the ring. One day I crawled under the fence to see them unload the animals and when I crawled back out, I was facing the shoes of the bullring impresario Livinio Stuyck, who couldn't have been more surprised to see me under his feet. My mother said I mumbled something like: 'A nice *novillada*, don Livinio, a really nice *novillada*!' It was actually a huge *corrida de toros*, with bulls weighing over 600 kilos!"

It is said that President Lincoln's ghost has been sighted wandering through the halls of the White House and by those illustrious guests who have slept in his bedroom. "I've never seen any ghosts in Las Ventas, but there are times when I walk through the dark patios and the *callejón* and get the eerie sensation that a bull might suddenly appear. On one occasion, I had a real scare: I had come back from a night on the town with my friends and as I parked my car in the patio, I turned my head to see a man pointing a pistol at me. He asked me where I thought I was going and I managed to stutter: 'A *casa* [Home]!', but he didn't believe me right away. Apparently, there had been a bomb scare and they'd had to evacuate the three families who live in the ring: mine, plus those of the *mayoral* and the other caretaker. Imagine a young boy coming home late after one drink too many and finding a policeman, gun in hand, waiting for him!"

The Horse Contractor

Article 60 of the *Reglamento Taurino* concerns the contracting of the stable of horses for the bullrings, and stipulates that it should be made up of horses which are sufficiently broken-in, trained, and with the necessary mobility to make them suitable for the *lidia*. There must be at least six horses, weighing between 500 and 650 kg in first-category rings, and four horses in the rest. The picadors choose their horses according to their seniority, from among the group that has already been approved by the veterinary surgeons.

José Salcedo
Madrid, 1921. Retired picador and owner of the stable of picadors' horses of the Las Ventas bullring

José Salcedo is another of the many exceptional personalities who live the Fiesta with devotion and passion. He is "second taurine generation", for his father was the horse contractor in the old Tetuán de las Victorias bullring in Madrid, destroyed during the Civil War. "I was 15 years old and in school when the war broke out. I would have liked to have studied Medicine at university, but as we had no money, I naturally decided to become a picador, growing up as I did, surrounded by horses."

He spoke often in the course of our conversation of his great love of horses and is grateful that he did not have to live at the time when they were not protected by the *peto* (padding), which was officially required in Spain from 1928. "It must have been a pretty ugly sight, with three or four horses lying dead or dying in the ring, waiting to be dragged out between bulls, while the torero was performing with the muleta. The *Reglamento* at that time called for 24 horses per corrida. It was not unusual in Madrid for all the horses to end up either injured or killed, and so it would be necessary to run out into the street to buy the old nags from the coachmen waiting in their carriages to take the spectators home. How sad! I hate to see anyone hurt a horse, because it is a very noble animal."

Salcedo's father not only supplied the horses to the bullrings in Madrid, but he also began to organise bullfights in small towns, after the civil war. Salcedo made his début as a picador on 25 July 1939 in Almagro. "I remember it as if it was yesterday. The reserve picadors always went out to give the first *puyazo* and then the one from the *cuadrilla* took over the picing, and that is how we learned the trade. Today the Ministry of the Interior gives credentials to anyone who asks for them, and then we see that they don't even know how to ride a horse. The end result is a sorry spectacle and it makes me furious. When the horses were not protected with the *peto*, the reserve picadors were always at the ready. If a horse was seriously injured or killed, and the picador was in the infirmary, another one would trot into the ring to replace him. When the *peto* was introduced, the old Unión de Picadores y Banderilleros agreed to have the reserve picador continue to give the first *puyazo*, as an excellent hands-on way to learn the profession. Obviously the *reserva* was injured every day, and if he was going to give the first *puyazo* on three bulls that meant being knocked off his horse three times. That was guaranteed!"

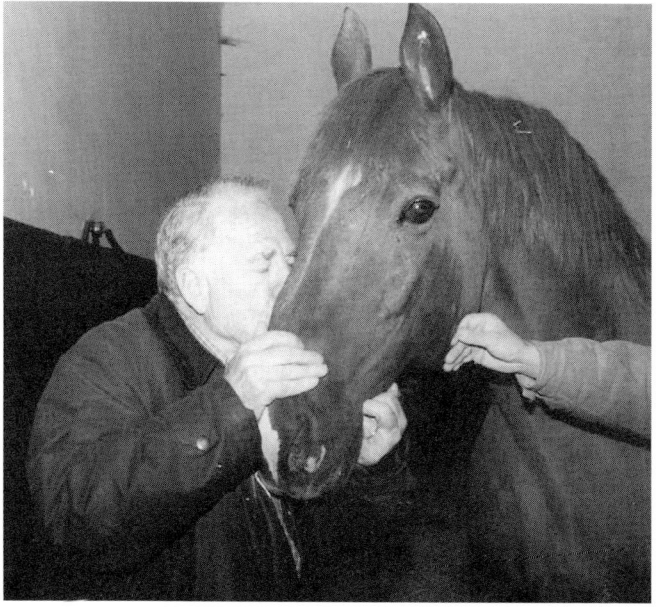

José Salcedo shows his dedication to his horses

"Furthermore," he continued, "no matter how good a friend you were, no matador would take you on as a picador if you weren't fully skilled and adept. Those of us who did not belong to a fixed *cuadrilla* would hang around two bars in Madrid's Plaza de Sevilla, El *Tropical* and *Riesgo*. The *mozos de espadas* would be there to hire the *cuadrilla*: 'Do you want to *torear* on Sunday?

How much do you want to earn?' Nowadays, they don't ask you what you want to be paid, they tell you to come along, knowing full well that you will settle for half of the stipulated salary. So, if you saw good picadors sitting on the side-lines while inexperienced clods were performing, it was obvious that they went through the *túnel*."

Salcedo explained the origin of the expression, the *túnel*: "One day I went to get paid by Curro Caro's sword-handler in the old café *Lyon d'Or*. He settled with four of us but not with the fifth, and when I asked why, he replied: 'I'll pay him when we go through a tunnel'. He was referring to the time when the toreros travelled by train and when it entered a tunnel the carriage went totally black and nobody could see what was going on."

Standards were high for picadors in Salcedo's time. His first corrida as the main picador did not take place until three years after his début, and then another ten went by before he became a fixed member of an important *cuadrilla*. "There were few plazas at the time, few corridas and no portable rings, so opportunities were scarce. *Novilladas* were not held in "portable" rings for the first time until the sixties." Salcedo went with such *figuras* as Curro Caro, *Gitanillo de Triana*, the *Bienvenida* brothers (Pepe, Antonio and Juan) and the *Dominguíns* (Pepe, Domingo and Luis Miguel). His last matador, in 1980, was Frenchman Christian Montcouquiol *Nimeño II*, who took his own life after never fully recovering from a tragic tossing in the bullring which had left him partially paralysed.

Pepe Salcedo shows incredible energy and vitality for a man of his age. "I've suffered considerable drubbings but I think on the whole I've been lucky. On the other hand, I took good care of myself. I was neither a drinker nor a smoker, and I'm actually one of the oldest professionals still involved in the bullfighting world, although I can't ride a horse any more. My brother Antonio made his début in the rings two months after I did, in September 1939, in Albacete. I have seen so much bullfighting over the years that I can tell just by watching the way someone walks, if he knows how to ride or not. In fact, the horse does four-fifths of the picing and the rider is responsible for only one-fifth. The first thing you have to do is look out for the horse, because he's your support, your pedestal, your protection, and if he falls you are cooked! That is why I get so angry when I see someone who hasn't got a clue about what he's doing and I get an irresistible urge to toss him in the water trough."

Though he talks with a gruff voice and dresses in worn jeans and an old sweater, Salcedo is a polite, educated, charming gentleman. "Wisdom is learned through living and as the old proverb says: '*Más sabe el diablo por viejo que por diablo* [The devil knows more because of his age than because he's the devil]'. I've seen a lot and travelled all over and if I hadn't learned something, I'd have to be pretty stupid. I know I'm somewhat unusual in that I must be the only Spaniard who doesn't like football, doesn't bet on the football pools or drop a coin in the slot machines in the local bar. I'm also deeply moved by all the tragedies going on in the world, affecting people and animals. For example, after the civil war, there was a lot of hunger in Spain. People would dig into rubbish bins to find something to eat, even banana and orange peels, which they fried and ate. At that time, there were no cats in the city for obvious reasons, yet we had an old hen in our house and neither my dad, my brother, nor I was capable of slitting that animal's throat."

The RSPCA might consider Salcedo a hypocrite. "I respect their opinions, but they also exaggerate. I don't like to see a bull take a long time to die, though that is its fate, and we do everything we can to make sure that the horses don't suffer. We shouldn't forget that in all of man's activities throughout history: travelling, waging war, working, the horse has been a loyal servant, even more so than a dog. A dog can be a 'best friend' but he does not render man a valuable service. I must admit that I even have difficulty watching a *corrida de rejoneo* because I'm afraid that the horse might stumble and get injured."

A picador's horse is often given a very mild tranquilliser, such as is prescribed for people with insomnia. Nevertheless, Salcedo looks for horses that are docile by nature, and so 90% of his stable does not require medication. The horse's eyes are covered with a cloth; the *Reglamento Taurino* stipulates that only one eye should be blindfolded, although some of the recent regional versions do acknowledge that both may be covered. "The horse can sense the presence of the bull, but if he were to see it, it would be impossible to control him. He cannot be forced to go against his natural instincts and stand firm awaiting the bull's bludgeoning charge. It's necessary to cover his eyes and we also use the *truenos,* folded-up newspapers, as earplugs for the same reason. However, my horses are obedient, agile and in good condition, so they do their job well and it's not easy to knock them over."

Pepe's son José Ignacio has not followed the Salcedo tradition and become a picador. He preferred to become a veterinary surgeon instead, and has taken over the family business. The horse contractor must also hire the *monosabios* and although only four are in the arena or *callejón* at any one time, two to guide and protect each horse, there are always more "in the wings" in case a horse is knocked over and it becomes necessary to pull it back on its feet, due to the heavy and cumbersome *peto*. "The job of the *monosabio* is to aid the picador when he loses his stirrup, needs a new *vara* or is thrown from his horse. He is the picador's assistant, and if at times the toreros do not succeed in drawing the bull away from a fallen horse and rider with their capes, the *monosabio* reacts instinctively to attract the bull's attention with his thin stick. There are a minimum of eight *monosabios* in Las Ventas but they don't get a salary; they offer their services gratis because they love what they do and it allows them to see the bullfight free of charge. They've all been with me for years and receive the appropriate social security and insurance coverage."

José Salcedo has many tales, but relates them reluctantly because he does not wish to hurt anyone's feelings. He had his confrontations with the police on a number of occasions as a picador. "We arrived at a bullring in the north of Spain in the morning, and the Police Delegate asked for our identity cards to record the information. I was tired and annoyed and I blurted out: 'Is this a jail? Have we committed a crime?' He replied that if he had to fine us during the corrida, he would already have our data. I said I thought everyone is considered innocent until proven otherwise. After the *paseíllo*, I went to the picadors' *burladero* and he was standing there. I couldn't help saying: 'This is for picadors only, so get out and find the one for the police!' Another time, we arrived at a ring after travelling all night and all I wanted to do was lie down and go to sleep. The president was nowhere to be found and after waiting around for some time, I said to the other picadors that we should leave, but they were afraid of being fined. The president finally showed up and started to tell us how to prepare the *puyas*. I was grumpy, so I snapped: 'Why don't you catch all the criminals on the street and put them away? We are all experienced professionals here, and we know what we have to do!' He was shocked and retorted: 'Don't come crying to me this afternoon about the fines and how your poor family needs the money!' 'My family's fine, thank you,' I replied. 'My kids go to the best schools in Madrid and are tired of eating prawns and lobster!' As it turned out, that afternoon, I piced a very brave Juan Pedro Domecq bull so well that the public applauded me and the president did not have the nerve to fine me. I heard he died a few months later and the local aficionados say it was because no-one had ever dared to confront him the way I did."

"On another occasion, some forty years ago, we were staying in a hotel in Seville, noted for its lousy food and skimpy portions. We left to fight in Palencia and on the way back we stopped at a service station and I ordered a *pepito* [a steak sandwich on French bread]. Well, they gave me a sandwich with five centimetres of meat poking out on either side. I ate the whole thing and then asked for another to take away. When we arrived back in Seville, I handed the hotel manager the sandwich. 'This is a *pepito* in Palencia, but here you would celebrate two weddings and three communions with this piece of steak!' He fell off his stool! The life of a torero is always full of stories."

The Bullring Musicians

The music in the plaza adds a touch of *alegría* (cheer) to a spectacle, which is already very much alive with colour, pageantry and excitement. Each plaza, no matter how modest it may be, is proud of its band, whether it be the municipal marching band, that of the village high school, or the rudimentary ensemble of the local *peña* (club), because the Fiesta needs its music not only for festive purposes but also for basic, functional reasons: the *timbales* and *clarines* (drums and bugles), signal the different *tercios* of the *lidia* and the orders issued by the president.

The *pasodoble*, the "military two-step", is the classic background par excellence to the Fiesta, although the spectacle can lend itself to other melodic accompaniments, such as the overture from Bizet's opera *Carmen*, which opens the *paseíllo* in some French rings, or the heart-rending, profound notes of flamenco guitar and *cante jondo* to accompany the performance of some gypsy torero in an Andalusian bullring.

However, very much to the regret of music-loving aficionados, the Las Ventas bullring, unique for many reasons, is the only one in the entire world where the band is not permitted to play during the fighting of each bull, but only in the intermissions. Although many people think this prohibition is due to the maximum category of the ring, the reason is quite different, especially if we bear in mind that music was played in the old Madrid plazas of the Puerta de Alcalá and Felipe II, and in Las Ventas itself until 24 May 1939. That was the day taurine activity was resumed after the Spanish civil war. Performing in that first bullfight, dubbed the "Corrida de la Victoria", were the rejoneador Antonio Cañero and the matadors Marcial Lalanda, Vicente Barrera, Pepe Amorós, Domingo Ortega, Pepe Bienvenida and Luis Gómez El Estudiante. Lalanda performed a great *faena* with a Carmen de Federico bull and so, at the request of the general public, the Municipal Band began to play the famous pasodoble written in his honour by the maestro José María Martín Domingo, *Marcial, eres el más grande* (Marcial, you're the tops). Everything was fine until this point; however, when Domingo Ortega performed another historic *faena* with his Antonio Pérez Tabernero bull, the public's request to hear the pasodoble *Domingo Ortega*, by the composer Ledesma y Oropesa, was not granted, for reasons unknown. The raging protests unleashed in the stands were such that the President declared: "No more music until further notice!" Unfortunately, that "further notice" never came, although there was one exception in that long period of musical "silence", on 16 October 1966, when matador Antonio Bienvenida killed six bulls all by himself. The matador placed his own sticks on the last bull, which he dedicated to his brother, matador Pepe Bienvenida, and the band began to play a pasodoble, composed in his honour, with the permission of the bullring president. This is how a temporary prohibition issued to avoid possible rioting in a politically sensitive and controversial period of Spanish history became an absurd tradition, which has lasted for seventy years. (The foregoing information was furnished to me by the conductor and composer Lorenzo Gallego Castuera.)

The Director of the Band: Lorenzo Gallego Castuera
Trujillo (Cáceres), 1931. Director of the Las Ventas bullring band

Lorenzo Gallego joined the band in 1978, following the baton of maestro Vaquero, whom he eventually replaced in 1990. Gallego is a charming, softly-spoken, extremely polite and educated gentleman, born in the small town of Trujillo, in the province of Cáceres, where he claims his love for the bulls was born, along with his love of music, at the tender age of 10. He got his start in the local band in Trujillo before deciding to follow a musical career in earnest, which prompted his moving to Madrid to study in the national conservatory. It was at this time that he began to compose his first "toys" as he calls them, his very first pasodobles. When he graduated from the Madrid Conservatory, he was immediately employed by the Menorca Symphony Orchestra and it was on that beautiful Balearic Island that he was inspired to compose his first tango, Sombra Querida.

Although he writes "melodic tunes" for mainly lucrative purposes, his real passion is the pasodoble. "The bullfighting pasodoble is our most characteristic, typical music. In fact, it dates back to the dances and theatrical tonadillas [songs] of the 17th and 18th centuries, and then to the pasacalles of the operas and operettas. The pasodoble was so popular that all the great Spanish composers such as Chueca, Chapí, Vives, Barbieri, Penella, Moreno Torroba, Gaztambide and Alonso included them in their zarzuelas [light operas]."

Maestro Gallego has composed about a hundred taurine pasodobles. "The bullfights and their music make up the historical and cultural memory of Spain. They form a major part of our customs and traditions and influence our language, define who we are and the way we think. In the end, they reflect our outgoing, cheerful nature. One cannot really conceive of a bullfight without its music because it is a picturesque, gallant, colourful spectacle and we cannot imagine the *cuadrillas* making the opening parade without a pasodoble."

The director of the band prepares a different musical programme for each Sunday corrida, well in advance of the date. "I actually give it a lot of thought, because I want my music to adapt to the programme, the toreros who will be performing, and the general mood which might reign in the bullring that day. I've written a pasodoble for all of the important and most of the less important toreros and so, if one of them is performing, I like to play it for him." The Las Ventas band has an extensive repertoire of some two hundred pasodobles, half of which were written by its director. Gallego adores his profession and possesses a great musical library, so that he can relate all the details of any particular pasodoble, its composer and the date of its composition.

Lorenzo Gallego Castuera directing the band at Las Ventas, tucked away—under cover—high in the gradas, during the paseíllo

Would he like the band to play during a good *faena* in Las Ventas? "Sincerely and unequivocally, yes! But with the permission of the impresario and the president, of course. I'd be delighted to do so. I firmly believe that the corrida needs its music, but I wouldn't dare to do it on my own for fear of the consequences." Gallego feels that music is always a good influence, for the public as well as for the torero. "It's a source of inspiration for the matador and is like a decorative fringe which envelops the art of *toreo*. I also wonder if the bull might not enjoy it as well."

A modest ensemble in a small-town bullring

The Las Ventas band is made up of eighteen musicians, and the director complains that such a monumental ring requires a bigger band so that it can be heard well throughout the plaza. Each musician brings his own instrument and his portfolio containing the complete repertoire of pieces with its corresponding catalogue number. The director has a list of the seven works he is going to play, written down with exquisite calligraphy, although he never took a class. "I always enjoyed drawing and sketching but I am not an artist. However, my handwriting does attract a lot of attention, even in the bank."

Corridas are held in Las Ventas in which the greatest ovation of the afternoon is often dedicated to the band. The public enjoys such lovely pasodobles as *Nerva* and *Espartero*, but which is Gallego's favourite? "The best pasodoble, in my opinion, is *Suspiros de España*, by Antonio Álvarez Alonso, and there is a little story behind it. Alonso was a pianist in the Café España, in Cartagena. One day, in the course of a discussion on the origin of artistic inspiration, his friends challenged him to demonstrate his ability to write a pasodoble in an hour. Disturbed by the lack of confidence of his friends, he accepted the challenge and went to sit in a corner where, in just half an hour, he wrote the music for this beautiful pasodoble. As he had time to spare, he left the bar to take a walk and stopped in front of a bakery selling the popular *Suspiros de España* pastries, and that is how one of the most beautiful pasodobles in the world got its title."

The dummers and buglers

José García Vázquez, Alonso Gallardo, Jesús Rubio and José María Silva
Timbalero (drummer) and clarineros (buglers) of the Las Ventas bullring

The responsibility for the functional music in the corrida rests with the *clarines y timbales* or bugles and drums. The *Reglamento Taurino* stipulates that these musicians should be seated directly opposite the presidential box, so as to be able to see the president at all times. Every bullring has its own traditions and customs regarding the notes played and the wardrobes of the drummers and buglers.

The *clarín* (bugle) is similar to the trumpet but has no valves, is somewhat smaller, with a conical bore and emits fewer notes. The bugles, together with the *timbal*, a hemispherical metal drum, signal the different stages in the course of the corrida and announce the orders of the president in a clear, precise manner.

The timbalero and clarineros of Las Ventas

José García, the *timbalero*, describes their role. "We are the *traductores* [interpreters] of the *corrida*, because we 'translate' or communicate the orders issued by the president with his handkerchiefs, so that the torero knows what he has to do and how much time he has in which to do it. When the ring is full and there is a lot of noise, sometimes the public does not see the president or hear us, and they do not know if the bull has been returned to the corrals or if the *tercio* has been changed. The *timbalero* is usually the most attentive to the president, although we are all watching. We have a signal among us: *¡Arriba!* [Up!] and when someone shouts it, we all grab our instruments. I remember one day a bull was about to jump the fence and somebody shouted without realising it: '*¡Arriba, arriba!*' and we almost began to play!"

There is a series of bugle calls which must be played when the president orders them: for the opening parade, for the bull to come out, for the picadors to make their entrance, to begin the *tercio de banderillas*, and then for the *faena*, which is the same as the one indicating the release of the bull. Then, of course, there are the *avisos* (warnings). José explains that they always have their instruments ready throughout the entire *corrida* and one of the *clarineros*, Alonso Gallardo, has his own chronometer for timing the *avisos*. "The first 10-minute period used to begin when the matador took the muleta in his hand, but now it starts when the *clarín* sounds: that's when the president sets his watch and we set ours."

José María Silva explains that the *clarín* is much more difficult to play than the trumpet. "You have to blow harder because the mouthpiece is smaller than that of the trumpet. As it doesn't have valves like the trumpet, you have to make a greater effort to force the sound out using your tongue and lips. The difficulty lies in getting accustomed to the mouthpiece and knowing how to make the *clarín* sound. I had problems at the beginning because I was used to playing the trumpet and my lip didn't adapt easily to the smaller opening of the *clarín*. I kept making burping sounds and it took me two full weeks to learn."

José García Vázquez became the drummer quite by accident. "I used to meet the *clarinero* José María Silva in the Metro every Sunday and he told me that they were looking for a *timbalero*, so why didn't I apply for the job? I didn't have any drums of my own so I practiced all week with a couple of spoons on an old pot. When I had to play for the first time, I was terrified because I had no musical background whatsoever." The instruments belong to the musicians and José keeps the *timbales*, according to tradition, in the bar *Los Timbales*, a little way up the street on calle Alcalá. "The impresario who took me on, José Luis Lozano, had these drums made to order because the original ones, which date back to the old bullrings of Goya and Tetuán de las Victorias, were bought by the impresario Manuel Martínez Chopera from the former timbalero's widow."

Seville's clarineros

The timbalero and clarineros sit in Tendido 4 and wear uniforms furnished by the Madrid impresarios. In Pamplona and Bilbao, they wear traditional regional costumes, but in Seville they have no formal outfits and only put on black *sombreros de ala ancha* [broad-brimmed hats]. Seville is also different in that there are only two clarineros. A clarín is more strident than a trumpet and that is why it was used to signal the charge into battle. When it rains, they have waterproof jackets but cannot take refuge under a canopy because it would block the view of the people seated behind them. "Our major concern is not to get our instruments wet."

They all give the same reason for explaining their profession. "You have to like bullfights and music because there is little financial compensation, and you have to bear in mind that you are a slave to your job every Sunday and holiday from mid-March to mid-October. Then, during the Feria de San Isidro, in May, there are 30-odd corridas in a row, so we have just enough time to come home from work, eat lunch, then rush off to the bullring."

Clarineros and *timbaleros* form a close-knit unit and are always very attentive to the president's indications. José García remembers one time when the president was very impatient, "He sent the *alguacilillo* over to tell us to pay more attention because we were taking too long to play. We didn't say anything but when the *alguacilillo* came back a second time and shouted up to us from the *callejón*: 'The president said you are all asleep'. I gave him a card on which I wrote: '*Señor Presidente*, we are not mechanical toys! We're four people and we have to synchronise ourselves and take a deep breath before we play'. What did he expect? For us to have the instruments in our mouths all the time?" I remember another incident when the bull was about to fall, but the president was determined to give the matador an *aviso*. We had to raise our instruments to our lips but the bull dropped immediately and all we had time for was a little 'peep'."

The Taxidermist

Thanks to the art of taxidermy the history of bullfighting has been preserved and immortalised. There are thousands of stuffed bulls' heads which bear witness to the triumphs and tragedies of an endless number of toreros. They adorn the walls of museums, bullrings and the homes of matadors and bull-breeders, and serve as impressive decorative motifs for bars and restaurants.

Justo Martín Ayuso
Galapagar (Madrid), 1938. Taxidermist

Justo Martín explains that his vocation as a taxidermist began as a hobby. An enthusiastic bullfight aficionado and a keen hunter of small game, he became interested in conserving his own trophies, and so he decided to study this difficult, complicated and lengthy process, which requires not only scientific and technical knowledge, but also artistic modelling, designing and composition skills. "A good taxidermist is really a sculptor. There have always been just a handful of professional taxidermists and they weren't anxious to share their secrets, so I had to do a lot of experimenting and investigating on my own. Unfortunately, the profession has been degraded because the new generation has not accepted the fundamental, handcrafted procedure and has opted for a less skilled and painstaking process, using polyurethane or polyester moulds. As a result, the animals look as though they've been mass produced and lack the life and distinctiveness which I have always tried to give each one of them."

Vital to Justo's professional history was the time he spent in Colombia, where he learned to dry and stuff not only bull's heads, which are his speciality, but also every variety of exotic animals. "Although I have done thousands of bulls," he says, "each one is different and poses a challenge. The bull is a unique, majestic species and I want to capture all that spirit in my work. I am proud of the fact that there is also a great deal of interest abroad, and I have shipped *cabezas de toros* [bulls' heads] to such faraway places as Lithuania, Japan and all over the United States."

Justo feels it is important to reflect the animal's bright, vibrant look in the final piece, and so he goes to the *apartado* in the morning to study the live bulls. "Each animal is different in terms of its size, horns, anatomy and, most importantly, expression. Furthermore, the bull varies greatly when it's in the country, in the corrals and in the ring. That means that if the *ganadero* asks me to prepare a bull's head, he generally wants a more noble expression on the animal's face than a torero, who prefers it to look fierce and aggressive, which is precisely the way he perceives it."

There are very few skilled taxidermists around today, although there are those who do a quick but superficial job in which sooner or later the bull's head breaks or the skin splits. This is unfortunate for a torero who took the *alternativa* or scored a great triumph with that bull, or for the *ganadero* who wants to keep one of his best animals on display.

The taxidermy process is not continuous, and involves a series of steps which represent 35 to 40 hours of intensive work, carried out over a six-month period. The taxidermist buys the bull's head from the butchers in the bullring. He removes the hide and sends it to the tanner's, where it takes months to dry. The skeleton of the head is cleaned very well and disinfected and then a model is made, first in clay and then in plaster, which is why Justo's bull's heads weigh so much. It is necessary to wait until the skin is totally dry before applying it to the mould. Then the horns and glass eyes are added. "I have so much work right now, including other animals, that it usually takes a year before I can deliver a commission. I know it would be easier, faster and cheaper to do it another way, but I prefer to create my own little 'work of art'. I study the animal carefully while it is alive and then in photographs, because if you are not careful, the dried skin might not fit afterwards."

Obviously, all this work has its price. "You must first distinguish the material worth from its historical significance, because the true value lies in where the bull was killed, by whom, from what ranch it came, on what occasion (the Seville or San Isidro ferias, for example) and finally whether the matador cut any ears. There are, of course, those 'other' bulls which I wished I never had to do: the tragic ones, like Burlero, which fatally gored poor Yiyo in Colmenar Viejo, on 26 August 1985, or the cow Conocida, which was responsible for Antonio Bienvenida's death in the little tentadero ring of a ranch. In general, the bull's head costs roughly 250 euros to cut and skin, and then my work can range between 900 and 1,200 euros, which means the final price is approximately 1,500 euros, plus any additional or travel expenses incurred."

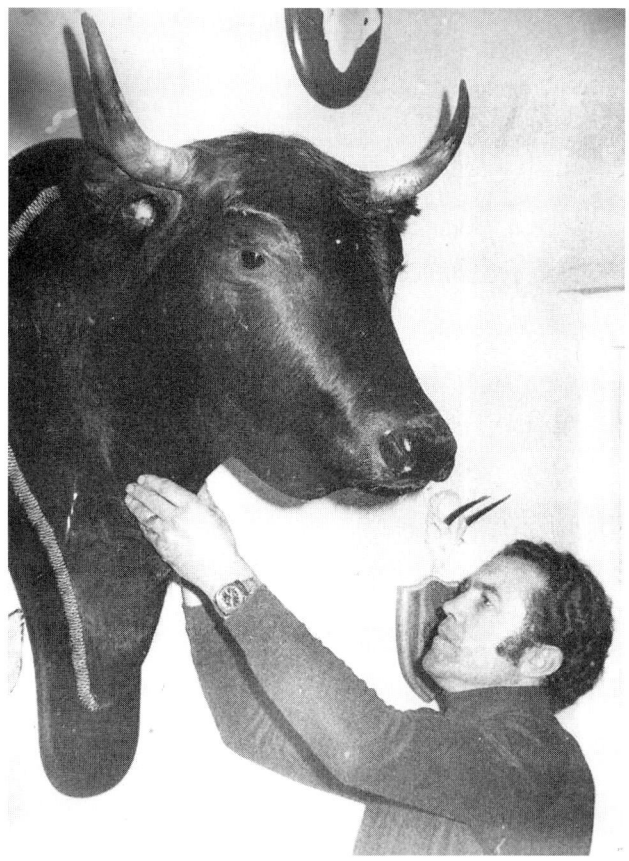

Justo Martín Ayuso with one of his cabezas de toro

Justo Martín Ayuso's "heads" are totally guaranteed and he is very proud of his work. Of the more than 3,000 cabezas he has prepared, not a single one has been returned to the shop for repairs. "The ones I did over thirty years ago appear the same as they did on day one, and this is due in part to the fact that they are not hollow inside, which in turn explains why they weigh so much. I also use the best tanner and don't skimp on any expenses to assure that the end result is the very best I can achieve."

He was the very first taxidermist to stuff a complete bull. "I have done seven up to now. The first was for Japan, oddly enough, and there is another in the Mijas bullring museum and, of course, the famous Belador, of the Victorino Martín ranch, fought by José Ortega Cano, which is the only bull to have been pardoned to date in Las Ventas. If both the matador and the *ganadero* want the bull's head, traditionally the *ganadero* takes priority, although if it marked a great triumph, like the time José Tomás cut two ears from an El Torreón bull in Madrid in 1998, the *ganadero* might let the matador have it. After the breeder and the torero, then the impresario can claim the bull, and finally any aficionado. There are people who prefer animals without their ears, reflecting a triumphant afternoon, and others who want the ears, because it makes them look more attractive."

Justo remembers fondly what Antonio Chenel *Antoñete* told him when he delivered the mounted head of the last bull he killed in Las Ventas in June 1998: "When I sit down to smoke a cigarette under this bull's head, I'll still be able to hear the applause ringing in my ears from that special afternoon when I was awarded both its ears."

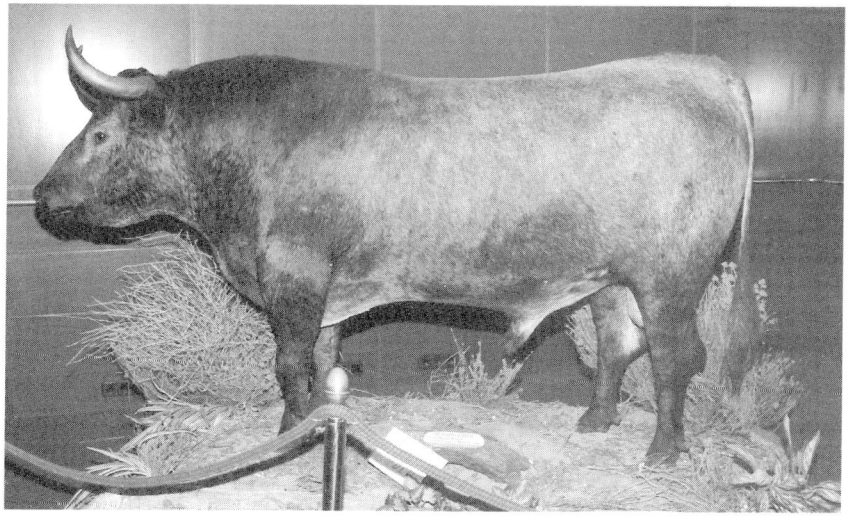

Martín Ayuso conserved the whole body of Belador, the Victorino Martín bull, the only one to be pardoned in Las Ventas to date

The Taquillero (Ticket Office Manager)

When bullfights were first being organised in village squares, there were no tickets as such. The spectators handed over a small coin to the gatekeepers controlling the entrance to the square, and then scrambled up on to the wagons and carts set up to form and close off the makeshift arena. With the construction of the first permanent rings, the need to distinguish the better seats from the less desirable ones led to the creation of a ticket system, and the first ring to sell tickets was Seville's La Maestranza, in 1738, although they called them *boletines* rather than *entradas*, the word most often used today. *Abonos*, season tickets, came into being in 1803, to reserve certain privileges for the more noteworthy spectators. In 1836, matador Francisco Montes, in his *Tauromaquia*, one of the most important "rule books" on bullfighting written by a professional, emphasised the importance of providing numbered tickets, "to avoid quarrels and the discomfort resulting from an avalanche of spectators". Melchor Ordóñez adopted Montes's suggestion in the first *Ensayo de Legislación Taurina*, published in 1852, and stipulated something sensible and elementary: "No more tickets will be sold than the number of people who can be seated comfortably inside the ring".

The manager of the bullring ticket office is responsible for the printing of the tickets for each corrida, according to Article 36 of the *Reglamento Taurino*, and he is obliged to retain 5% of the total capacity of the plaza for sale to the public on the day of the *festejo*. In addition, and according to the category of each ring, up to 10% of the total capacity of the plaza can be reserved for sale by the authorised, privately-owned ticket offices, which are entitled to add a 20% surcharge to the face value of the ticket. Section 5 of Article 36 clearly prohibits the resale of any tickets, referring specifically to touts.

Iñaki Veiga
San Sebastián, 1935. Ticket-office manager, Las Ventas

Iñaki Veiga was for many years the ticket office manager of the Las Ventas bullring, in addition to other plazas managed by the José María Jardón-Livinio Stuyck duo, including that of his native San Sebastián and those of Valencia, Gijón, Castellón de la Plana, Alcalá de Henares, Talavera, Aranjuez and Colmenar Viejo. Although he was an aficionado from the time he was a child and accompanied his father every Sunday to the bullring, when Iñaki moved to Madrid in 1968, he was somewhat hesitant about giving up the security of his "day job" in the bank to take over the position at Las Ventas.

The *taquillero*'s job is a lot more complicated than many people may imagine, although computers have facilitated the work a great deal and the impresario can now verify the status of the *abonos* and daily ticket sales directly from his own office. "Before the 'computer era', the impresario used to come to my office and ask me what the status of ticket sales was on any particular date. I had my own system and would keep notes which worked out very effectively." Another major difference prior to computers was that the tickets had to be ordered from the printers well in advance, and now they are printed directly on the computer as they are requested. "That isn't all that great", complains Veiga, "because the aficionado is a romantic at heart and very frequently a collector of memorabilia. The old-fashioned tickets were beautiful and featured colourful drawings by famous artists. Now they're all the same and you can't tell them apart." One thing computers have not been able to do is avoid the fact that people tend to show up at the last minute and long lines are formed half an hour before the corrida begins. "It becomes a madhouse and this is where the computers tend to slow things down. When a customer asks for two seats in Tendido Bajo of 7, by the time you find them on the screen and tell him or her what you have and he or she asks the price, another employee has already sold them to someone else in his queue! And if they want to pay with a credit card, forget it! Sometimes the 'good ol'days' were better. However, there is no doubt that it is a clean, simple, transparent system, which can be easily monitored."

The real capacity of Las Ventas is almost 24,000 seats, although not all go up for sale. "There are some courtesy passes for government officials, police, veterinary surgeons, press, etc., which leave about 20,000 available to the general public. However, the San Isidro *abono* is the 'dream' of any taurine impresario, because it means a guaranteed 80% of the ring capacity sold. There are almost 18,000 *abonos*, plus those of the senior citizens, and the young aficionados, under 25 years of age." The *abono* is personal and non-transferable, and if a title-holder cannot come and collect it personally at the *taquilla* (ticket office) because he is ill, disabled, travelling or working, a signed authorisation is necessary, with the signature endorsed by the bank. "Years ago", says Iñaki, "there was not much concern about the *abonos*, but as the demand increased dramatically in the 1980s, when Manolo *Chopera* was the impresario, it became necessary to include the clause 'personal and non-transferable.'"

Despite modernisation and the strict controls on the sale of *abonos*, exorbitant re-selling still runs rampant. Iñaki responds: "First of all, we must make clear that there are a dozen official agencies which have existed for many years, and they hold legitimate rights to approximately 2,000 seats, which is not a lot, although they are the best seats in the house. If they

Iñaki Veiga, Director of taquillas at Las Ventas

weren't—if they were in the upper tiers of the sunny section—it would not be much of a business for the agencies, would it? What they do with their tickets once they pay for them at the bullring ticket office is their problem. If they sell a 50-euro ticket through 'freelancers' for 200 euros or more, it has nothing to do with the bullring and becomes a police matter. It is also a question of supply and demand. I remember some time ago the bullring impresario issued an *abono* card rather than individual tickets, so what did the touts do? They took the driving licence and car keys of their clients to make sure that the card would be returned. Furthermore, you can't prohibit someone from effecting a sale at the legal price. During the Feria de San Isidro Fair in May, bullfights are held every afternoon for a month, and aficionados with *abonos* may well not be able to come every day! One thing is clear, there are touts all over, in luxury hotels, and offices, and now they operate through their mobile phones. When I went to Paris to see Plácido Domingo, I wasn't going to spend the whole night waiting in a queue, so I bought a ticket from the touts—who happened to be Japanese! They were carrying around signs saying: 'Opera tickets for sale'".

Even though most bullrings are now computerised and tickets can be purchased online, Iñaki feels that the Fiesta is still very antiquated and is in need of an urgent face lift. "The posters, the terminology, the printed matter, etc., have not changed and their language and presentation are archaic. There's a desperate need to adopt a new marketing strategy. In the advertising world, image is everything, and nothing is being done to revamp bullfighting. The local Telemadrid television station films the morning's *apartado* and shows it on the midday news, which creates interest in the afternoon's corrida, but aside from the two or three toreros who are in the glossy gossip magazines, you don't find too many matadors with whom the general public is familiar. The impresario orders the same standard advertising and posters, which they hand out to 'volunteers' to hang up in local bars and that's it! I think it unforgivable that a concierge of a major hotel will call up to ask if there's going to be a corrida on Sunday: he should know that from the second Sunday in March until the second Sunday in October, a bullfight is scheduled every Sunday and holiday! You don't call up a cinema to ask if they are showing a film, although you may ask which one is playing. This shows that the current advertising system is not working."

Iñaki has another interest in addition to the bulls: painting. He was a student at the San Sebastián School of Fine Arts and, aside from designing posters, he likes to paint impressionist landscapes. He won first prize for the best *cartel* for the Corrida de la Beneficencia in 1983, as well as other important awards. "The poster, no matter what it's for, has to be like a 'punch in the eye'; it has to attract your attention, with striking colours that call out to you. You can't have a grey poster in the city because it would go unnoticed. There have been good poster painters who haven't been good artists, and vice versa. For example, Picasso was a genius, but he couldn't paint a good poster, yet the most glorious epoch of bullfighting posters was that of Roberto Domingo, who was an extraordinary painter and the best poster artist ever."

Now Iñaki works less and enjoys his *afición* more. "I like to go to the corrida with my friends and my cigar. When I was in the *taquilla* I couldn't enjoy the bullfight because I was in the office. Even though latterly I was able to watch it on a closed-circuit television, it wasn't like being in the plaza."

Iñaki once asked the impresario he worked for to contract a good friend of his for a corrida, the matador Ireneo Baz *El Charro,* who was from a town near San Sebastián. "It was the first and last time I've done anything like that! We both had the misfortune of suffering a very serious goring. I say 'we', because I felt responsible. If I had stuck to my tickets, maybe nothing would have happened to him."

Veiga's life as a *taquillero* was full of memorable moments. "One day a friend of mine came to ask me for a favour. He said: 'I have a problem: I need two good tickets for Friday's corrida!' I replied: 'You have a problem? You're creating a problem for me! If you were a pharmacist and I asked you to give me a prescription drug, I would be creating a problem for you'. I suppose this is part of the Spanish picaresque. I even had to go to court on several occasions, because a boy stole his father's *abono* card and sold it without his permission. Or when the *abono* was registered in the wife's name, and after the divorce, the husband wanted it back. We at the ring have to respect the name appearing on the card. Relatives of people would come to pick up *abonos* with duly signed authorisations when I knew for a fact that the title-holder had long since passed away."

Some (but by no means all) of the employees of the Las Ventas bullring

Miscellaneous Sales Personnel

Blas Romero El Platanito
Castuera (Badajoz), 1945. Lottery seller and retired comic torero

*In later life, El Platanito retains the good humour
he showed when in his prime as a torero*

Blas Romero's story deserves a book in itself, rather than just a brief reference in this chapter. Today he sells lottery tickets with the same good humour he displayed when he was a comic bullfighter in the sixties and seventies and filled the rings with his entertaining antics. He amassed a considerable fortune and even starred in the film of his own life-story, *Jugando a morir* (Playing with Death), directed and produced by José Hernández Gan. But the bullfighter's money is often just a chimera and Blas Romero lost it all. He supports his family by selling state lottery tickets.

Manuel Cicerone
Madrid, 1946. Souvenir salesman

Manuel sells all kinds of taurine souvenirs to aficionados and tourists and has been a fixture in front of the bullring for over forty years. He sets up his municipally licensed stand between the Puerta Grande [main gate] and the *patio de caballos* and also has his own print shop for bullfight posters, while his wife embroiders the tiny *capotes de paseo* which people hang from the rearview mirrors of their cars. He declares: "I'm a dedicated fan of El Juli and I've followed his entire career from the time he was 13!"

Spectators who have arrived early inspect Manuel Cicerone's wares

Félix Reyuerta
Madrid, 1932. *Seller of refreshments*

Félix Reyata is one of the most veteran soft-drink and beer sellers in Las Ventas. In fact, he possesses Las Ventas bullring employees' identity card no. 8. He also happens to be one of the most gracious. His grandfather used to bring the mule team to the bullring after the Spanish civil war, and both his father and uncle sold drinks in the plaza. In 1955, Félix decided to continue the family tradition. Although he possesses his own senior citizen's abono, he prefers to sell refreshments in *Las Ventas*, although he does not do the same in the Santiago Bernabeu football stadium, unlike many of his colleagues.

Of the many memorable afternoons he has witnessed, he recalls the corrida in which Gregorio Sánchez, as the only matador, cut seven ears; Antoñete's famous *faena* with the white Osborne bull in 1960; the double session—morning and afternoon—of Antonio Bienvenida, and the last time a horse was killed in the ring, because they didn't wear the ultra-protective 'underpants' they do now.

Félix saves all the bullfighting programs and has a vast collection of curiosities and trophies, which he has placed in an album, entitled Mi vida en Las Ventas. He has many stories to tell. "Tourists never stop eating during the whole corrida. They can't resist munching on sandwiches, crisps, sweets, ice cream ... while Spaniards tend to chew pipas [sunflower seeds] and drink. I also get to see a lot of famous people. I remember Yul Brunner, who was much, much shorter than I expected, and the Mexican actress María Félix, who was thin and drawn from so many face-lifts. She came often, and always pulled out a cigar and waited for some gallant gentleman to light it for her."

Simón Rodríguez
Badajoz, 1932. Seller of posters, magazines and miscellaneous items

Simón and his wares in the tendidos of Las Ventas

Simón has been selling anything and everything related to bullfighting in Las Ventas for the past 45 years; he has been on the payroll since he was 26. He was a *novillero* and got as far as performing with picadors. He claims to have taken part in *tentaderos* with *Antoñete* and Dámaso Gómez. Now he sells the bullfight magazine *Aplausos* in the *tendidos*, together with a wide variety of taurine memorabilia.

There is an infinite number of curious and wonderful personalities, devoted aficionados all, who deserve to be included in this book, although this is obviously not possible.

Chapter 5. On the Sand

The Alguacilillo

During the 16th, 17th and 18th centuries, the first duty of the *alguaciles* or *alguacilillos* (constables) was to clear the ring of the spectators who gathered in it before the beginning of the spectacle, especially when a corrida was held in small-town rings. The presence of the *alguacil* in the ring coincided with the arrival of the authority in the main box (*palco*), and he was responsible for executing the president's orders. Mention was first made of their duties during the reign of Isabel la Católica, in 1503. Nowadays, their job is to lead the opening parade, collect the key to the *toriles* from the president and then cross the ring on horseback to deliver it to the *torilero*, supervise the correct progress of the *lidia* according to the authority's orders and finally, the happy task of presenting the matadors with any trophies awarded: ears and tails. At present, in major bullrings they wear traditional attire corresponding to the epoch of Felipe IV: a black velvet suit, short cape, starched white collar, high, black riding-boots and a hat called a *teja*, crowned with feathers, most often red and yellow, which add the only note of colour. In provincial rings, they may be dressed in *traje corto* and *zahones* (chaps).

Teodoro Martínez Meco
Madrid, 1927. Alguacilillo of the Las Ventas bullring

Teodoro Martínez joined the Las Ventas payroll when he was aged 26, thanks to his friend, Paco Llorente, who was one of the *alguacilillos* at the time. "Paco asked me if I liked the bulls and I replied jokingly: 'Of course, it's my favourite dish!' Paco found me a job in the ring, first as a doorman, and I cannot forget one dreadful afternoon when I was stationed at the main gate. An older woman approached and said she had come to meet her husband. I told her I was sorry but I could not allow her to come in without a ticket. I made her wait outside for half an hour until her husband showed up; it was Livinio Stuyck, the impresario! I was horrified at my stupidity, but when my superior arrived, he said: 'Don't worry. You did just what you were supposed to do'."

One day, the head of personnel asked if he knew how to ride a horse and Teodoro did not hesitate to rise to the occasion. One of the *alguacilillos* had suffered a stroke and they needed a substitute immediately. "He was a huge man and when I put on his outfit, the hat slipped down to my nose and I had to wrap the jacket around my waist twice! They had a proper suit made by the following Sunday."

The alguacilillos *await the entry of the toreros in the Las Ventas ring*

The *alguacilillo* is an employee of the impresario, although his responsibility is to carry out the president's orders, which include the following duties, according to Teodoro: "To supervise the *suerte de varas* and make sure that the bull, the horse and the toreros are all positioned correctly; if a bull is returned to the corrals, to instruct the toreros to retire to the *callejón* so that the tame steers can come in; to clear the ring of toreros if the president orders the third *aviso*; in summary, we have to enforce the *Reglamento Taurino*".

The *alguacilillos* kick off the corrida by cantering across the ring to salute the president, and then they return to the *puerta de cuadrillas* to lead the *paseíllo*. If it is a *novillada*, they will return to the patio entrance side by side, but in a *corrida de toros* they will each circle back along the *barrera*. The senior *alguacilillo* receives the key to the toril symbolically from the president and then hands it to the *torilero*.

Madrid is the only ring in which, due to its category, the torero is obliged to request a change of *tercio* (from picing to placing banderillas or from the latter to the *faena*) from the *alguacilillo* instead of directly from the president, because, according to Teodoro, tradition dictates that the matador can take off his *montera* only if he is going to dedicate the bull. "According to the new *Reglamento Taurino*, in a first-category ring the bull must receive at least two *puyazos* and preferably three. If the matador requests the change after the first pic, I must inform the police delegate and he telephones the president, but I know he will not grant the request. I have learned a lot from Llorente, who spent more than 50 years in this ring; he began as a *monosabio* when he was just 14 years old, because he wanted to become a picador like his older brother."

The torilero receives the key from the alguacilillo

The *alguacilillo*'s responsibility begins with the *paseíllo* and ends when the mules drag out the last bull. He is also particularly concerned about his wardrobe. "We are the image of the bullfight, and the first ones to appear on the screen during a televised corrida. My wife made sure that my outfit was impeccable, my cape pressed and my collar starched, but when it rained, the feathers got wet, and red and yellow streaks stained my clean white collar."

What Teodoro loved best is the granting of trophies. "Traditionally, the senior alguacilillo gave the ears to the torero, until one day I asked him if we could take turns. The first matador to whom I gave an ear was Andrés Vázquez, although I'll never forget the afternoon of 22 May 1972, when I presented Palomo Linares with the two ears and the historic, controversial tail. Thirty-six years had passed since they had granted a tail in Las Ventas [to matador Curro Caro]. I was delighted, although they dismissed the president Juan Antonio Pangua the very next day and black mourning ribbons were hung from the balconies of the more demanding sectors of the ring. What I do remember is that the whole plaza had been clamouring and waving their handkerchiefs for the tail. I was as nervous as Palomo was and he hugged me so tightly that he covered my suit with blood. To this very day, I get goose pimples when I think about that afternoon."

Sebastián Palomo Linares with the controversial tail

Teodoro made his last *paseíllo* in a festival held in February 1998, in honour of Doña Maria de las Mercedes de Borbón, King Juan Carlos's mother, and he could not stop the tears from flowing down his cheeks. "The impresario said I had to retire because I was 72 years old. I told him I would do it for nothing but he insisted, because he was afraid that I would get thrown from my horse or a bull would jump into the *callejón*." Nevertheless, Teodoro did not stop riding and he helps Carmelo Caballero, his substitute, with the cattle he has on his ranch. All this *afición* is not surprising because as an adolescent Teodoro worked as a ranch hand on the Duque de Tovar's *ganadería*, which today is Peñaflor, between Torrejón de Ardoz and Mejorada del Campo, to the east of Madrid.

Teodoro's "day job" was with Iberia Airlines, where he worked the early morning shift for 41 years. When his boss wanted to switch him to afternoons he replied: "There is only one thing that I care more about than my life and that is my job as *alguacilillo* in Las Ventas. Either I continue with the morning shift, or I quit!" He was lucky, and his boss agreed.

There is one afternoon he does not remember fondly. "I was in the *callejón*, standing beside an *arenero* and a banderillero, and I turned to warn them not to move because the matador was going in for the kill. The sword hit bone and flew out of the matador's hand and ended up stabbing me in the foot. I saw my boot slowly filling up with blood as they rushed me to the infirmary. I begged the doctors not to give me an injection, because I hate needles, but they insisted on an anti-tetanus shot and I had to sit down in a *burladero* because I started to feel faint."

The Monosabio

The term *monosabio*, according to Luis Nieto's *Diccionario Ilustrado de Términos Taurinos*, is applied to the "mozo [lad] who aids the picadors and whose only defence is a thin stick". The work of the *monosabio* begins with the general tasks of any stable-boy: cleaning the stalls, feeding the horses, grooming them, warming them up, saddling and bridling them, and attaching the protective *petos*. In the ring, he helps to place the picador's horse in the proper position and gets both horse and picador back on their feet if they are toppled to the sand. This is a difficult task, due to the weight of the cumbersome *peto* and the heavy armour the picadors wear on their legs. Prior to 1928, when the *peto* was introduced in Spain, the *monosabios* also carried a small *puntilla* or dagger in their sash, with which to give the coup de grâce to a seriously injured horse. Fortunately, it is very, very rare indeed to see a horse hurt nowadays.

The *monosabios* also take very seriously their role of protecting the horse and rider. As they are usually young and agile "lads", they are ready to make a life-saving *quite* (taking the bull away from the horse or a fallen rider), with their staff, cap or even their own body. They are also the first ones to jump into the ring to pick up an injured torero and rush him to the surgeon's capable hands in the infirmary.

Seven monosabios, keeping one eye on the bull, attempt to raise a fallen horse

It cannot be said that the *monosabios* had very glorious beginnings, and as their work in the stables was neither lucrative nor easy, they would appear in the plaza wearing the dirtiest, scruffiest attire, until in 1840 the Madrid impresario decided to furnish them with a uniform: dark blue trousers and shirts, with a red sash and cap, an outfit which has not varied much over the years. However, it was not until 1874 that they earned their unusual nickname, which translates as "wise monkeys". It seems that a travelling troupe of trained monkeys had a very successful booking in Madrid's Apollo theatre. The monkeys happened to be dressed in outfits similar to those worn by the bullring employees, and as the stable boys jumped in and out of the arena with the same agility as a monkey, they become known as *monosabios*.

Throughout the history of *toreo*, many a picador has begun as a *monosabio*, such as José Marquetí, as have toreros like Felipe García, and, more recently, the rejoneador Basilio Barajas and his brother, matador Faustino Barajas, both of whom were predecessors of the famous *Pimpi* dynasty of picadors.

Luis Durán
Madrid, 1959. Monosabio of the Las Ventas bullring

Luis Durán's maternal grandfather owned a small stable of horses and was responsible for the immense *afición* of both Luis and his older brother, Manuel, a well-known photographer, director of the graphic art and documentation department of the Espasa-Calpe publishing company, and author of several books on bullfighting. Luis used to break and train the horses on his grandfather's ranch, and in his spare time he loved to run the *encierros* of the nearby towns and practice the art of *recortes*, jumping over and feinting before 300-kg *novillos*. When he was called up for his military service at the age of 20, he served in the northern provinces of Zaragoza and Navarra, where he was able to participate in the local *capeas* to earn a few extra coins. "I have enough courage to run with the bulls and jump over them, but not the skill or art needed to *torear*, and I couldn't be a rejoneador because we didn't have enough money in our family to buy an expensive string of horses."

Being a *monosabio* is more than just a hobby for Luis Durán, who has been working with Pepe Salcedo for more years than he can remember. Wherever the Salcedo stable went so did he: Toledo, Ciudad Real, Guadalajara and, finally, Madrid. In his free time, he attends to his "day job", his own locksmith's shop. "During San Isidro, I am at the shop at seven in the morning and I organise and prepare the work for my two employees. I head for the ring at three in the afternoon, with barely enough time to grab a sandwich, because I have to put on the horse's stomach linings and the plastic gaiters which protect the hocks from the hooves. The other *monosabios*—we are usually eight in all—put on the rest of the *peto*, the harness and the saddles." There are lesser-known, behind-the-scenes aspects of the preparation of the picador's horses which help to make them more suitable for participation in the corrida. First, the newsprint *truenos*, the "ear plugs", are prepared, and then stuffed into the horses' ears so that they cannot hear the bull approaching. The daily sports papers *As* and *Marca* are preferred, according to Durán, because they have a smaller format than the broadsheets of the popular dailies *El País* and *El Mundo*, which are too large to be folded easily. "It's important for the horses not to hear or see the bull's approach, because they'd get frightened and try to run away, and as their eyes are covered with a cloth, they could smash into the fence and get hurt. Even though the Reglamento Taurino followed in Madrid says you can only cover the right eye, we really have to cover both or else they will bolt. In some rings, mild tranquillisers are administered to the horses, but Salcedo chooses well-trained, obedient animals making the use of sedatives unnecessary most of the time", says Luis. "I think the horses should go out into the ring with all their wits about them, so that they too can show that they are 'toreros'."

Whenever a bullfight is scheduled, the veterinary surgeons remain on call to attend to an injured animal. The horses may suffer bumps and bruises, but very rarely do they receive a serious goring. Despite the indications of the Reglamento, Durán feels that the *monosabio* should stand no more than two metres away from the horse's head so as to be able to grab its bridle and prevent it from being knocked over, avoiding at the same time a goring to the animal or the man. "You have to react in a fraction of a second, and I think my most important job is to make sure that nothing happens to either horse or rider. Also, you have to consider the damage that a 500-kilo horse can do if it falls on top of a man or if the man is left lying on the ground, defenceless, and at the mercy of the bull's horns. You have to stroke a horse and treat it right and it makes me sick to see a *monosabio* beat a horse with a stick in other rings."

Durán might be considered over-zealous in carrying out his work. "I feel our role in the bullring is important and I may not always be standing strictly where I'm supposed to. I have been fined three times by a president for trying to save a horse, but I don't care. The picador and his horse weren't injured. I watch everything closely and if a matador or a *peón* is gored, I automatically rush in to the ring to help them as well. I feel this is part of the job of a *monosabio*, an *arenero* or a *portero* [doorman], who is in the ring every Sunday and has a sixth sense about what is going to happen."

The *monosabio* is not an employee of the plaza, but is contracted by the owner of the stable and Durán insists that one is a *monosabio* out of *afición* for the bulls and the horses, because there is no real financial compensation.

Memorable afternoons? "Absolutely all of them because I love what I do. A couple of years ago, a horse was gored in El Tiemblo, in the province of Ávila, and I had to stitch up the animal myself. Another time, I was working with a novice picador in Buitrago. He was really nervous and had a little too much to drink before the corrida. When I led him out of the ring after he did a lousy job of picing, we had to go through a dark tunnel and under a low arch. I warned him to duck, but he didn't, he hit his head and then vomited all over me. I got so angry I whacked him with the *garrocha*. We're the best of friends today!"

Fermín Vázquez
Las Palmas (Canary Islands) 1954. Monosabio and artist

Stranger still is the great *afición* which Fermín Vázquez professes for the bulls, as he was born on the self-proclaimed "bullfight-free" Canary Islands. "I became a *monosabio* quite by accident, through my friendship with a couple of neighbours in Getafe where I live, the picador José Alba *Cotón* and veteran monosabio Germán Mencías. One day they saw my taurine sketches and were so impressed that they encouraged me to get closer to the bullfighting world than being just a mere spectator in the stands. When I walked into the *patio de caballos* with Germán, I discovered a whole new world, buzzing with excitement and filled with colour, activity and inspiration for my paintings."

Germán Mencías exercises one of the picadors' horse in the patio de caballos

Fermín remembers his very first day in the *callejón*. "The bull smashed into the *barrera*, sending the wooden slats flying in the air everywhere. It was a miracle it didn't jump the fence. From that moment on, I was hooked! I hear comments and 'pillow talk' all the time, which afford me a closer and more intimate look at the Fiesta. I am not interested in depicting great faenas; other painters and even photographers can do that. The man, his fears, his emotions and how he expresses them fascinate me. It can be a *figura*, a *subalterno*, a *novillero*, a *monosabio* or a *mulillero*, but his work is his passion and his face reflects the history of his unique life. I find it exciting and challenging to try to capture that personality, the experiences, the hopes, the dreams and all that literature, written all over his face."

Despite his great *afición*, Vázquez never wanted to be a torero. "I was focused on studying Fine Art from the time I was a child. I am actually a rather restless person: I like to write, mostly treatises on painting, and I also did theatre, radio announcing, sang in *zarzuelas* (including several performances with the great Alfredo Kraus in the Tenerife Opera House) and I love to go horseback riding. When I discovered the complex world of bullfighting, I found everything I was looking for, particularly for my canvases, because I live, dream and breathe art. Even though I may not be holding a brush in my hand, I am still 'painting' in my mind's eye."

For years, Vázquez had to devote most of his time to commercial graphic art. "It was a great sacrifice for me, but I had to earn a living and it did help me to improve my technique. You have to dominate the technique first in order to be able to produce art. It is true of painting, and poetry—you have to learn metre and rhythm—and as a writer, you need to be familiar with grammar and semantics to be able express an idea." His greatest admiration is for the painter from Fuendetodos. "Goya always fascinated me, as did Beethoven; similar lives: both geniuses who became deaf and isolated in their own little world, while they poured out their emotions for the rest of us to share: one on his canvases and the other in his music."

Fermín Vázquez considers himself old fashioned. "I was born a hundred years too late. I am a man who likes tradition and I hate modern inventions like television and mobile phones. I think that's why I'm drawn to the horse world, because you still have to shoe, saddle and bridle them in the same old way. I hate the internet and there is nothing like writing a letter with your own hand and calligraphy."

It is also that sincere, authentic and romantic spirit which brought him to the world of the bulls. He remembers the afternoon his dear friend, picador *Cotón*, retired during a Victorino Martín corrida, in the Autumn Fair of 1998, performing in Luis Miguel Encabo's cuadrilla. "The public applauded as he rode through the *callejón*, in recognition of his thirty-odd years of professional dedication. I knelt down to wash the blood off of his armoured leg, the *gregoriana*, with soap and water, and tears rolled down my cheeks ... and his. It was my tribute to a great torero, although he still continues to act like one. He strides down the street like a *figura*."

Fermín in front of one of his extraordinary canvases, a tribute to the great aficionada Doña Maria de las Mercedes de Borbón

Fermín laughs when he recalls his début as a *monosabio*, which took place in the new Torrejón de Ardoz ring in 1997. "Germán [Mencías] told me to position myself in the middle of the opening parade. I was so nervous that I didn't see where I was stepping and I tripped over this huge steel ring which is used to secure the doors. I took my very first step into the ring and nearly fell flat on my face. I thought to myself: 'Fermín, this is one hell of a beginning!'"

The Arenero

The role of the *arenero* is to clean and smooth the sand and remove the excrement of the horses and mules after the *paseíllo* and between the lidia of one bull and the next. Prior to the introduction of the *peto*, the *areneros* had the even more unpleasant task of gathering up the offal and remains of the horses killed during the *lidia*. Although this job may seem trivial, it is not, as evidenced by the fact that they are not treated as simple "sanitary workers", but make the *paseíllo* with due solemnity behind the matadors and their *cuadrillas*. After saluting the president, they proceed to smooth out and restore the sand of the arena, a task laid down in Article 47 of the *Reglamento Taurino*.

The Las Ventas areneros in action

César Palacios
Madrid, 1937. Arenero of the Las Ventas bullring and artist

César Palacios's employment in Las Ventas dates back to 1962, when he began as an *acomodador*, showing spectators to their seats. "I wanted to attend the corridas, and as I had little money, it was a good way to see them free of charge. People don't want to give up all their Sundays and holidays, unless they have true *afición*. I have good memories of that time and besides, between my meagre salary and tips, I would make 29 pesetas [15p] every Sunday, which was not bad in those days. The first year, I was a 'reserve' and I was sent high up to the *gradas* and *andanadas de sol* [the cheapest seats in the sun], but then I was admitted to the permanent staff and assigned to a *tendido*. They eventually wanted to promote me to 'Inspector' but I refused the post, because I was afraid it would lead to conflicts with colleagues and I don't like giving people orders. I decided to become an *arenero*, because you get to experience a lot more and besides, as an *acomodador*, I used to miss the *paseíllo*, which is so beautiful."

He explained that the *arenero*'s job is important because if the blood, excrement or other refuse is not removed from the arena and the sand smoothed, the situation could become dangerous: someone can trip over a hole or slip, or a bull can adopt a *querencia*—a favoured place in the ring—because of the smell, and keep returning to that spot.

In Las Ventas, where approximately 80 *festejos* are celebrated every year, there are nine *areneros*, plus the *hondero* or "slinger", Constantino Iruelas Tino. His job is to place the rope around the dead bull's horns and hook it on to the ring fixed to the bar on the harness of the mule team, so that they can drag the animal out. Tino explains that you have to be nimble and able to get out of the way quickly. "If not, the mules just take off and could drag you along with them. Some people don't want to be there, in front of the bull, even if it's dead ... because it may only appear to be. It happened to me once that the bull suddenly raised its head and hit me in the leg. I wasn't hurt but it scared the hell out of me!"

The *areneros* divide the ring into three sections and work in threes, supervised by the chief, Rafael Rivas. The first group clears up the area extending from the *burladero* where the capes are hung in Tendido 9 to the *puerta de arrastre*, through which the dead bull leaves the ring, the second between Tendidos 7 and 9; and the third from Tendido 7 to the *toril* gate. The *areneros* are somewhat specific about which are their terrains, but as the *toreros* usually fight more in the shade than in the sun, except under exceptional circumstances, they tend to go wherever they are most needed. In each team, the newest to join the group is the one responsible for filling the basket with sand and pouring it over the puddles of blood. Then he scoops up the sand with the refuse and excrement, and empties it below the *estribo* (the "stirrup" or ledge on the *barrera*), while the rest of the *areneros* smooth out the sand of the arena with their rakes.

The *areneros* have their own uniform, as do the *monosabios* and *mulilleros*. Their costume consists of blue trousers, a green shirt with red collar, cuffs and ribbing, a red sash and a cap to match. They wear black slippers similar to those worn by the *toreros*, whereas the *monosabios* opt for normal running shoes. The position of *arenero* has traditionally been passed on from father to son, and they have usually had previous experience as *acomodadores* or *porteros*.

Monosabios, areneros and toreros together rush an injured torero to the infirmary

Another task of the *areneros*, although unofficial, is, together with the *monosabios*, to carry injured toreros to the infirmary. "It's an instinctive reaction," explained César, "because we don't have any obligation to do so. The younger ones are usually the first to jump into the ring and if necessary they apply pressure to the wound or make a quick tourniquet to stop the bleeding. They know that the characteristics of the *cornada* determine how to carry the victim and there is also a good rapport between the *areneros*, *monosabios* and medical team, and we run right into the operating room and help to undress the torero. We know what has to be done and how to do it quickly, which is a big help to the doctor who is busy scrubbing up."

Despite the seriousness of the matter, César adds jokingly: "The worst thing that can happen to an *arenero* is to have to rush a picador to the infirmary, because they are usually older and a lot heavier, not to mention their metal-plated boots. I have done so often and I thought I would collapse under the weight ... and the doctor would have to operate on both of us!"

As the *areneros* and *monosabios* are very attentive to everything that happens in the ring, they have become famous for their opportune "*quite de la gorra*", although Palacios insists that you have to know how to toss your cap at the bull; otherwise you could make matters worse.

He felt a bit like a torero when he put on his *arenero* uniform and black slippers and waited in the *patio de cuadrillas* to begin the *paseíllo*. "You can really sense the toreros' fear, and yet they seem outwardly very calm and in control. It makes me realise that they are made of different stuff from the rest of us mortals, and that's what I try to capture in my canvases."

The *areneros* have to enter the plaza an hour before the commencement of the corrida but César preferred to get there much earlier. "I like to just sit in a *burladero* to get into the mood and I almost always find something to sketch in my notebook. On corrida days, my wife says I should set up a bed in the corrals, because I start off the day at 10 in the morning, drawing the bulls before the *reconocimiento*, and after lunch I am back in the ring."

César Palacios: a self-portrait—with bulls

César Palacios was born in the calle Bocángel, across the road from Las Ventas, and his first childhood memories revolve around the unique, picturesque experiences of the bullfighting world, which he witnessed at first hand. The whole neighbourhood would become totally transformed on the day of a bullfight. "I used to see the toreros ride down the avenue in their carriages to the bullring, with an admiring public lining the streets and the picadors trotting down the calle Alcalá on horseback, with the *monosabios* mounted behind them. They looked like heroes to me. If I didn't have the money to go to the plaza, I would wait outside, and I can remember seeing toreros being carried on shoulders up to the Plaza de Manuel Becerra, and an enthusiastic crowd taking Antonio Bienvenida all the way to his home at number 3, calle General Mola [today Avenida Príncipe de Vergara]. Unfortunately, the world has lost its sense of romanticism and now they won't stop the traffic on Alcalá for a torero, but they will do it for a marathon, a political rally, or a gay parade. All I can say is that this taurine painter was born watching the toreros arrive at the bullring in their horse-drawn carriages and later in their Hispano-Suiza cars, and the whole show enchanted a twelve-year-old boy."

Since his father was a good friend of Paco Parejo, the bullring mayoral and brother-in-law of Antoñete, as a young boy César had the opportunity to spend a lot of time in the corrals contemplating the bulls before he ever saw his first corrida, and that is why, pen or brush in hand, he feels more torista (follower of the bulls) than torerista (follower of the toreros). "The truth is that the animal has always fascinated me more than the man, although I adore the corrida and think it the most profoundly dramatic and beautiful spectacle there is. I never tried to be a bullfighter because I didn't have the courage ... that is one thing about which I was sure. I was incapable of picking up a capote in a fiesta campera! I feel a profound respect for the bull when I am sitting in the callejón, because you never know when it will try to jump into your lap. The bulls can be dangerous even after they are dragged out by the mules, and we areneros always worry when an inexperienced banderillero gives the coup de grâce because we wonder if he's done the job properly."

César has many tales to tell, but his favourite brings to mind the late matador Enrique Vera, who starred in several important films, such as Tarde de Toros, El Niño de las Monjas and El Último Cuplé. "When I finished sweeping the sands and slip back into the callejón, I liked to say 'Suerte' ['Good luck!'] to the toreros. Most of them nod or say 'gracias', although they may not even hear what I say. One day, Vera, who had a great sense of humour, was standing in the burladero and I said, 'Suerte, Enrique', and he replied: 'You're the lucky one, maricón—you're going back inside!'"

César Palacios is known worldwide for his artistic talents. He describes the classes he attended at the Academia de Bellas Artes as "cold and boring", and considers himself self-taught. Even though he always preferred an impressionistic style, his innate restlessness has inspired him to seek different methods and formulas for expressing himself.

As might be expected, his favourite toreros are those of "arte y pellizco" ("art and goose pimples"). "I would follow them all over if I could, even though many people don't understand that it's impossible to create a work of art on a specific day and at a specific time and with a very difficult medium, the brave bull. Even if I was paid a small fortune, there is no guarantee that I'd be capable of painting a truly great canvas at a given moment with an audience watching. In bullfighting, as in painting, the heart and one's innermost feelings are what ignite the magical flame of artistic inspiration."

"El patio de caballos", by *César Palacios*

César and his little sketchbooks are inseparable, and he has about a hundred of them in his home. "I can't stop drawing wherever I am: in the Metro, having a beer in a bar, sitting on a bench waiting for the bus ... When people see me drawing, they ask me to give the page to them, so now by using a small 5 x 9 cm notebook, I have the excuse that I can't rip out the pages. I don't just depict bullfight themes ... I sketch everything I see, from the face of an old man, to a child, to a puppy. It's a kind of intimate, graphic diary."

The Mulillero (Muleteer)

The *mulilleros* bring up the rear of the *paseíllo* in most bullrings, with the exception of some "portable" ones, where for economic or strategic reasons, the mules are replaced by a tractor or similar system, a modern technological advance perhaps, but also rather sacrilegious. The brave bull does not deserve the ignominious end of being hoisted up on a mechanical shovel like some useless débris, rather than being taken out in a more dignified manner by a team of mules, adorned with colourful flags, ribbons and bells, and maybe even receiving a lap of the ring for a good performance.

The mules were even more important prior to the introduction of the *peto*, for at that time there were two sets of mules, one to drag out the bulls and another to drag out the dead horses.

In the first-category rings, and in many others, the *mulilleros* have a uniform. In Madrid, they wear grey trousers, a light blue shirt and a dark blue sash and cap. As is the case for almost all of the professionals of the plaza, a certain hierarchy is respected in regard to seniority.

Juan Anchuelo
Anchuelo (Madrid), 1934-2007. Owner of the Las Ventas mule team

Juan Anchuelo happens to be from a *pueblo* also called Anchuelo. He became involved in the bullfighting world when he was 12, helping his father deliver the straw and feed to the contractor of the mules of the Madrid ring. When the old muleteer retired, Juan took over, and found he loved the job. "It was hard work taking care of them and on the day of the corrida I had to bring them right across Madrid. I did it for almost 50 years, but I loved every minute of it. I was studying to be a doctor, and when I had two years left I decided to give it all up to continue in the world of the bulls with my mules. I haven't become rich, but I have been happy, and that's a lot to achieve in today's world."

Juan adores his eleven mules and his horse, each with its own very torero name: *Romero, Gallito, Jesulín, Litri*, etc. "They're all named after bullfighters, but I don't think the matadors would mind. My horse *Perla* [Pearl] is a jewel, and not just because of her name, and I love her more than anything in the world. She could drag out a bull in the *pueblos* all by herself and she understands me with just a nod. She is far more intelligent than the mules and is wonderful company. We're both old now, and when one of us dies, the other will be very lonely, her or me. After spending so many years in the plaza, I know male mules are better than females, and better still is the cross between a female donkey and a stallion."

Juan encounters a lot of problems nowadays finding new mules because they are no longer needed on the farms, as they were replaced years ago by tractors. "It's a hybrid line which is in danger of extinction. There are still some left in Andalusia but none at all in Castile. Their only task is to drag the bulls out of the arena on Sunday afternoons. The rest of the week they are in the stables, eating, drinking and resting ... so they live much better than I do!"

Juan usually brings two teams to the plaza, although only three mules are needed to drag out a 600-kg bull. He signed a contract with the impresario, and the muleteers who assist him are all family members (brothers and cousins) or friends, with the most varied professions in real life. "My brother is a civil engineer who heads the hunting and fishing department in Segovia, but that doesn't stop him from running with the mules. I worry about the future because my nephews prefer football to the bulls—and believe it or not, they're afraid of my poor little animals, that wouldn't hurt a fly." During the week, Juan takes care of the mules by himself. "I love to be with them and they've never kicked or bitten me. They're noble, tame animals as long as you don't mistreat them. I bring them bags of sweets, which they love."

Juan Anchuelo with one of his mules, ready for action

He suffered polio as a child, which left him with a slight limp, "but it never prevented me from riding. It's what I most love to do. I never felt afraid and I suppose I was a daredevil at heart." He remembers nostalgically how he used to bring the mules to the bullring from the stables in the Parque del Oeste in the southwest corner of Madrid, along the boulevards: San Bernardo, Bilbao,

Alonso Martinez, Colón, Goya and Alcalá to Las Ventas. "I used to lead all six of them across the city and I never had a problem, not even with the buses. It was probably the last image of the old bullfighting world that still existed. They are clean, obedient animals and the children used to get all excited when they saw us. Every once in a while, though, some idiot out strolling with his girlfriend would say: 'Look at that country bumpkin with his mules,' and they would laugh at me! But we didn't care, my mules and I just continued on our way to the bullring."

José Antonio Tamayo
Peralejos de las Truchas (Guadalajara), 1954. Mulillero

José Antonio Tamayo has been an aficionado all his life, and confesses, "I think that beneath the uniforms worn by everyone working here in the plaza is a frustrated torero. Why didn't we become professionals? We obviously lacked the courage, the knowledge and the madness to pursue a career as a torero, because, believe me, they are crazy!"

Tamayo became a *mulillero* twenty years ago, because Juan Anchuelo is his wife's cousin. The *mulilleros* and the *monosabios* are the only "protagonists" in the plaza who do not get paid. "We do it out of goodwill, as a hobby, and because it's a way to get to see the bulls close up. And the look in the bull's eyes tells you everything, if it is noble, brave, or has evil intentions. You see everything much better from the *callejón* than from the *tendido*, of course."

José Antonio's situation is unique, in that he lives in Valladolid, almost two hours northwest of Madrid, and he is the director of a home appliance chain for the Castile-León region, with a number of stores and employees under his management. Nevertheless, he manages to come to Madrid every Sunday and holiday and every day during the Feria de San Isidro to attend to his mules. Of course, he arrives in sufficient time to harness up and deck out the mules, an operation which takes about half an hour, because all ten *mulilleros* pitch in. Each one has an assigned position although they can interchange posts at will. "Nevertheless," according to José Antonio, "those who take the lead of the mules have to be extremely fit and actually run the greatest risk, although there have been times when those of us who run behind the animals have been knocked over by the bull. There is always some danger involved when you are in front of the bull, even if it is dead."

One *mulillero* takes the lead, together with two others who pull on the animals' halters. In order to ensure that the mules run together, they are harnessed to an iron bar. If they were not firmly secured to one another, it would be almost impossible to control them, because they are young, strong

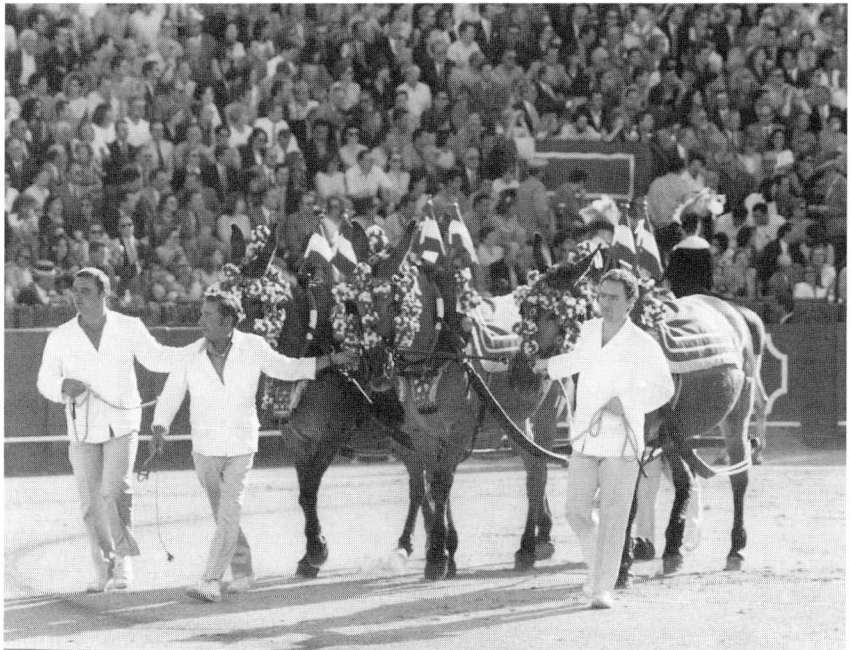

A contrast in styles: top: the Las Ventas mulilleros, José Antonio Tamayos second from left; bottom: mulilleros in La Maestranza, Seville

and spirited animals. Sometimes, they get frightened when they see the dead bull and so a mulillero brings up the rear carrying the bolea, the iron bar which has a hook to snap on to the ring of the hondilla or sling wrapped around the bull's horns. Thus, there are at least six mulilleros: one with the hondilla, one with the bolea, the two who pull on the halters, one who directs the team and another alongside to make sure the animals do not bolt off.

Mules, like all animals, have a natural querencia. "We have to position the animals well or else it would be impossible to restrain them. Once they are turned in the direction of the patio, they break into an uncontrollable sprint. Sometimes people think we stall to see if the president will grant the matador an ear, but that's not the case. It is just difficult to manoeuvre the mules and get them to stand still long enough to hook the hondilla on the bull's horns. We are good aficionados and like to see the torero triumph, but we obviously don't have any personal interests. We obey the president's decisions, but sometimes he pulls out his white handkerchief at the last minute to grant an ear or the blue handkerchief to grant a lap of the ring. In 1995, we had to drag a Dolores Aguirre bull back out of the patio de arrastre because the mules broke into a gallop and there was no way to stop them."

The mulilleros leave their burladero at Tendido 2 to get the mules ready and bring them out of the patio de arrastre when the matador goes for his killing sword.

José Antonio keeps in good form by playing football, jogging and horseback riding. He also has stories to tell. "I always try to get here around five in the afternoon in the summer [when the corridas start at seven], but one time I had an important business meeting in Ibiza and at six in the afternoon I was still in the airport in Ibiza. I don't know how, but at 7.03 I was making the paseíllo in Las Ventas: I had a friend waiting for me at Madrid airport and while the alguacilillos were getting things started, I managed to jump into my uniform and slip into the last row of mulilleros." He also remembers the time a bull was dragged to the desolladero, but the tercero had not done a good job of finishing off the animal with the puntilla. When the mulillero at the back went to remove the hondilla, the bull, which had incredible horns, raised its head. "Everybody was off, running in different directions and I was left all alone at the front holding back the mules and had no clue as to what was going on. Fortunately, the bull just lifted up its head and then collapsed ... I hate to think what would have happened if it had managed to get back up on its feet."

Will the mules ever disappear? "I sincerely hope not, especially in the first-category rings, because their image, their colour and the sound of their bells is an important part of the tradition and ritual of the bullfight."

The Puntillero

The *puntillero* or *cachetero* (a term common in the 19th century, and used by the matador *Pepe-Hillo* in his *Tauromaquia* of 1804, appearing thereafter in several English-language texts) is in charge of finishing off a dying bull, once it has collapsed on the sand. In most of the smaller rings, the so-called *tercero* or third banderillero can also give this coup de grâce to the animal. It is a skill of great importance, considering that on many occasions it can determine whether a matador is awarded an ear or not. The *puntillero* in Madrid customarily wears a suit of lights because in the early 20th century the matadors had four *subalternos* in their *cuadrilla*: three banderilleros and a *puntillero*. Eventually, the position of *puntillero* disappeared and the role was assumed by the *tercero*.

The *puntilla* is a dagger with a wooden handle and steel blade approximately 3 cm wide and 12 cm long, which ends in a lancet, used to administer the coup de grâce to the bull, by severing its spinal cord. There are two kinds of *puntilla*: one with a pear-shaped blade, which has more weight on the tip and so can be handled with more precision, and a straight-bladed knife, which is used to finish off an already dying animal. There are also two ways to hold the *puntilla*: grasping it in the fist, which allows for a more powerful blow (as below), or in the *ballesta* fashion, where it is pressed against the palm of the hand.

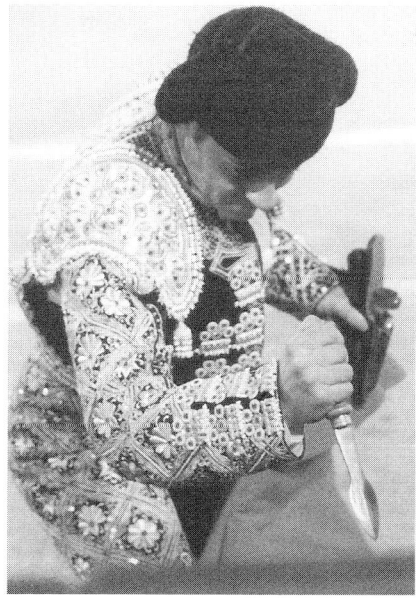

A puntillero *at work*

Agapito Rodríguez
El Pardo (Madrid), 1923-2002. Puntillero

Agapito Rodríguez became an institution in Las Ventas, as he was the official puntillero from 1955 to 1982, the year in which he was replaced by Antonio Medina. Even though there were no taurine antecedents in his family (his father was a butcher employed in the El Pardo slaughterhouse and later in Madrid), Agapito decided to pursue a career as a torero. He described his eight years as a novillero, using the professional name El Niño de la Perla: "I had a daring, tremendista [flashy] style like El Cordobés, but that wasn't popular in my time, the early 1940s. My manager, Isaac Fernández, who ran a ticket office in Madrid, was afraid that I would get myself killed one day and make him feel guilty for the rest of his life, so he tried to persuade me to become a banderillero. I didn't like the idea of having to walk behind the matador, so I decided to hang on to my old job at the slaughterhouse and become a puntillero."

Agapito began as the puntillero in Madrid's second ring, Vista Alegre, until there was an opening in Las Ventas in 1955, when he jumped at the opportunity. As he had had experience in the slaughterhouse since the age of 10, when he could barely hold the knife, he not only knew how to apuntillar (pith) the animals, but also the entire process of skinning, stripping and cutting them up. "The public was afraid I'd get seriously gored one day because it seemed as if I was overconfident, but really I was just doing my job. Sometimes you have to stand in front of the bull even though it is not mortally injured and before you know it you have been caught and tossed in the air."

As a novillero, Agapito suffered a major goring which affected his femoral artery, along with several other injuries, and as a puntillero he was seriously hurt by a big Ceballos bull. "I was thrown three times into the air and landed flat on my back. I somehow managed to get to my feet and was dizzy and aching, but I ran after the bull like a drunk, and killed it in front of Tendido 5!"

What was Agapito's secret formula for handling the puntilla so well? Should you do it from in front of the bull or from behind? "It all depends on the position of the animal and on the trajectory of the sword. It's also important for the matador to stand in front of the animal to focus the bull's attention, so that the puntillero can hit the right spot. I almost always used the puntilla from behind if the matador was distracting the bull, but there were times when they would walk away in triumph, thinking the bull was dead when it was not. I think that killing the bull from the front detracts from the matador's performance, because that is his place. I remember great matadors like Bienvenida, Ordóñez and Camino, who said to me, 'Take your time. Don't worry'. Others less experienced, got nervous and shouted: 'Hurry up and kill the bull!'. But I always followed my instincts, because you have to be able to see the exact spot: 4 to 6 cm behind the nape of the neck. If that spot isn't totally exposed, it makes no sense to jab away. I know that, because I had been killing sheep and rams when I was seven. You don't need a great deal of strength; you just have to be accurate. If you miss, the animal is left stunned or dazed. The dagger has to penetrate 8 to 10 cm to sever the spinal cord, in which case the bull instantly feels nothing, even though it may keep twitching on the ground."

Agapito insisted that the great skill he displayed in Las Ventas, and which so endeared him to the public, was the result of having killed many, many animals and being familiar with their anatomy. "This is very important for the *puntillero*. Most toreros have no idea what organs the sword has affected, and you hear them say: 'Don't pull out the *espada*. It won't do any damage in the sheath'. The sword is well located if it slips in between the shoulder blades, and death is instantaneous if it pierces the heart or liver, but if the animal vomits blood, it is because there is internal bleeding or the lung has been affected. At times, I have had to argue with matadors about whether it was wise to remove the sword or not."

He became so popular that he used to be "loaned out" to the plazas of Pamplona and Bilbao, where the bulls are especially large and serious. Now, the *Reglamento Taurino* stipulates that all first-category rings must have their own official *puntillero*.

Agapito Rodríguez retired at the end of the 1982 season after many decades of working 16-hour days. "I spent all morning in the slaughterhouse and drove a taxi in my spare time, when I was not in the bullring. In winter, I had a lot of extra work too, because I would accompany hunters to skin their animals." He calculates that he has despatched some 15,000 animals, between *novilladas* and *corridas de toros*, and is fully aware of the importance of his job. In his 35 years of professional activity, he remembers with special fondness when Pepe Luis Vázquez decided to make a comeback. He appeared in Madrid and performed an extraordinary *faena*, but when he went into kill he left a half-sword. "The bull stumbled and fell to the sand and I ran in and gave it the *puntilla*, and the matador was awarded the two ears. He hugged me and said: 'You've made it possible for me to sign a lucrative professional tour of Spain this season. Thank you!'."

During his long career in Las Ventas, Rodríguez had to kill half a dozen bulls from the *burladero*, at considerable risk, because the animals were very much alive and refused to follow the *cabestros* back to the corrals (this was before the time of Florito). One of his many anecdotes is classic. "I was having breakfast with my co-workers one morning in a bar, when a bull escaped from the slaughterhouse. I ran after the animal all the way up to the Plaza de Legazpi and then along the broad avenue of the Paseo de las Delicias. I grabbed a raincoat from a passer-by and tried to torear the beast and prevent it from fleeing towards the pavement, where a lot of children were on their way to school. I managed to lead it up to the Avenida de la Ciudad de Barcelona and into an abandoned warehouse, by which time I was exhausted. Fortunately, Antonio Medina, my successor in Las Ventas, arrived with the police, who finished the animal off."

Curiously enough, Agapito's brave deed never made the newspapers, because it occurred at the same time as a major political event, the assassination of the President of the Government, Luis Carrero Blanco. "Not only that; the authorities decided not to make the incident public because they were afraid it would stir up a wave of fear and panic among the local residents that something like this could happen again." That may be true, but a similar incident occurred way back in 1928, when matador Diego Mazquiarán *Fortuna* killed on Madrid's Gran Vía a bull which had escaped from a slaughterhouse; he was granted Spain's highest civil distinction, the Cruz de Beneficencia.

In his other job, as a taxi driver, Agapito also had some memorable experiences and had to act as a "midwife" on several occasions. He remembered one in particular. "We were on our way to the hospital and I had to pull over quickly to deliver the baby all by myself. The car was a mess, but it was worth it. I still keep in contact with that little girl."

Antonio Medina
Madrid, 1936. Puntillero

Antonio Medina, who replaced Agapito Rodríguez, had followed in his mentor's footsteps, working in the slaughterhouse from an early age. He describes his method as follows, "You have to keep the *puntilla* very straight and extend your arm. I prefer to kill in the *ballesta* style because in this way I do not expose my forearm to the bull".

He claims that 90% of the bulls collapse on the sand not because they are dead, but because they are injured, fatigued or simply *mansos* (tame or cowardly). For this reason, he does not understand why a matador would risk a triumph in an important ring like Madrid by leaving the job to an inexperienced *tercero* so as not to pay for Antonio's services. "If I were performing in San Isidro I would make sure that I had a good *puntillero* in my *cuadrilla* to finish off the animal. An ear or two in Madrid could be equivalent to hundreds of thousands of euros and a whole season of contracts."

Antonio also has his stories. "On one occasion Curro Romero couldn't kill a bull in Madrid and heard the three *avisos*, and I had to finish it off from the *burladero*. Far from being angry, when I entered the *callejón*, Curro, being the wonderful person he is, said to me: 'Maestro, you should come to my hotel and we can share my fee, because I killed one bull today and you killed the other!"

The Torilero, Chulo De Banderillas and Carpenters

A first-category ring like Las Ventas has approximately two hundred devoted employees on its payroll, each with his own special job to do, and together they make it possible to stage the bullfight. One thing becomes quite evident when you talk to them: they are in it not for the money, but for their *afición*. The bullring staff includes a wide variety of positions, some of which have already been described: the *chulo* or *mozo de banderillas*; the *mozo de puyas*, who furnishes the pics; the *corralero*, responsible for unloading the animals from the lorry, providing them with food and water, and generally taking care of the corrals; the *mayoral*, who tends to the *cabestros* in the first-category rings;

the *clarineros* and *timbaleros*, who transmit the president's orders; the chaplain; the *porteros* (doormen); the *acomodadores* or ushers; the sellers of cushions, drinks, sandwiches, ice cream, posters, souvenirs ...

Marcelino Saboya (left) and Francisco Sanz,
when they proudly wore the suit of lights

A first-category ring like Las Ventas has approximately two hundred devoted employees on its payroll, each with his own special job to do, and together they make it possible to stage the bullfight. One thing becomes quite evident when you talk to them: they are in it not for the money, but for their *afición*.

The bullring staff includes a wide variety of positions, some of which have already been described: the *chulo* or *mozo de banderillas*; the *mozo de puyas*, who furnishes the pics; the *corralero*, responsible for unloading the animals from the lorry, providing them with food and water, and generally taking care of the corrals; the *mayoral*, who tends to the *cabestros* in the first-category rings; the *clarineros* and *timbaleros*, who transmit the president's orders; the chaplain; the *porteros* (doormen); the *acomodadores* or ushers; the sellers of cushions, drinks, sandwiches, ice cream, posters, souvenirs ...

Marcelino Saboya
Madrid, 1947. *Torilero of Las Ventas*

The *torilero*, as his name implies, is responsible for opening and closing the *toril* gate and making sure that the ring is empty and the *lidiadores* are in place when he releases the bull. At the end of the *paseíllo*, the *alguacilillo* requests the key to the *toriles* from the president and in a symbolic ceremony, hands it to the *torilero*. Marcelino Saboya is a bus driver in "real life" and gets up every Sunday at five in the morning to cover his route Madrid-Tres Cantos-Soto de Viñuelas. He has the morning shift and when he arrives at the bullring on Sundays and holidays, he has driven some 300 km. He got his start in the bullring as a *monosabio* and moved up to *chulo de banderillas* when there was a vacancy. He already had his own suit of lights hanging in the closet because when he was young, he wanted to be a torero and had participated frequently in *capeas* in Teruel, Castellón de la Plana and Valencia. According to tradition, the *chulo de banderillas* becomes the *chulo de toriles* and both are employees of the Comunidad de Madrid.

Marcelino was delighted by the opportunity of getting to wear a suit of lights. "This is the first ring in the world and I was actually baptised in the Church of Covadonga, right up the street in the Plaza de Manuel Becerra, so who could ask for anything more in life? I won't deny that I have had my share of scares, like the time the bull jumped the fence right where I was standing." (It was decided in 2015 that it was more appropriate for the *torilero* and *chulo de banderillas* to wear *traje corto* rather than a suit of lights.)

The *torilero*'s first job is to check that all the padlocks on the doors to the individual *chiqueros* (the pens in which the animals are kept until it is time for them to make their entrance into the ring) are open and then he is attentive to the president's white handkerchief to signal the release of the first bull. Before doing so, he makes sure that no one is in the ring who should not be there and that there is a banderillero ready in the *burladero* below the president's box. He carries out his job with absolute solemnity. "My position inspires a great deal of respect because you know that behind that wooden door is a ferocious animal and that the slightest mistake could result in serious consequences. I have to open the door quickly, so that the bull is scarcely aware of any movement. For example, if I do not slip the bolt correctly, the bull could slam up against the door, hurt itself, damage a horn or even break down the door."

Francisco Sanz
Madrid, 1960. Chulo de banderillas and artist

Francisco "Paco" Sanz has been employed in the bullring since the age of 12, when he was in charge of opening the door to the bullring chapel. "Of course, I didn't get paid for doing it, but I got to see the toreros close up and also saw the corrida for nothing. Then I became an *acomodador*, after that an *arenero* and finally a *chulo de banderillas*." He went from *acomodador* in the stands to *arenero* in the arena for the same reasons as César Palacios: "To see the Fiesta close up and to participate in the corrida more directly, albeit in a very minor way". Paco inherited his *afición* from his father, Mariano Sanz, who was a plaza inspector for 35 years. Francisco requested the job of *chulo de banderillas* in 1998, when the previous *torilero* retired and a new *chulo* had to be employed. "As an *arenero* for so many years, I had shown that I was reliable and also knew how to react in the *callejón*."

The *chulo de banderillas* hands the sticks to the toreros and prepares four pairs for each bull, 24 pairs in all, although there are always spares. He removes them afterwards from the dead bull because they are recycled and he has another task as well. "I take over the position of *torilero* on the fourth bull—for practice—so that I can replace him whenever necessary. I have to be very careful because, if I mess up, the bull could escape into the *callejón*. When the president sends a bull back to the corrals, you have to release the *cabestros* and then make sure that they all retreat along the passageway leading out to the corrals and that the bull is not left 'hiding' behind the door. That is what happened a few years ago, when the *toril* gate was opened and two bulls appeared in the ring instead of one!"

In "real life", Paco is a laboratory technician and, in his spare time, a fine painter. "Like most young people, I tried giving *capotazos* in village *capeas*, but I hadn't got the talent to become a serious professional. Besides, even though my father is a great aficionado, he didn't support my efforts because he was afraid that something would happen to me."

As he wore a suit of lights, just like the *torilero*, until 2015, and is young and slim, he was often confused with a member of one of the *cuadrillas*, hence the following story. "As I like to arrive early in the patio, when José Tomás made his formal presentation in Madrid, I happened to be standing next to Jesulín's *banderillero de confianza*, Carmelo. José Tomás shook my hand as if I were another torero and wished me luck!"

Sergio Sánchez-Monje
Madrid, 1970. Carpenter, lawyer, writer and flamenco guitarist

From the beginning of the Fiesta, the presence of a carpenter was essential, as the old rings were made of wood or wagons and carts forming a circle in the main square of the towns. When permanent, solidly built rings were put up, the carpenter's role became less significant, although the maintenance of the ring, the fence around it and the *burladeros* is still necessary. According to the *Reglamento Taurino*, two carpenters are stationed at each door to the arena, not only to repair damage to the fences but also to control the access to the ring, a job of considerable importance and not lacking in risk. "I used to watch the corrida from right up in the *andanadas*, but one day I wanted to get a lot closer," explains Sergio, as the reason a young lawyer would put on a blue peaked cap and spend all his Sundays during the bullfight season in the bullring. "I was lucky to get the job because it is usually passed on from father to son or through recommendations."

There are a dozen carpenters in Las Ventas who make the rounds of the six doors: that of *cuadrillas*, Tendido 6, picadors, Tendido 9, *arrastre* and *toriles*. If a bull is returned to the corrals, the carpenters of Tendidos 6 and 9 have to go to the *chiqueros* and are supplied with hammers in case the boards must be repaired. There is more wood and extra tools in the carpenter's room. As in everything related to the bullfighting world, there is a respect for ranking, seniority and the experienced supervisor.

Sergio's family was taken aback when he graduated from law school and, while working on his doctorate, became so involved in the bullfighting world. In fact, he starts Sundays off with the *apartado* in the morning and then spends the rest of the day there. "My family was surprised and my grandmother lamented: 'Such a nice normal boy and a good student .... and now this!'" He actually has two passions: bullfighting and flamenco, and is an accomplished guitarist.

Sergio Sánchez-Monje (left) with Julián López El Juli,
on the day of his presentation in Madrid

Nevertheless, there have been times when Sergio has had his doubts. "One afternoon a bull jumped into the *callejón* three times! We carpenters don't have a *burladero*, because we have to man the doors. On the third jump, I thought: 'What the hell am I doing here?' I also remember the time that two bulls were let loose by accident in the ring. Everybody was shocked and said: 'Thank God; what if the matador, Vicente Barrera, had gone out to do a *portagayola* [receiving the bull initially by kneeling down in front of the gate]?' But I also thought what would have happened if the poor *mozo* had closed the door after the first bull? The second would have slammed right into him!"

Víctor Ruiz
Madrid, 1966. Carpenter

Víctor Ruiz started out in Las Ventas as a *mulillero* for pure "love of the art", but in 1998 he switched to being a carpenter. "I discovered I was allergic to the horses but my allergy has not prevented me from running with bulls from the time I was eleven. My family actually knew nothing of my penchant for running in the *encierros*, nor for seeing the bulls close up. I just said I was off to see a corrida. They found out when they saw me running up front in a televised *encierro* from San Sebastián de los Reyes. Boy, did they get angry! You're scared when you run, but then the feeling of exhilaration is a fantastic compensation; the more harrowing the experience, the greater the satisfaction you feel afterwards. I never thought of being a torero, never picked up a cape or *muleta*. I have enough with the *encierros*!"

Víctor runs up the dangerous calle Estafeta every day in the *sanfermines* of Pamplona. "When you run regularly, you begin to feel more comfortable and you do it better. On 11 July 2012, a good friend of mine, Brooklyn-born Joe Distler, a highly respected runner, celebrated his 45th anniversary in Pamplona without having missed a single *encierro* in all that time. I have been going to Pamplona faithfully since 1989." What is the secret to running well? "It's not just waiting for the bulls to arrive but finding a position alongside one of them and there are a lot factors to take into account, like the number of people in the street that day. Saturdays and Sundays are without a doubt the worst. You have to know how to make your way to the middle of the street, because if you keep to the side, the flood of people and the bulls will swallow you up. You have to aim for the centre, put up with the pushing and shoving and when the bulls reach you, you have to hold your ground. No matter how many times you do it, seeing those animals close up never ceases to impress you. It's very difficult to keep your position while continuing to look in front of you as well as behind, and bearing in mind at all times the presence of the bulls. You have to be especially careful about the runners in front because if they fall, you can trip over them. More than a race, it seems like a street brawl."

Work for the Las Ventas carpenters

Víctor Ruiz has suffered several injuries, the last on 24 August 1997, during the *encierros* of San Sebastián de los Reyes. He actually studied classic languages, but admits: "There is no relationship. I am also a swimming referee and I help organise *encierros* in the Comunidad de Madrid, as a *pastor* [shepherd]. I don't like to be a 'shepherd' in Pamplona, because that is like New York's 'Met' or Milán's La Scala and so it's where I must run myself. The same is true of San Sebastián de los Reyes: I want to participate in the *encierros*, not organise them." A story: "Once, in a small town in the sierra outside Madrid, a bull escaped and headed for a group of private homes. It ended up in the swimming pool and they had to call the *Guardia Civil* to pull it out with a rope. I thought to myself that was 'above and beyond the call of duty' for the *Guardia*".

Jesús Pérez El Suso
Madrid, 1971. Las Ventas bullring employee

Spectators can't help noticing Jesús Pérez because he is the only one in Las Ventas who sports a real pigtail. He has practically grown up in the bullring, distributing publicity material and hanging up posters in the streets, because that is what his father did. He also lends a hand as an *ayuda*, assisting the regular sword-handler, drives the bullring advertising van with a loudspeaker announcing the corrida and runs assorted errands. But perhaps the job he enjoys the most is hoisting up a triumphant matador on his shoulders and carrying him around the ring. "It's difficult and requires strength and a certain amount of skill. I'm not a messenger and I'm not delivering a package. That is why, when the toreros cut ears, their *mozos de espadas* come and fetch me because the matadors want to be carried out by someone they can trust and who knows what they are doing. I also feel happy because I consider it an honour."

Suso continues, "It's difficult to make a lap of the ring with the matador on your shoulders and the crowd pressing against you from all sides, but the worst part is going out of the Puerta Grande. It's horrible: I've been pushed, stepped on by the horses, lost my shoes and almost been knocked over with the matador on my back. Everyone wants to touch the torero, shake his hand or yank a *macho* tassel off his suit and it's almost impossible to control the situation."

Jesús Pérez is proud of the fact that he has never dropped a matador and that such a triumphant photo is very important to the bullfighter. The tips are attractive as well. "It depends on the torero. A *figura* can give you as much as 300 or 400 euros, but a *novillero* obviously doesn't have that kind of money. Nevertheless, being carried out through the Puerta Grande in Las Ventas for a *novillero* is like winning the first prize in the national lottery."

Suso cannot forget the highly successful opening of the Leganés plaza, in the suburbs of Madrid. "I had to carry out José Miguel Arroyo *Joselito*, who happens to be my favourite torero. In the end, all three matadors, *Joselito*, Enrique Ponce and Rivera Ordóñez, left on shoulders. We made a lap of the ring but when we reached the Puerta Grande, it was locked, because they were waiting for the Condesa de Barcelona to leave the ring first, according to protocol. So we all took another turn of the ring, but when we reached the Puerta Grande again it was still closed. *Joselito* peeked down at me from above and said: "Well, shall we go around one more time?"

Antoñete is paraded around the ring on shoulders
after a triumphant performance

Chapter 6. The Taurine Media

The Journalist and Bullfight Critic

According to Luis Carmena y Millán, taurine journalism came into being with the reports on the very early royal *fiestas de toros*; the first documented chronicle dates back to the coronation of Alfonso VII in 1135. Taurine journalism developed along with the spectacle, and as it gradually passed from the nobles on horseback to the common people on foot, the accounts in the chronicles of the time also took on a more popular, down-to-earth, informative nature. This style became more established in 1820, when the very first taurine weekly, *Cartel de Toros*, appeared. In 1882 one of the best taurine journals ever, *La Lidia*, was published, featuring some very noteworthy writers—Luis Carmena y Millán, Pascual Millán, Sánchez de Neira, Peña y Goñi and Mariano de Cavia—and the best graphic illustrators and painters of the time: Lizcano, Ferrant and, above all, Daniel Perea, whose centrefold plates are highly sought-after today. Taurine journalism has never ceased to be at the forefront of the Spanish media, due in part to the desire for immediate news and the illustrative support furnished by the latest photographic advances; hence its important presence today on the internet.

The veteran: Rafael Campos de España
Zaragoza, 1920-2008. Journalist and author

Rafael Campos de España was born in Zaragoza, where his father was a professor at the University, although most of his family came from Alicante. He was studying medicine in Valencia when his father died, thus forcing him to abandon his medical career with the qualification of "physician's assistant", a profession he practiced only during the civil war. He pursued further studies in business administration and philosophy and, as he was the nephew of the director of the daily newspaper El *Correo de Alicante*, he finally opted for a career in journalism and found a job in Radio Alicante, where he was eventually appointed the station manager. At the same time, he passed the official civil service examination and, as a result, began a long and very fruitful career in the Ministry of Information and Tourism. From his position in that Ministry, he did everything he could to promote the Fiesta, particularly through a series of excellent taurine publications. He was also responsible, as Head of the Departamento de Espectáculos Varios, for having created the famous *Festivales de España*, an important calendar of cultural events featuring star performers of ballet, opera, modern dance, music, etc., from all over the world, although, he admitted, "I was really only interested in bullfighting".

He was later designated taurine critic of Radio Nacional de España, and of the state television network by Minister Manuel Fraga Iribarne in 1965. "I created the programme *Cartel de Toros*, which was more than a news programme and really the first general-interest, variety programme on bullfighting, and it proved to be a difficult but very gratifying experience. Unfortunately, we had to televise in black and white, because there was still no colour television in Spain at the time."

Campos de España was also responsible for organising the taurine documentary material in NO-DO, the film archives of all the newsreel material shown in cinemas, and he produced seven excellent documentaries on the Fiesta which won international acclaim. "I spent hundreds of hours viewing and cataloguing the fantastic footage which NO-DO had of bullfights in Spain, France, Portugal and Mexico. We transferred all the old, highly inflammable celluloid material to non-flammable 33 mm film."

Rafael's parents were responsible for his *afición*. "My father took me with him to the bullfights, but my mother rarely came, for at that time women never travelled outside their home town! That was certainly not my case: I always took my wife Fina with me, and we enjoyed our trips to the different bullfight fairs immensely."

Rafael preferred spoken journalism to written and, in view of his many posts, was lucky to be able to count on the help of a "super-efficient secretary", his wife, who helped him type up his manuscripts. Fina Marceli was an opera singer before the couple married, and while he brought her into his bullfighting world, she also introduced him to the opera.

Rafael had been a trailblazer in trying to transfer the responsibility for the Fiesta from the Ministry of the Interior to a more logical state body: at the time, the Ministry of Information and Tourism, and today, that of Culture. "But it has been a losing battle," he said in 2007. "I hope we have not lost the 'war', but until now we have not won any significant victories. As it is, it seems as though the Ministry of the Interior has worried more about fines and controls than about the promotion, defence and cultural preservation of the Fiesta. I should add, however, that the reason it was supervised by

Interior in the first place was the fact that anything which was not specific, like education, health or public works, was dumped in the lap of the Interior Ministry. Historically speaking, the king was considered the first president of the corrida. When bullfights were held outside Madrid or Aranjuez (where he had his summer palace), he was replaced by the Governor or *Corregidor*, who in modern times delegated his powers to the local police chief. However, now that there is a Ministry of Education and another of Culture, with their corresponding secretariats for Spanish cinema, theatre, fine arts, literature, etc., it is absurd that there is no department specifically set up for bullfighting. I am optimistic, and still have hope that this will happen soon."

Rafael Campos de España

Campos de España was very clear about the fact that bullfighting is a reflection of the true social, political and historical circumstances of Spain. "The situation of the Fiesta mirrors the situation of the country. The essayist

Ortega y Gasset wrote: 'The history of the Fiesta consists of three or four millennia of Spanish men confronting Iberian bulls', which underwent a logical metamorphosis over the centuries. I think the toreros are performing better than ever; in fact, the enhanced aesthetic and artistic content of the Fiesta nowadays can be extended even to the newest and youngest students in the Escuelas de Tauromaquia, who are light-years ahead of the *novilleros* in my day. What does concern me is the bulls, which get bigger and bigger, but display less *casta*. Bravery and *casta* have nothing to do with size, weight and volume. It's like a vintage wine: if you add water instead of maintaining the initial pure stock, in the end the contents of the barrel will be inferior. As in any art, bullfighting without emotion ceases to be art. If a person looks at a painting or listens to a few bars of Puccini and is not moved, it's because either the artist is bad or the aficionado is."

Rafael's undoubtedly favourite matador was Manuel Rodríguez *Manolete*. "I had the great pleasure of meeting him and if he was a great torero, he was an even greater human being. He might have seemed cold and unfriendly, but that was not the case, he was just extremely timid, and I remember something that defines his personality very well. He liked to spend part of the winter in Salamanca, on the ranch of Antonio Pérez de San Fernando, not just to participate in the *tentaderos*, but also to relax and contemplate in solitude the bulls grazing in the fields. One day, he was with his cousin, *Cantimplas,* who was also his banderillero, and they stopped on a hill to smoke a cigarette. *Cantimplas* said: 'Manolo, this is just great! It's really paradise', to which *Manolete* solemnly replied: 'Yes, but if we didn't talk, it would be even better!'"

Rafael insisted on the importance of respecting the magic and the ritual in the Fiesta. "Bullfighting resembles a religious ceremony: religion has a God and bullfighting has a torero who is transformed into a demi-god. The dressing of a bullfighter reminds me a lot of how the priest prepares for Mass. In all the sacristies, there is a large mirror so that the priest can make sure his attire is in order before he approaches the altar."

The general public has changed: the more devoted and knowledgeable aficionados are gradually being replaced by mere spectators. The press has also changed, because journalism in general has. "The style has grown more informal and colloquial. There are certainly good critics and bad ones now, as there were many years ago, except that the critics in the thirties and forties wrote their reviews in thoroughly literary, grammatically correct Spanish. I am referring to intellectuals of the calibre of Mariano de Cavia, Gregorio Corrochano, Curro Meloja, José de la Loma *Don Modesto*; in fact, all the leading journalists at the time happened to be outstanding intellectuals."

During his many years as director of the programme *Clarín* of Radio Nacional de España, Rafael gave very eloquent accounts of the corridas and never spoke badly of any torero. "You can always find something nice to say if you try hard enough! Of course, I had my preferences, including *Manolete*, Juan Belmonte, the dominating skill of Domingo Ortega, the variety of Marcial Lalanda, the valour of Luis Gómez El *Estudiante*, the presence and profundity of Antonio Ordóñez, the celestial grace of Pepe Luis Vázquez, and even Manuel Benítez El *Cordobés*, of whom the distinguished member of the Academia Española José María Pemán, said: 'He is precisely the vitamin the Fiesta needs'. Of today's toreros, we cannot forget the extraordinary Enrique Ponce, José Tomás—very reminiscent of *Manolete* —and El Juli. I remember Julián when he was a student of mine in the history classes at the bullfighting school. He was extremely bright, but as nervous as a mosquito. He never sat still and from the very beginning he showed he was extraordinarily gifted."

Rafael's wife added her own little account of her husband's *afición*. "The other day my children Rafael *hijo* and Pilar asked us where we wanted to be buried. Rafa replied immediately: 'On a ranch, so that the brave bulls can step on my remains for all eternity!' I was a little taken aback at first, but then he explained: 'When I visited the Monastery of Yuste, I learned that Carlos I wanted to be buried under the altar so that the priests would be walking over him continually when they said Mass.' That shows the degree of my husband's *afición*!" laughed Fina.

Rafael Campos de España's last wish was fulfilled and his ashes were buried on the brave bull-breeding ranch of a close friend.

The contemporary: José Luis Ramón
Madrid, 1960. *Torero and journalist*

Today José Luis Ramón is a highly respected taurine writer and journalist and the director of the weekly bullfighting magazine *6 Toros 6*, but he learned his job from the ground up. He began his career in the bullfighting world as a torero and even made his début with picadors in Madrid, a kind of aristocratic title one has the right to brandish for life. He inherited his driving *afición* from his father, banderillero Manuel Ramón Bermejo, as did his older brother Manuel, also a journalist, specialising in financial and economic matters, although he, too, tried his hand at bullfighting. The three men grew up as a close-knit family, as the boys' mother died when José Luis was nine years old. "I don't know the precise moment when I decided to become a bullfighter, as the taurine world always formed a part of my life. I do remember that my father was very good with his hands and he made us a miniature wooden bullring to play with, including all the participants in the corrida, instead of a Wild West fortress with cowboys and Indians. Besides, after our mother died, Dad had to be both father and mother to us. We had a very tight relationship, and sometimes we even went with him when he had to *torear*. When he needed to pay more money into the social security system, he performed in comic taurine spectacles. My brother and I really enjoyed that because we would travel on the bus with the troupe and the clowns and we had a ball!"

José Luis Ramón in traje corto, as a novillero, with his father

Oddly enough, when José Luis decided to become a bullfighter he had his sights set on being a banderillero, like his father. "I loved him so much, I just wanted to follow in his footsteps, but once you put on the suit of lights, your dreams change and your goal is to make it right to the top." He became a student in the newly-created bullfighting school of Madrid in December 1976, which he considered a fundamental, endearing experience. Like many beginning bullfighters, he also obtained valuable experience in such comic taurine spectacles as *Fantasías en el Ruedo, El Bombero Torero, El Gran Kiki* and *El Chino Torero*. He fought in about 80 *novilladas* without picadors, and made his début with horses on 26 April 1978, in Plasencia, with Pepe Luis Vargas and Juan Mora. However, a few days later his luck changed, and he suffered a major goring in a *novillada* without picadors in Lillo (Toledo). "The *cornada* was so serious that I could not torear again for a whole year. I was anxious to get back in the ring but I also ran the risk of ending up lame for the rest of my life. This interruption in my career made it very hard for me to get back on my feet, literally! I was finally signed for a *novillada* in the Feria de Otoño of Madrid on 12 September 1982, with Curro Durán and Luis Miguel Campano; Campano cut an ear and I was applauded and had to salute on both of my animals, but without an ear my career was stalled."

It was at this point that he began studying journalism, something that made his father very happy. "I didn't want to waste another year of my life waiting for an opportunity to *torear* again, and live with 'maybe next time', so I became totally focused on my studies. Years later, I found out that after that *novillada* in Madrid, an important *apoderado* wanted to manage me, but my father said 'No'. Now I'm grateful he did that, but had I known at the time I would've been furious. I remember a wonderful short story written by the American *matador de toros*, a great writer and painter, Robert Ryan, which won the first Hotel Tryp Short Story Prize [Ramón was in second place], and which revolved around the repetition of the painful question to which there may be no real answer: 'When will you fight next?' or 'When is your next corrida?' 'I've been promised an opportunity in Huesca, in Calahorra, ...' False promises! I didn't want that future for myself!"

José Luis Ramón graduated from the Universidad Complutense in 1986, and obtained ample radio experience with *La Voz de Madrid*. Following this, he worked at the newspaper *Diario16* in its exemplary taurine supplement and other sections. Now he is really in his element as editor-in-chief of the taurine weekly *6 Toros 6*. He obtained his doctorate and published a book *Todas las Suertes por sus Maestros*. "I'm sad my father didn't live to see my book published, although I dedicated it to him. Actually, what I wrote in that book was a lot of what he had taught me, and much of what I put into my articles and short stories is the baggage of his rich experiences which he passed on to me, the result of an entire life devoted to the Fiesta. I felt his experiences were a lot more interesting to relate than my own. I can remember him leaving the house to fight—when mobile phones didn't exist—and we didn't know how he was until he could get to a public phone or return two days later with his suit covered with sweat and blood. The life of a banderillero then was not as easy as it is today."

José Luis explains that his experience as a torero was fundamental to his training as a taurine critic. "It's helped me understand the bull and bullfighting, and how difficult it is to be out there in the ring. Those who are up in the stands may have their ideas and criteria, but the only one who really

Ramón with his first book, in the Madrid Feria del Libro

knows what the bull is like is the man standing in front of it, because he can read the message in the animal's eyes. The fact that a little-known *novillero* comes to Madrid in the hope of finding his big break is no reason to criticise him unmercifully. Life and the *toros* he encounters will put an end to his bullfighting career, as it did to mine. I remember beginning the *paseíllo* and thinking: 'The critics are going to compare me, who's fought the grand total of three *novilladas* with picadors, with the others who've fought close to 50, and that's not fair'. And I try to bear all of this in mind when I sit down to write up my reviews."

Maybe we should put some bullfight critics in front of a bull, so they might learn something? "I don't think it is necessary, because a critic is a critic, and a torero, a torero. Just as an art critic does not have to be a painter or a literary critic, a writer, although it could be better if they were!"

Nowadays, José Luis Ramón keeps busy with his bulls "on paper" and his wife, Mercedes, and two daughters, Andrea and Paula. He likes to play football but almost never picks up a *capote*. He said he was not superstitious, but he did discover a coincidence which repeated itself throughout his career as a *novillero*: "Every time I went to *torear*, if I forgot something—a shirt, a *muleta*, a sword—I had a good afternoon. In fact, one time we forgot the whole *fundón* and another torero had to lend me his swords. In San Martín de Valdeiglesias I forgot my tie and I had a great afternoon." Then, when he suffered the serious goring in Lillo, did he not forget anything? "In Lillo, I forgot to run ... because it was a really dangerous *novillo*."

The Bullfight Photographer

The presence of the photographer in the bullring has made it possible to preserve the changing image of the bullfight world over the years, and has provided for posterity some of the most beautiful, dramatic and tragic images which make up the truth and essence of the Fiesta. Nevertheless, even before the proliferation of digital cameras—everyone has one now— and home videos, bullfight photographers were highly underrated and are now almost a "species in danger of extinction". They definitely deserve more admiration and respect than they currently receive.

Photography was invented in 1839, when Louis-Jacques Daguerre presented a process that reproduced an image on a metal surface coated with silver and iodine, which was developed when exposed to mercury vapour. One of the first metallic photographs of a taurine subject was an interior view of Seville's Maestranza bullring, taken by E. K. Tennison in 1853. Another foreign photographer, this time French, Jean Laurent, also showed great interest in the spectacle.

It became a popular custom at the end of the 19th and early 20th century for the toreros to sit for studio portraits, and among the most famous photographers were Emile Beauchy, in Seville, and Alfonso Sánchez García *Alfonso*, Baldomero Fernández Raigón *Baldomero*, father of the exceptional Pepito Aguayo, and the Calvache brothers, Diego, José and Antonio, in Madrid. They captured the history of *toreo*, along with other great names such as Serrano, Mateo, Joaquín and Manuel Sanchís Blasco *Finezas* and *Finezas II*, Ampuero, Luis Arenas, Francisco Marí, Cervera, Paco Cano (the only photographer to witness the death of *Manolete* in Linares, and an outstanding participant in the past seventy years of tauromachy), Diego Rodríguez Vallejo *Diego*, José María Lara, Alberto and Arturo Lendínez, father and son, Martín Sánchez Yubero, Miguel Martín, José Rubio, and the more contemporary professionals, Pedro Vega, Julián Madrigal, Jesús Rodríguez, Emilio Cuevas and his son Antonio, the Botán agency (Fernando *padre e hijo* and employees Santos Martín *Santi* and Domingo Álvarez), Pepe and Agustín Arjona (father and son), Damián Gil and his son Ismael, José Pozo Boje, Carlos Arévalo, Juan Miguel Sánchez Vigil, Manuel Durán Blázquez, the Americans Roberto Vavra, Lyn Sherwood, Jim Cornfield, Michael Crouser, José Ramón Lozano, Julián López, Alfredo Arevalo, Paloma Aguilar, Juan Pelegrín, Alvaro Marcos, Alcolea, Constante the French Lucien Leclergue, Maurice Berho, Christine Spengler and a long *et cetera*.

An early studio portrait of Aguayo,
who later became a highly respected taurine photogrpher

The first studio portraits of toreros were published in the magazine Blanco y Negro in 1893 and photographs taken directly in the bullring appeared in Nuevo Mundo in 1894. The work of such prestigious photographers as Baldomero and his son Aguayo should be highlighted, due to the circumstances under which they had to work: the glass plates, the low-sensitivity emulsions and much slower shutter speeds. Furthermore, the photographers at the time had to carry around a set of heavy glass plates, plus the cumbersome camera and the indispensable tripod. It was not easy to single out just one person to personify the classic taurine photographer, but I opted for Francisco Cano *Canito*.

Francisco Cano *Canito*
Alicante, 1912-2016. Former torero and photographer

Francisco Cano was the son of the torero Vicente Cano *Rejillas*, who was forced to retire prematurely due to a serious goring. Like many noteworthy bullfight photographers, such as Aguayo and Antonio Calvache, Paco Cano sought a successful bullfighting career before he concentrated on his cameras.

Paco Cano's life could easily lend itself to a film, for not only did he try to be a bullfighter in his youth, but was also a football player, swimming instructor and lightweight boxer; the latter vocation is not without its entertaining tale. "I got into a street fight, as young kids are likely to do, but without knowing it I had raised my fists to the regional boxing champion of the Levante. I initially held my own but ended up with a fine thrashing. In the end, my opponent and I became good friends and he introduced me to his world of amateur boxing. I finally gave up a relatively promising career in boxing to pursue my passion for *toreo*."

He made his début in his hometown ring of Alicante, precisely with two toreras, sisters Enriqueta and Amalia Almenara, the *Hermanas Palmeño*, in 1935, and eventually appeared in 39 *novilladas* without picadors and half a dozen with. The outbreak of the Spanish Civil War found him in the Republican zone, and he got a good scare when a group of armed militia showed up at his home one day. It turned out they only wanted him to perform in a series of *festivales* to support their cause, an offer that Cano "could not refuse". Unfortunately, in the course of one of those *festejos* he suffered a serious goring in the testicles. "They operated on me in Alicante and then transferred me to Madrid in one of their convoys. However, I lost my documentation in the process, which posed a serious problem. I wasn't a Republican, a Communist or a Fascist. We were and still are all just Spaniards."

When he reached Madrid, a good friend, Gonzalo Guerra Banderas, took him in, and Cano remained in hiding for three long years in a fourth-floor apartment on the calle Ventura de la Vega. "Gonzalo risked his life to save me and I can never forget that." It so happens that Guerra not only saved Cano's life, but as he was a skilled chemist and worked in the popular Heno de Pravia perfume factory, he introduced him to the world of photography. "He taught me how to take photos and then develop them. We assembled a really rudimentary camera, with a second-hand lens bought in the Rastro and a metal tube cut to size for attaching the shutter. We welded it all together with a small tape measure on which the different distances were marked: 10 metres, 20, 30 ... I took my first photos with that ridiculous gadget in the Madrid bullring in 1942. Since everyone knew me as a bullfighter, when the other photographers saw me with that poor excuse for a camera, they roared with laughter. I took some twenty photos of the Peruvian matador Alejandro Montani and when his manager saw them, he ordered a dozen of each, postcard size, at two pesetas per dozen. A litre of olive oil cost 30 céntimos then, so I was in business!"

Canito ready for work, as always (Photo by the author)

Cano fought another thirty *novilladas* after the war, and combined the *muleta* with the camera. "I performed in a *novillada* in Alicante, and when I'd killed my animal, I picked up my camera and continued shooting again from the *callejón*." One of his most important reports was when *Manolete* broke his collarbone while performing in the Alicante plaza. The photos were published in the prestigious taurine weekly *Dígame* in 1945, and marked the beginning of a close friendship with the famous *diestro* (matador).

Curro Toro, Cipriano Velázquez and El Vito with "don Ernesto", captured by Cano

In fact, Paquito was famous throughout the bullfighting world, not just for his talent and his charm, but also because he was the only photographer present in Linares on that fateful day—28 August 1947—when *Islero* inflicted the goring which put an end to the life of the most internationally renowned torero of all times, *Manolete*. "I actually went to Linares with Luis Miguel Dominguín, for in that epoch, the top figuras used to have their own photographers travel with them to all their corridas, so they could send photos back to the national newspapers. Luis Miguel owed me a lot of money and I was angry with him—he always paid up in full in the end, but he enjoyed seeing me suffer. We met at a bullfight and he said I should go round the next day with my bills and a suitcase. I showed up and he waved

One of Cano's most famous images: Paquirri with an Osborne bull in Valencia

his bills aside and said: 'Get in the car, we are going to Linares, Almería, Granada ... and I'll pay you for everything all at once'. That's how I ended up in Linares on 28 August. I wanted to stay for the funeral because Manolo was a friend of mine, but Luis Miguel wouldn't hear of it. He said: 'Who hired you, Manolete or me?' He was scheduled to fight the next day in Almería and he was great. I don't know what happened when I developed the film, but I ruined all the photos. Luis Miguel got really furious and thought I'd done it on purpose. No matter how angry I was with him, I would never have deliberately destroyed a roll of film of a corrida in which he cut a tail! I attributed it to divine punishment."

What was the secret to being a good bullfight photographer? "First of all you have to know the torero and what is the best moment to shoot him before the bull: at the beginning of the pass, in the middle, or at the end. Of course, with today's motorised, digital cameras, you can take five or six photos one right after another, but when you were shooting with film, that was unheard of because of the cost. In fact, almost anyone can take a picture nowadays. I have a rich friend who has much more advanced photographic equipment than I do."

Who was the most difficult torero to photograph? "On one hand, Luis Miguel, because he was so tall, but on the other, he was such a good lidiador and so elegant, it didn't matter. The most photogenic without a doubt was Manolete, because he appeared in the paseíllo straighter than a telegraph pole and everything he did was smooth and graceful. He knew how to take advantage of each and every bull that came into the ring."

Of the millions of photos he has taken, with four or five rolls of 36 frames per corrida, could he single out just one? "I have lots of photos of Dominguín with famous people because he and his family were always throwing big parties: Dr. Alexander Fleming, the discoverer of penicillin, Ernest Hemingway, Orson Welles, Ava Gardner, Lauren Bacall, Gary Cooper, etc., but the most important photo for me was the one which shows Manolete being carried to the infirmary in Linares." Cano would not single out any modern bullfighters as his favourite because they were all good friends of his, although he did prefer those who demonstrate profound art more than those who just display great courage.

He resisted the move from black-and-white to colour, because, apart from being a creature of habit, he liked to develop his own film in the bathroom of the hotel where he was staying. He would get up at 7 in the morning to send off photos to the newspapers, attend the apartado and pay a visit to the toreros in the hotel. After a couple of drinks and lunch and a half-hour siesta, he would go to the corrida. From there he would go back to his room to develop the film. "If Maruja, my wife, was with me, she would lend me a hand. She had no choice", he added jokingly, "because I feed her well!"

In the more than 85 years he spent watching bulls close up, he saw how the Fiesta had changed a lot. "The toreros definitely fight much better now than ever before, but a bull with 600 kilos can barely move, let alone charge bravely. Toreros like *Manolete* and Arruza performed extraordinary *faenas* because the bulls had mobility and were able to follow the cloth over and over again. Now, after one or two *puyazos* the animal can barely move."

Canito at an advanced age, still full of youthful enthusiasm

Had bullfight photography lost some of its importance? "In the past, toreros really valued their photos and used to give them away frequently to their admirers and to the local bars. Now, they take one portrait photo and make thousands of postcard copies to distribute for public relations."

Cano respected all the superstitions of the toreros—careful with the salt, never leave a hat on the bed, avoid the colour yellow—but his characteristic white cap had nothing to do with superstition; it was more like a talisman. "My eldest son lives in Germany and works in a car factory and every time he comes to visit with his wife and four kids, he brings me a cap. Those caps are expensive: 750 euros—because getting one means I have to feed six people for a whole month."

He had thousands of tales to tell. "One day *Manolete* asked me what kind of torero I had been, and I answered: 'Very bad, because I was gored a lot!', and he responded, 'You were caught because you stood still'. That conversation took place on the morning of the day he was killed."

The Bullfight Cinematographer

Everyone knows the ancient proverb: "One picture is worth a thousand words", but when applied to such a visual, ephemeral art as bullfighting, this saying takes on extra significance. Unlike painting, in which one can admire the same masterpiece by Goya or Velázquez at any moment by visiting the Prado Museum, aficionados cannot enjoy or even be familiar with the *toreo* of *Joselito* or *Manolete*, if they did not live in that era. For that reason, the taurine film archives take on special relevance. Nevertheless, it seems odd that such a photogenic world as that of the bulls, which is indeed dramatic, artistic, impassioned and colourful, has not occupied a more fitting place in Spanish cinema, similar to that of the western in Hollywood, which has even surpassed the borders of the Old Frontier in order to become a totally universal, epic genre.

In general, Spanish bullfight films have tended to be trite, following the same basic argument: the torero born in the most abject poverty—better still, as an orphan—who, after much struggle and suffering, manages to triumph and marry the daughter of the rich rancher and live happily ever after—or to be killed in the ring. Rarely did the films deviate from that classic formula, although sometimes the cinema served as a vehicle for promoting or launching the popular toreros of the moment, such as Manuel Benítez *El Cordobés* and Sebastián Palomo *Linares,* each of whom starred in two films.

The fascinating bullfight world did not escape the imaginative creativity of certain foreign directors, especially in the United States, France and Italy. However, in order to make a valid, genuine film about bullfighting, or any specialised theme for that matter, one must possess a profound knowledge of the subject so as not to end up with a superficial, frivolous product.

The first metres of celluloid filmed about bullfighting were for a brief documentary entitled *Arrivée des Toréadors*, by Albert Promio, for the extensive catalogue of the inventor of the movie camera, Frenchman Louis Lumière, in 1896. The very first film starring a Spanish torero was *La España trágica* (1918), featuring *novillero* (and photographer) Antonio Calvache. Then came the first of the four versions of *Sangre y Arena*, whose script and direction were the work of the author of the novel on which it was based, Vicente Blasco

Ibáñez. It was produced in Spain in 1916, although Hollywood would become enchanted with the story line and make three more versions: the first, *Blood and Sand* (1922), with the silent-film idol Rudolph Valentino in the role of matador Juan Gallardo; then that of Russian director Rouben Mamoulian (1940), with Tyrone Power and Linda Darnell, as the protagonists; and finally, the last and least successful attempt (1990), a Spanish-U.S. coproduction with Sharon Stone and Chris Rydell.

Perhaps the best taurine film ever was *Torero* (1955), starring Mexican matador Luis Procuna and directed by Carlos Velo, a Spanish university professor exiled in Mexico. The film focused on a very human story and is a study of how the matador deals with his fears and anxiety before a corrida.

In Spain, one must highlight *Tarde de Toros*, which relates in a brilliant manner the story of three toreros at different stages of their respective professional lives—the beginner, the universally recognised *figura* at the height of his glory, and the veteran about to retire—interpreted by Enrique Vera, Antonio *Bienvenida* and Domingo Ortega, respectively. The film was directed by the Hungarian director Laszlo Vajda in 1955, and obtained special recognition in the Cannes Film Festival.

Curiously enough, in the United States—defying major attacks by animal-rights associations, which do not know or appreciate the true significance of the Fiesta—a variety of full-length bullfight films have been made, not to mention countless shorts, including such comedies as *The Toreador* (1920) by Jack Blystone, *The Bullfighter* (1927) from the studios of famous producer Mack Sennett and the feature-length *The Kid from Spain*, starring Eddie Cantor.

The U.S. film director Budd Boetticher was a great bullfight fan, and thanks to him we have a number of fine films in English, which also became popular in Spanish-speaking countries: *The Bullfighter and the Lady* (1950), with Robert Stack and Gilbert Roland (whose real name was Antonio Alonso, and who was the son of a Palencia-born torero living in Ciudad Juárez, Mexico, Francisco Alonso *Paquiro*), *The Magnificent Matador*, with Anthony Quinn and Maureen O'Hara, and *Arruza* (1972), a posthumous tribute to his close friend, Mexican matador Carlos Arruza.

Aprendiendo a morir (1962), by Pedro Lazaga, told the life story of the popular matador Manuel Benítez El Cordobés and also revealed the torero's natural dramatic talent (enabling him to make another movie a year later, *Chantaje a un torero*), and the same was true of El Cordobés's major rival in the ring, Sebastián Palomo Linares, who also starred in two films: the autobiographical *Nuevo en esta plaza* (1966), and *Sólo los dos* (1968), a musical with pop singer *Marisol*. Many other bullfighters have also appeared on the big screen, beginning with José García Algabeño (*La medalla del torero*, 1924), Marcial Lalanda (*Viva Madrid que es mi pueblo*, 1928), and Nicanor Villalta (*El suceso de anoche*, 1928) in silent films; and even Manolete began a project with French director Abel Gance in 1944, until the producers unfortunately ran out of money. Then there were, among many others, Mario Cabré (*Pandora and the Flying Dutchman*, 1951, with American actress Ava Gardner, and *La mujer, el torero y el toro*, 1950), Rafael Albaicín (*La fiesta sigue*, 1948), rejoneador Ángel Peralta (*La novia de Juan Lucero*, 1958, and *Cabriola*, 1965), Antonio Borrero Chamaco (*El traje de oro*, 1959), Miguel Mateo Miguelín (the noteworthy Spanish-Italian production *El momento de la verdad*, directed by Francesco Rosi, 1963, and the third version of *El relicario*, 1968), Gabriel and José Luis de la Casa (*Cuando suena el clarín*, 1965, directed by José H. Pepe Gan), Luis Miguel Dominguín (*Yo he visto la muerte*, 1967, together with Antonio Bienvenida, Álvaro Domecq Romero and Andrés Vázquez), Paco Camino (*Fray torero*, 1966), Ángel Teruel (*Sangre en el ruedo*, 1968), the comic torero Blas Romero El Platanito (*Jugando a morir*, 1968, also directed by Pepe Gan), and *Tú sólo* (1982, focusing on the story of the students of the Madrid Bullfighting School, such as José Miguel Arroyo Joselito, José Pedro Prados El Fundi, Lució Sandín, Luis Miguel Calvo, José Antonio Carretero, etc.).

Mexico showed the same passion as Spain for making bullfight films and in addition to the extraordinary *Torero*, other top bullfighters starred in their own films: Rodolfo Gaona (*El último día de un torero*, 1925, and *Oro, sangre y sol*, 1926), Antonio and David Liceaga (*¡Que Viva México!*, directed by Russian film genius Sergei Eisenstein, 1931), Jesús Solórzano (*Ora Ponciano*, 1936), Lorenzo Garza (*Novillero*, 1936, and *Un domingo en la tarde*, 1936), Juan Silveti (*El brillo de los caireles*, 1941, and *Toros, amor y gloria*, 1944), Pepe Ortiz (who also wrote the script for both *Ora Ponciano* and *Seda, sangre y sol*, 1941, *Un corazón en el ruedo*, 1949, and *Maravilla del toreo*, 1944, with the incomparable Peruvian rejoneadora Conchita Cintrón), Alfonso Ramírez Calesero (*El precio de la gloria*, 1948), Manuel Capetillo (*¡Viva Jalisco que es mi tierra!*, 1960), Carlos Arruza (*Mi reino por un torero*, 1943, and *Sangre torera*, 1949), and Luis Procuna (who, in addition to starring in *Torero*, participated in *El niño de las monjas*, 1944, and *Sol y sombra*, 1945), and one should, of course, not forget the comic bullfighting antics of the inimitable Mario Moreno Cantinflas.

José Hernández Gan

Córdoba, 1916-2002. Producer and director, and founder of Filmoteca Taurina Gan

The person who did most to preserve the history of bullfighting on celluloid was without doubt José Hernández Gan, whose film archives were located for more than half a century in the very centre of Madrid, in calle Espoz y Mina. After Gan's death, his close assistant and protégé, Domingo Estringana (Castilmimbre, Guadalajara, 1947), whom he had taken on as an apprentice at the age of 18, continued to carry out his maestro's invaluable work with the same passion and enthusiasm until he himself became ill.

José Hernández Gan with one of his unwieldy 35 mm cameras

The person who did most to preserve the history of bullfighting on celluloid was without doubt José Hernández Gan, whose film archives were located for more than half a century in the very centre of Madrid, in calle Espoz y Mina. After Gan's death, his close assistant and protégé, Domingo Estringana (Castilmimbre, Guadalajara, 1947), whom he had taken on as an apprentice at the age of 18, continued to carry out his maestro's invaluable work with the same passion and enthusiasm until he himself became ill. This library preserves more than 500,000 metres of film documenting the most brilliant moments in bullfighting history. "The contents could line the AVE train tracks from Madrid to Seville," Gan said jokingly, about what represents a whole lifetime devoted to the cinema and the bullfighting world.

Born in Córdoba in 1916, José Hernández Gan had a boyhood playmate who would mark the future course of his life. A neighbour, Angustias Sánchez, had a son who became Gan's closest friend, Manolete. "Doña Angustias, the widow of two toreros, would throw out all of her son's bullfighting paraphernalia because she did not want him to be a torero too. So Manolo had no choice but to use his jacket to torear during his clandestine excursions to the ranches. The garment suffered the consequences and Manolo, fearing his mother's stern punishment, would take refuge in my house and ask my mother to mend his clothing. At the same time, I would help him with his homework—though neither of us was a genius."

Gan had other fond memories. "As children, we used to dig into our pockets and pool our loose change so that we could go to the neighbourhood cinema. We particularly loved the westerns, and after we saw the film Broken Arrow, Manolo had the bright idea of slitting our forearms to make us blood brothers forever."

Gan confessed that he was not particularly attracted to bullfighting or film when he was young; it was a late-blooming *afición* in both cases, which led to over sixty years of highly fruitful production. After finishing his business administration studies, he decided to become an actor. "But as I was short and not the leading-man type, I did not foresee a great future for myself on the screen. Nevertheless, I did everything from dubbing and announcing to ballroom and tap dancing. I wanted to become an assistant director but as nobody showed any confidence in me, I had to get my license as a director." Among his first shorts, which total more than 150, were Estampas campesinas (Country scenes) and Estampas taurinas (Bullfight scenes), and he made seven full-length films on taurine or folkloric themes, including Jugando a morir, with comic torero Platanito, and Cuando suena el clarín, with bullfighting brothers Gabriel and José Luis de la Casa. "I was convinced that it was better for me to deal with subjects with which I was thoroughly familiar, and just as the Americans had universalised their own genre, the westerns, I wanted to do the same thing with bullfighting. Nevertheless, when I presented the films for the censor's certificate, they would laugh and say: 'What, Gan? Another film with toros and toreros?' I asked them if they wanted me to shoot westerns too."

What did he consider his best bullfighting film? "The truth is that each one seemed important to me at the time because I immerse myself totally in everything I do, even though I might single out Sangre en la arena, with Ángel Teruel. It was meant to be the rebuttal to an English film, which represented the corrida as a barbaric martyrdom of poor, defenceless bulls in the ring. I wanted to show that *figuras* like Joselito and Manolete also died in the plaza and

Pepe Gan with his close collaborator Domingo Estringana

that it is both a magnificent and a dramatic Fiesta, in which death is ever-present."

He regretted not having found enough support to have made more feature-length bullfight films, because there were a lot of stories to tell. "During the celebration of the *Oportunidades* (novilladas for beginners) in the old Vista Alegre ring, the postman delivered an urgent letter to a young boy, who refused to open it. When I asked him why, he replied: 'It's from my mother, and I know if I read this letter I'll end up going home. She was running behind the lorry shouting: 'Hijo, don't leave! Come back!' But I want to be a torero!' I've witnessed many unique moments like that one. For example, I wrote a script for a film called *Ruedo sangriento* and I wanted Francisco Rivera *Paquirri* to star in it, but eventually his *apoderado*, Manolo Camará, said no, because he didn't like the story: it ended in tragedy. Everyone wants the same clichés: the torero is carried out of the bullring triumphantly and marries the beautiful ganadera. In the end, I did not make that film, while in real life poor *Paquirri* died tragically in the Pozoblanco bullring."

José Gan considered *Torero*, directed by Carlos Velo and starring Mexican matador Luis Procuna, to be the best taurine film. "Velo filmed in black and white; he didn't need colour because he was telling a very real, vital, profound story. He focused on an aspect of a torero's life which people do not usually get to see—their fear—because the bullfighters don't talk about it except within their most intimate circle of friends."

The success of Gan's films and documentaries lies in his personal style of working. He lived the corrida intensely, beginning with the *sorteo* in the morning to study the bulls close up and then a visit to the toreros in the hotel to wish them luck. "I discovered that the torero's mood would affect the corrida later on. They had their worries, about the weather, the wind, and a change in the bulls, along with other personal or family problems. At times, because they were so nervous, either they barely said anything or they never stopped chattering away about nonsense. This reminds me of the true story of a lad in the *patio de cuadrillas* who was so scared that when a man came over to him and asked him how he was doing, he replied like a robot: 'Fine, thank you. Have you seen my father?' And he was talking to his father!"

Part of Gan's success also lay in his special, innovative way of filming, using agile, rapid framing and interchanging close-ups with wide panoramic angles of the ring, creating the sensation of time and emotion and trying to involve the spectators in a corrida with a view which cannot usually be obtained from the stands. While today they tend to film and televise with half a dozen cameras and the latest technological advances, José Gan had to make do with just one camera and the problem of the high cost of the film. "I couldn't afford to waste footage because I had to pay for it out of my own pocket. It didn't take very long to put together the film because I'd paid extra special care during the shooting, and of a 60-metre roll, I wasted 4 or 5 metres at most, due to a bull falling down, a *pinchazo* [an unsuccessful sword thrust], etc. If I hadn't had that type of vision, I'd have gone bankrupt very soon. When I saw that a bull wasn't going to let anyone triumph, I had already used up half a roll and spent a nice amount of money. The 16 or 35 mm film wasn't like video: you couldn't erase it and begin again."

Another problem Gan had to deal with in the beginning was the heavy 35-mm camera and, if the corrida lasted longer than usual, he encountered a new problem: his battery running out. He even remembered when he had to continually stop shooting to wind up his camera. However, José Gan travelled all over Spain on his Vespa, with the heavy equipment piled on the back, filming corridas from the humblest to the most important. He began in the Valdemorillo fair, in February, and ended in Zaragoza, in October. He also liked to film the alternativas for posterity because he considered them to be a torero's "first communion". "Very often the torero never even asked me to do it and then he was pleasantly surprised with the recording of his doctorate. On the other hand, after I'd travelled to the other end of the country, the new matador in question never even bothered to come round and watch what I'd done. And then there were also those cases, like a second-rate torero who made a lot of money as an *apoderado*, and begged me to look in my archives to see if I could find some footage of him as a torero to show his grandchildren."

An affectionate cartoon portrayal

Who was his favourite torero? "I was friends with all of them and they evoke very fond memories, but if I had to single out one because of his courage, merit and our personal friendship, I would have to say *Manolete*. I sincerely regret not having followed his career more closely at the time, but I was involved in other ventures. I liked to joke with him, and I said: 'You're a good torero but too serious!' and he replied that he did not see any reason to laugh when he was standing in front of a bull. I also picked on him by saying that he never did anything spectacular like a defiant *desplante* on his knees and he said: 'I do kneel down, Pepe, but when nobody sees me! I kneel down before the Virgen de los Dolores to pray'. What I most valued about him was that I first knew him as a child and that fame and fortune never made him pompous or conceited."

José Gan was reluctant to buy a video camera at first, although he recognised that it was a great invention and one which would definitely serve to promote the Fiesta. "There's no comparison between the heavy old 35 mm cameras and the video cameras of today. You can watch the pictures at home, without a projector and you don't even have to turn off the lights." He transferred much of his extensive collection to VHS cassettes and then his assistant Domingo Estringana kept up with the times and recorded the material on DVDs.

The plaque commemorating José Gan:
"With our gratitude for his taurine film legacy on behalf of our Fiesta"

Among the many awards, medals and multitudinous tributes which José Gan received, he was most pleased with the commemorative plaque which was put up at the entrance to Tendido 8 where he had his *abonos* and did most of his filming. "I was so moved", he said, "that they put up the plaque in this incomparably beautiful, awesome monument, the plaza of Las Ventas. It's wonderful to be recognised while still alive. I've never done anything heroic, nor even taken a lap of the ring. I was simply in the 'backroom' of *toreo*, but I feel I have been very lucky for having been able to live so intensely this fantastic world."

His greatest concern before his death on June 14, 2002, was to guarantee the future of his Filmoteca and of his collaborator Domingo Estringana, who was like a son to him, but he hated to talk about its value. "Several years ago I had to renew my insurance policy: 200 rolls at so many pesetas, but what price do you put on a historic, once-in-a-lifetime *faena* of Joselito or Belmonte?" Fortunately, fifteen years after pepe Gan's death, the Filmoteca Nacional Española reached an agreement with his heirs to acquire the Filmoteca Taurina Gan of unquestionable artistic and historical value.

Radio and Television

Although the Fiesta is an important part of Spanish cultural heritage it does not receive anywhere near the attention it deserves in the media, particularly on the radio and certainly not on the television, either public or private, where every minute counts ... and a lot! Despite the dearth of serious bullfight reporting in the media in general, the lack of immediate information and news has certainly been filled in this modern age of the internet, with the ever-growing number of taurine websites. Nevertheless, here is an interview with the leading icon of corrida broadcasting in Spain, Matías Prats. Earlier famous broadcasters were Pepe Alameda, in Mexico, and for English-speaking bullfight aficionados the retired matador from Brooklyn, Sidney Franklyn, and Lyn Sherwood. Nowadays, major corrida broadcasters are Manolo Moles, Chapu Apaolaza, David Casas, Miguel Cuberta, Germán Estela, Maxi Pérez, ... (Canal+), Fernando Fernández Román and Federico Arnás (TVE), Miguel Ángel Moncholi (Telemadrid), José Luis Benlloch (Valencia), Enrique Romero and Juan Antonio Romero (Canal Sur and Andalucia), Julio Téllez and José Mata (Mexico, with the longest running bullfight TV show in history: over thirty years) and also Heriberto García, Guillermo Leal, Pepe Mata (Mexico) and Magaly Zapata (Peru).

Matías Prats Cañete
Villa del Río (Córdoba), 1913-2004. Journalist

This legendary radio and television personality was loved and admired by bullfight fans and sports enthusiasts and by every Spaniard, not only because of his extraordinary journalistic talent, but for his open, friendly nature and his exceptional culture and refined education.

He grew up in the small town of Villa del Río (Córdoba) surrounded by animals, and though he loved country life, he also had an endless thirst for knowledge. He initially studied Industrial Engineering at Málaga University, although he later opted for Philosophy and Letters. His first efforts in the journalistic world were poetic, but he does not wish to recall them. "I knew the technique, the metres and how to write a sonnet, but I did not possess the profound inspiration of those great Andalusian poets Manuel and Antonio Machado or Juan Ramón Jiménez, whom I admired so much."

The truth is that Matías earned his fame with his voice, not his pen, and his unmatched ability to broadcast any sporting or entertainment event. Nevertheless, he began to write his memoirs. "More than anything, I wanted my children to know something about my life and the definition of my experiences and what I have learned: my youth, the wars, my studies, my friends, my visits to Madrid and the impression I had the first time I walked into the National Library. I am working on my fifth volume now, but I don't want to bore them to death!"

He set out on his journalistic career by obtaining a post in Radio Nacional de España, in Málaga, in 1939, after successfully taking some very tough official examinations. "I got the coveted post because I had a melodic voice, spoke well, and at 25 years of age I had a certain amount of experience and acquired culture and knowledge from the time I had spent in Madrid. It was a 'gift from heaven', because my happiest moments were furnished by my personal and professional relations on the radio. The fact of the matter is that at that time radio was a relatively new invention: it did not appear in Spain until 1924."

Matías Prats was an institution, synonymous with the ideal model of a professional commentator. "I don't think I was the best, I was just lucky. To be a good radio announcer and commentator, you have to be naturally endowed with a pleasant voice—for that's your means of expression—a facility for improvisation, a good memory and adequate intellectual background. There was no school at the time where you could learn this. You were just given a microphone and the question was: 'Does that individual who talks so much also express himself well and know his grammar? If so, we can give him a chance'. But what was most important then was the quality of the voice."

Prats stressed the importance of the cultural background, because specialisation would not be required until much later on. "When I first started out in the radio, I did a little bit of everything: sports, cultural activities, politics, religion, but it eventually became obvious that you couldn't keep the whole world in your head and that a certain amount of preparation in a specific field was necessary."

Did he prefer spoken or written journalism? "The radio, above all, which should have taken more seriously its responsibility for training qualified journalists who could express their own thoughts and opinions with their own voice, because in the beginning they structured the radio programme like a newspaper, with people who wrote the news and announcers who read it with their 'nice voices'. I was successful because I had a satisfactory oral 'calligraphy', which is what I like to call it. The calligraphy of the way we write, and the way we speak."

His first live broadcast was neither sporting nor taurine, but ecclesiastical. "It was the canonical coronation of Nuestra Señora de la Victoria, the patron saint of Málaga. Amidst 150,000 spectators filling the park, there I was alone with a microphone and absolutely no idea at all of religious ritual, so I just tugged on the sleeves of all the soutanes I saw passing by and had the priests and even the bishop relate to the listeners exactly what was happening. The idea is for you to talk as little as possible and let the microphone do the rest."

Little by little, Matías specialised first in sport and then in bullfighting. "When I broadcast a football match, I described the field, who ran, where he came from and where he was going, trying to give the listening public coordinates with which to follow what I was saying." According to Matías, it was far more difficult to broadcast a *corrida de toros*. "It is the most difficult of all, both for radio and television, although television should be much simpler if you are guided by your own prudence and let the beauty unfolding on the screen envelop the spectators. You only have to add or highlight something which cannot be seen or understood easily. You should never talk about what people are seeing with their own eyes, but you can say the name of the picador, his background, whose son he is, where he was born, etc., etc., and adorn the details a bit. This is particularly true for the knowledgeable aficionados: for them, the less said, the better."

Matías Prats had the extraordinary ability to communicate to both ends of the spectrum: the aficionados and the simple spectators. "I know some people bragged that they turned the sound down on the television so as not to hear me, arguing: 'You're saying what we all know!', but I would reply: 'You may know it and you are right to turn off the sound, but there are a lot of people out there who need some aural references'." He was able to fill in the "lulls" better than anybody. "I did my homework. I could describe the corrida, but I really needed to know the players, so part of my preparation for the broadcast was to gather all the details I could. Of course, I knew all the matadors, but they had five other toreros in their employ, each one with his own story, and you have to find out their names and colour-code them to the suits they are wearing that day in order to identify each one of them in the ring."

When Matías transmitted his first corridas on television, he would show up at the ring five hours in advance, asking questions, taking notes and

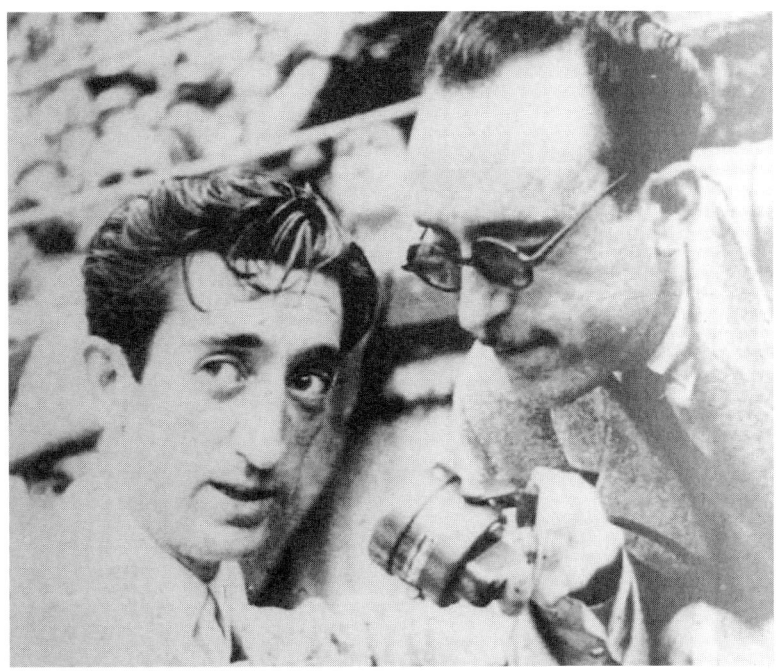

A young Matias Prats interviews Manolete "el monstruo" in the callejón

experiencing first-hand all of the prolegomena of the spectacle. "With all of this preparation, I found myself more relaxed when the corrida began. However, one day during the Feria de San Isidro, I got to the plaza just as the picadors were making their entrance into the arena, because I was caught in an immense traffic jam; I tried not to panic and managed to get through it somehow."

Even though he was a pioneer in television sports and bullfight broadcasting, his first love was radio. "On the radio, we have to keep talking and never stop, because the audience only 'sees' what we're telling them. You have to talk fast and have no time to get involved in detailed descriptions. However, with television, you have to fill in the gaps or expand upon some finer points, but then you run the risk of creating a conflict between the commentator and the spectator in his home, because he is watching what is happening and can form his own opinions. Every once in a while, you could hear a booming voice in the stands: 'Matías, this is a lousy corrida! Don't try and make it seem otherwise!' I was intimidated at the thought that everyone was listening to what I was saying until we were put into soundproof cabins and I was able to breathe a little easier."

Matías did not feel that too many corridas are televised, as some people would argue. "The aficionado who wants to go to the plaza will go, because nothing can compare to the live spectacle. We should bear in mind, too, the old people who can't get around easily and appreciate the possibility of watching a corrida on TV, and the aficionados in the *pueblos* who do not have an opportunity to see the *figuras*. Television also creates new aficionados. Obviously, a corrida is an expensive spectacle to organise, but neither radio nor television are prejudicial to the impresarios' interests. On the contrary, they can serve as a valuable source of publicity. After a good televised bullfight, people will try to see another corrida, but in the plaza itself. I think this conflict of interests really ends up as a draw, leaning more in favour of television's promotional capacity on behalf of the Fiesta."

Matías Prats in later life, still manifesting his pride in his birthplace

He was confident about the future of the Fiesta: "Those who think it's sliding into decadence are quite mistaken. As long as the bull enters the ring with its kilos, its *trapío* and its horns intact, the Fiesta will never disappear.

The fundamental element is not the torero, but the *toro*, for this brave animal is the significance and sustenance of the spectacle, which can never become routine and monotonous because each bull and each bullfighter is different."

I wondered if this great master of journalism maintained a lively conversation in the intimacy of his own home. "I'm noted for being rather quiet. I charge my batteries in my armchair. I'm almost always reading the newspaper or listening to the radio."

Contrary, too, to what many people might think, he much preferred bullfights to football matches, and did not limit himself to watching the bulls from the *barrera*. He took an active part in *tentaderos* as often as the opportunity presented itself. "I was once tossed really badly by a cow, and as if that were not enough, she shat all over me—pardon the expression—and then bit me while I was lying on the ground. She would have killed me if two footballers had not come to my rescue."

Matías Prats even made the *paseíllo* in Las Ventas once. "It was in 1962 and I participated in a charity bullfight. They left the last and smallest animal for me and I didn't do all that badly, if I say so myself. I actually felt pretty pleased with myself despite the protests I heard from one sector of the stands. It turned out to be my wife encouraging everyone to boo me out of the ring. She was afraid that I would get too enthusiastic about my performance and want to do it again."

Chapter 7. The Aficionado

The aficionado and spectator have their rights and obligations clearly established in Chapter II, Article 33, of the *Reglamento Taurino*, and among those rights is the one considered essential: to receive the spectacle in all its integrity and in accordance with the terms and conditions announced in the programme. The rights also include reimbursement of the price of the ticket if the corrida is cancelled or postponed, or the *cartel* (the announced combination) is modified as regards one of the matadors or half the number of bulls of the *ganadería* announced. The obligations are covered in the first paragraph of Article 34, and every ticket also has printed upon it: "The spectator is not permitted to leave his seat during the *lidia* of each animal".

It is customary for aficionados to group together in clubs or *peñas*, particularly in view of the fact that bullfighting is seasonal—although less so since modern indoor rings have been built, unattractive as some of them may be—and fans need some way to keep the "flame of their *afición*" kindled during the long winters. Consequently, bullfight clubs have been created throughout the world: there are approximately 650 in Spain, vast numbers in all the other taurine countries, Mexico, Colombia, Peru, Ecuador, Venezuela, Portugal, and France. Special mention should be made of the foreign aficionados, who really deserve their own book, because they are indeed meritorious. They save their money to make their "pilgrimages" to their favourite ferias in Spain, France or Latin America, and during the rest of the year they meet regularly in their local taurine venues. There are approximately fifteen associations in the United States (particularly active are those in New York, Chicago Los Angeles, San Francisco and Miami) and other enthusiasts in Italy, Sweden, Finland, Germany, etc.

Of exceptional merit is the Club Taurino of London, founded by George Erik in 1959, which has full programme of activities, monthly meetings and an exceptional newsletter. As well as a banquet in the winter in London to honour a top bullfighter or bull-breeder, the CTL also celebrates an annual lunch in Madrid during the San Isidro Fair, which is attended by leading personalities of taurine society from all over the world. Another brilliant undertaking of the Club Taurino of London is its publication of taurine books in English, including this one, for which I am extremely grateful.

These "expatriate" aficionados also dedicate their spare time to their bullfighting-related hobbies: subscribing to bullfight magazines, putting out their own newsletters, collecting books, tickets, posters, photographs and other assorted taurine memorabilia.

It would be an impossible task to try to name even a few of the most outstanding and knowledgeable of foreign aficionados, although obviously one must refer to Ernest Hemingway, whose true merit lies in the fact that he introduced the art of bullfighting to the English-speaking world with his books, Fiesta (also issued as The Sun Also Rises), published in 1926, Death in the Afternoon, (1932) and The Dangerous Summer, which first appeared in three instalments in Life magazine in September 1960. It would also be unforgivable not to cite another prolific American taurine author Barnaby Conrad, who has written a total of ten books on the subject, among his many other literary endeavours.

Mariano Aguirre Díaz
Casavieja (Avila), 1943. President of Spain's Real Federación Nacional de Peñas Taurinas

Mariano Aguirre presenting the annual awards of the Real Federación Taurina

Mariano Aguirre joined the Peña Taurina de Usera, the oldest club in Madrid, founded in 1945, when he was a 15-year-old schoolboy. In 1981, he founded the Peña Taurina Los Amigos in his home town, Casavieja, where, with just 1,400 inhabitants, they organise an annual fair of five *novilladas*, the proceeds of which go to charitable causes such as repairing the local church. The 240 members of the Peña Taurina take on all the tasks: contracting *toros* and *toreros* (a task for Mariano himself), ticket sales, doormen, cleaning squad, etc.

Aguirre graduated from being president of the Peña Taurina Los Amigos de Casavieja to President of the Real Federación Nacional de Peñas Taurinas, made up currently of 648 *peñas taurinas* from all over Spain, grouped together in 16 territorial federations. He jokes: "The Federación represents between 400,000 and 500,000 aficionados, making us the third largest organisation in Spain after the two leading political parties PP [the right-wing "Popular" Party] and PSOE [Spanish Socialist Workers Party], and we were particularly proud of the fact that King Juan Carlos, an excellent aficionado, granted us the right to use the word Real [Royal] in our title."

Aguirre is devoted to defending the rights and obligations of aficionados. "We have the absolute right to demand the corrida offered on the *cartel* in its unadulterated form, and the moral 'obligation' to take our children and grandchildren to the plazas, in order to perpetuate the future of this unique cultural manifestation 'forever and ever'. Our responsibility is to pay for our tickets, to be honest in our demands and judgements, and to be aware of the need to reward 'a job well done'. We should never fail to respect anyone who wears a suit of lights."

As for the problem recently created in Catalonia, where certain regional politicians have managed to ban the Fiesta, totally ignoring the desires of the vast majority of the local citizens, the president of the Federación says: "The situation in that region is absurd. In fact, the wild auroch, the ancestor of today's fighting bull, is believed to have entered the country from northern Europe through the Pyrenees, and today there are many excellent aficionados in that part of the country. Kings and popes have tried to do away with bullfighting, to no avail, so I don't think the Catalan Government will have any better luck, and they will eventually be obliged to accept the will and respect the freedom of the people".

According to Aguirre, matador Marcial Lalanda defined a good aficionado as: "One who is capable of appreciating the largest number of *toros* and *toreros*". Nevertheless, when his rival, Domingo Ortega, heard the customarily excessive protests coming from Tendido 7 and was asked who was right, he replied: "They are! Because they're the ones who paid for their tickets."

Mariano admits that he would have loved to have been a torero, but that he lacked the necessary courage from the word go. "I tried to give a few passes once to a calf: one, two ... and on the third I had to toss the muleta aside and run for my life! I think there is a torero deep inside each Spaniard. The last time I fought was in a tentadero on the Bernardino Piriz ranch, where Rafael de Paula was extraordinary with a great calf. I got so carried away that when he offered me the muleta I took it. I positioned myself, cited the animal and that tiny calf charged straight at me and broke two of my ribs. Paula came running over to see how I was, shaking his head and mumbling to himself at the same time: 'It was such a good calf! How did you manage to mess up like that?'"

José Luis Moreno-Manzanaro
Madrid, 1938. Lawyer and some-time President of the Unión Taurina de Abonados de Madrid

As a lawyer and aficionado all his life and the founder of the Unión Taurina de Abonados (season ticket-holders) de Madrid in 1992, José Luis Moreno-Manzanaro does not believe that the current *Reglamento Taurino* can cover all the needs of the Fiesta, and feels that aficionados and their associations have a moral obligation to support and defend its future, with what he liked to call their "unwritten right to veto". The Unión Taurina de Abonados de Madrid set the example for similar associations in Seville, Zaragoza, Málaga, Algeciras, Granada, Valencia and Córdoba, with a number of goals, including:

to defend the fundamental values of the Fiesta, above individual interests;

to promote and defend the *Fiesta de los toros* as a popular cultural manifestation and spectacle;

to collaborate with all the professional and regional associations in the promotion of the Fiesta;

to promote and support taurine culture in all its manifestations; and

to collaborate in the artistic and personal preparation of young people with a taurine vocation.

Moreno was anxious to minimise the distinction often made between spectator and aficionado as something disrespectful. "The worst thing that can happen to the Fiesta is that people stop going. It's not a problem that there are more 'mere spectators' attending the corridas; what is alarming is that there are fewer aficionados. What worries me is that the mass can 'devour', the ring and impose its criteria over those of a knowledgeable minority, and the Fiesta can end up distorted and adulterated in the process."

Another noteworthy aficionado who actively defends the Fiesta from his organisation, the Federación Taurina de Madrid, is **Jorge Fajardo**.

Las Ventas full "up to the flag".
The picador is in the centre; the aficionados in Tendido 7
(on the left) are well placed to assess the tercio de varas

Salvador Valverde Salva
Santa Cruz de Retamar, 1968-2010. *Tendido 7 season ticket-holder*

A large number of the seasoned aficionados in Las Ventas dislike or reject the perennial protesters in Tendido 7, but while some think they come predisposed to attack the *figuras* and intentionally spoil or put a damper on the most promising afternoons, in fact, the great majority are enthusiastic aficionados, although clearly with strong opinions of their own. However, they have their place in the plaza and hence in this book. Salvador Valverde Salva was one of their most noteworthy representatives, but outside the ring he was by no means the loud, boisterous, belligerent soul he appears to be in the arena; simply an impassioned aficionado.

"When I protest, what I am really trying to do is defend the purity of the *toro de lidia*. We consider ourselves, instead of the RSPCA, the ASPBB, The Association for the Protection of the Brave Bull. I sincerely believe that if we aficionados are not willing to fight for the integrity of the *toro bravo*, it will end up disappearing, together with the Fiesta. Personally, I protest the presentation of the bull, rather than attack the toreros. I have been fined twice for insulting the authority—it cost me 250 euros each time—which was preferable to the 6,000 euros of the initial fine. Three years ago, I paid yet another fine of 1,500 euros, but I admit that I made a mistake that time, because I shouted gross and impolite insults at the female veterinary surgeon. We really 'put our hooves in our mouths' that afternoon, but I think it is ridiculous that we pay for our tickets, feel cheated, protest and voice our opinions and then, on top of it all, are financially penalised as well."

Salvador, who has had his *abono* in row 14 of Tendido 7 since 1982, regrets that the seasoned and serious aficionados of the *tendido* are decreasing in number, even though they continue to publish a periodical entitled *La Voz de la Afición*, of which they print 4,000 copies.

He insists that "Los del 7" are not seeking notoriety, even though they have achieved it, and some have even been given their own nicknames. "Our one goal is to defend the *toro de lidia* and its integrity. We want to respect the bullfighter but if the bull is small, or has shaved horns, or is weak, we can't. It's like a housewife who goes to the butcher's and asks for a kilo of meat: if the butcher gives her 800 grams, she'll complain, and rightly so. You have to give me what I'm paying for!"

Salva puts theory into practice

Salvador is anxious to reaffirm that they are not concerned with the kilos but with the *trapío* and presence of the animals and if they protest as soon as a bull comes into the ring, it is because they have already seen it in the morning *apartado* and considered it unsuitable.

He has really fond memories of the baptism of his first son, which was held on the ranch of the Cura de Valverde. Where else? This ranch raises difficult, aggressive animals and is a veritable nightmare for toreros. "The invitations to the baptism were bullfight *carteles*," says Valverde, "and the *ganadero* himself—el cura [the priest]—performed the ceremony. Afterwards, we organised a *tentadero* for two hundred guests." Would he want his son to become a torero? "No way! I know it's a very hard life, beginning in the *pueblos*, with big bulls and little or no money. It would cost me at least 200,000 euros just to launch his career, and with no guarantee that he would be successful or happy. I will be satisfied if he is a good aficionado, but better than his father!"

Glossary

(Italicised terms also have their own entry)

Abono A season ticket or a series of tickets for an entire bullfight fair

Acoso y derribo: Testing of cows or bulls in the open country. *Acoso* pursuit, and *derribo* knocking down

Afición: A love or passion for something, in this case, bullfighting. Also, "la *afición*": *aficionados* as a collective group

Aficionado/a: A lover or fan, in this case of bullfighting

Alamares: Decorative tassels on the suits of lights

Alguacilillo: A mounted constable, classically dressed in a plumed hat and black velvet seventeenth-century costume, who is responsible for carrying out the president's orders in the ring

Alternativa: The formal ceremony in which a *novillero* or *rejoneador* graduates to full *matador* status

Andaluz: Someone or something from the Andalusian region of Spain.

Andanadas: Uppermost tier of seats in the bullring. In Madrid, they are found above the *gradas*

Apartado: The separation of the bulls into their individual pens, after the *sorteo*

Apoderado: The manager of a *torero*

Arena: Literally, sand. The sandy area in a bullring. Also, the building itself

Arenero: Someone who smoothes and cleans up the sand, before each bull is released into the arena

Asesor: One of two advisors to the president of the bullring: a veterinary surgeon, an expert in the behaviour of brave, fighting bulls; and a retired *torero* or respected *aficionado*, who will evaluate the *torero*'s performance

AVE (Alta Velocidad Española): Acronym for the Spanish "bullet" trains, such as the one which connects Madrid and Seville

Aviso: The call on the *clarín* which warns the *matador* that the 15 minutes allotted for the *faena* are being used up. In Spain, the first sounds 10 minutes after the *matador* takes the *muleta* in hand, the second follows three minutes later, and the third *aviso*, two minutes after that, signals that the *matador* must retire behind the *barrera* and allow the bull to be taken out of the ring. This ignominious finale is considered a major disgrace for a bullfighter

Ayuda: Help; the imitation sword, made of wood, aluminium or even carbon-fibre, carried during the *faena*. Also the assistant to the sword-handler

Banderillas: The 75 cm-long wooden sticks with steel barbs at the end, which are thrust into the bull's back in the second *tercio* of the *corrida*. Banderillas de fuego: Sticks with fireworks, which exploded when placed on the bull's back, used until 1930. Banderillas negras: Sticks decorated with black paper, with slightly larger barbs, placed on a cowardly bull, which cannot be piced

Banderillero: A member of the matador's *cuadrilla*, who assists him in the ring with the cape and places the *banderillas*

Barrenar: To drill: twisting around the pic while picing the bull. It is not permitted and the *picador* can be fined

Barrera: The wooden fence encircling and enclosing the *arena*, and separating it from the stands. Also, the very first row or rows of ringside seats. The row(s) immediately behind is/are *contrabarrera*

Becerro/a: A calf, one to two years old. *Becerrada* a bullfight featuring such animals in which would-be *toreros* perform

Berrendo: A mottled bull. Berrendo en negro: mottled in black. Berrendo en colorado: mottled in brown

Bravo: Brave or wild

Brindis: The dedication the *matador* makes to a friend or important personality, or (*brindis al público*) to the audience before he starts the *faena*

Burladero: The fence in front of the openings in the *barrera* surrounding the ring, behind which a torero in danger can seek refuge. Also, similar protective shelters within the *callejón*

Cabestro: Tame steer. Cabestrero: The person who directs the *cabestros*

Callejón: The passageway between the *barrera* and the public seating

Calzona: The light beige chamois-leather leggings worn by the *picador*

Campero: Country-style

Cantaor: A flamenco singer

Cañada: A route used for transporting livestock cross-country

Capa, capote: The *torero's* big fighting cape, made of silk in the past and heavy percale nowadays, magenta on the outside and usually yellow on the inside; also called *capote de brega*. Capote de paseo: The heavily embroidered dress cape, made of fine silk, and worn only during the *paseíllo*. Capa may also refer to the colour of the bull's hide

Capea: A village free-for-all in which an animal is let loose in a makeshift ring and anyone daring or "foolish" enough can go out and give it a few passes

Capilla: Chapel

Capotazos: Passes with the cape

Carioca: A manoeuvre invented by *picador* Miguel Atienza to pic a cowardly bull. The picador moves the horse out to block the *toro*'s natural line of exit, so that he can pic the animal. It can be abusive if used with a brave bull

Cartel: The poster advertising the *corrida*; the line-up of bulls and bullfighters. Also, a colloquial expression referring to a good reputation: "That matador has *cartel*"

Casta: A particular strain of bull. Also, the bull's innate bravery

Castañeta: False pigtail worn by the *toreros*

Castoreño: The *picador*'s wide-brimmed beige hat, made from beaver skin

Chaleco: The *torero*'s waistcoat

Chaquetilla: The lavishly embroidered jacket of the suit of lights

Charlotada: A comic bullfight

Chiqueros: The individual pens in which the bulls are kept in the bullring until they are released into the arena

Clarines y timbales: Trumpets (actually bugles) and drums

Cogida: Being caught by the bull, from the verb *coger*, to catch; to be tossed or injured, not necessarily gored

Coleta: The small pigtail worn by the bullfighter, which Juan Belmonte replaced in the 1920s with the *castañeta*, a small hairpiece attached to the back of the head. When the *torero* "cuts his *coleta*", it indicates his retirement

Colleras: When two rejoneadors perform together with the same bull

Conocedor: The ranch hand who knows everything there is to know about the bulls; from *conocer* to know

Cornada: A goring or horn wound

Corral: Corral where the bulls are kept in the bullring when they arrive from the ranch, until the *sorteo*

Corrida: Literally "running": the bullfight. A *corrida de toros* involves fully grown 4- and 5-year-old bulls; a *corrida de novillos* or *novillada* involves 3-year-old animals

Crotal: Identifying metallic plate clipped onto a calf's ear when it is a few months old

Cuadrilla: The *matador*'s team of assistants consisting of three *banderilleros* and two *picadors*

Descabello: The short sword with a crosspiece near the end used to kill the bull rapidly by severing its spinal cord; *descabellar:* to kill using this sword

Desolladero: Slaughterhouse patio where the dead bull is cut up and prepared for shipping to the butchers

Desplante: A daring pose in which the matador challenges the bull to charge

Diestro: Right-handed; dexterous; a *matador*

Divisa: Coloured ribbons identifying the ranch from which a bull comes

Empresa: A company; one which organises a bullfight or has leased out the bullring for a number of seasons.

En canal: Weight of the carcass of the animal after it has been killed

Encaste: The breed or strain of bull. *Encastado* brave, with *casta*

Enchiqueramiento: Placing the bulls in their individual pens before the bullfight

Encierro: The running of the bulls through the streets, the most famous being those held in Pamplona in July. Also, the string of bulls for a *corrida*

Enfermería: The bullring infirmary

Escuela de Tauromaquia or *Escuela Taurina:* Bullfighting school

Espada: Sword. Also, the man who wields it, the *matador*

Espontáneo: A would-be bullfighter, who jumps into the ring with a *muleta* or large cloth with the intention of fighting the bull. Doing so is illegal and nowadays can result in a stiff fine and a ban against performing professionally for two years

Esportón: The large rectangular leather case, in which capes and *muletas* are stored, often hand-tooled with the name of the *matador*

Estribo: Stirrup: the small step jutting out from the *barrera*, making it easier to vault over it

Faena: The final act of the fighting of each bull, when the *matador* fights the bull with the *muleta*

Faja: The silk sash of the suit of lights, which usually matches the colour of the tie

Farpa: (Portuguese) A *banderilla*-like weapon put in by the *rejoneador*

Feria: Fair, during which one bullfight or a series may be put on

Festejo: A bullfighting event

Festival (pl. *festivales*): A fight, usually for charity, in which the bullfighters wear the *traje corto* and the tips of the animals' horns have been removed

Fiesta, fiesta brava, fiesta nacional: Spain's "national spectacle", the bullfight

Fiesta campera: An informal event organised by or for *aficionados*, where they can have fun caping small calves

Figura, figura del toreo: A major star in the bullfighting world

Forcados: The men who form a line and try to dominate a bull during the performance of a Portuguese-style *rejoneador*. The "captain" of the group literally grabs the bull by the horns and the rest try to restrain the bull until another grasps the tail and swings around with the animal

Fundón: Long leather case for the *matador*'s swords and *muleta* sticks

Ganado: Cattle, in this case the brave bulls and cows (*ganado bravo*) *Ganadería:* A bull-breeding ranch. *Ganadero:* The owner of a bull-breeding ranch

Garrocha: Pole used to manoeuvre the bulls on the ranches. Also, the wooden pole on which the *puya* is mounted, used by the *picador*

Grada: The upper tier of the stands, above the *tendidos*; in the Levante, a row of seats in the *tendido*

Gregoriana: Protective metal covering worn on his right leg by the *picador*

Guayabera: A short, loose-fitting cotton shirt with four large pockets in the front, popular in Mexico and other Latin American countries and frequently worn by *taurinos*

Herradero: Branding session of the animals when they are approximately nine months old

Jijona: Breed of bulls dating back to the 18th century

Lance: A pass with the cape

Lidia: The way the bull is fought, from lidiar, to fight. *Lidiador:* A bullfighter, especially one used to dealing with difficult bulls

Macho: Male. Also, the tassels hanging down from the shoulder pads and *taleguilla* of the suit of lights

Maestro: A highly experienced *matador*

Maletilla: An aspiring *torero* who would hitchhike across the country in the hope of participating in *tentaderos* and village *capeas* in order to give a few passes. This colourful figure has all but disappeared thanks to the proliferation of bullfighting schools

Mansedumbre: Cowardliness or tameness. *Manso:* A cowardly bull, also "tame" cattle; sometimes used for a *cabestro*

Matador de novillos (toros): A *novillero*

Matador de toros: A killer of bulls who has taken the *alternativa*

Mayoral: Ranch or bullring foreman

Metisaca: Slipping the sword in and pulling it out, without letting go of the hilt, usually because the *matador* realises it has entered at a bad angle

Mimo: Pampering

Miura: A bull from the 150-year-old ranch of Eduardo Miura, noted for its difficult and dangerous animals, which have killed more *toreros* than those from any other ranch

Momento de la verdad: Moment of truth, when the *matador* attempts to kill the bull

Mona: Picador's leg armour

Monosabio: "Wise monkey"; the costumed ring attendants who assist the *picadors* in controlling and protecting their horses

Montera: The black astrakhan hat worn by the *matador* and *banderilleros*

Morrillo: The hump of muscle on the bull's neck

Mozo de espadas: The *matador's* sword-handler, who also acts as a valet, personal secretary and confidant

Muleta: The red flannel or serge cloth hanging on a stick, with which the *faena* is performed. *Muletazo:* A pass performed with the muleta

Mulillas: The team of mules used to drag the dead bull from the ring

Mulillero: The muleteer, the person who guides the mule team

Natural: The basic, left-handed *muleta* pass, when the sword is held in the right hand

Novillo: A three-year-old bull. *Novillada:* A bullfight in which *novillos* are fought. These can be *con picadores* (with larger and somewhat older bulls) or *sin* (without) *picadores,* in which the *novilleros* do not have the benefit of the *picadors* to weaken and temper the animals. *Novillero:* A junior professional *matador* who has not yet received the *alternativa*. *Novillero sin picadores* is the first stage in which the would-be professionals fight smaller animals without the benefit of a *picador's* intervention. A *novillero con picadores* performs with horses and fights larger animals until he or she acquires enough experience to take the *alternativa*

Olé: Shout of approval, "Bravo!"

Padrino: The "godfather", the *matador* who bestows the *alternativa*

Palco: A separate box of seats in the bullring. The president has his own *palco*, before which the Spanish flag is hung; there may also be a *palco real*, or royal box

Pañoleta The narrow silk tie, usually red, green or black, worn by the *torero*

Pase: A *muleta* pass

Paseíllo: The colourful, opening parade of the bullfighters and their entourage across the ring at the start of the bullfight

Pasodoble: A lively two-step, played in the bullring during the opening parade, during the second *tercio*, when the *matador* is placing the *banderillas*, or when the *torero* is executing a good *faena*

Patio: A yard *Patio de arrastre:* Yard to which the dead bull is taken from the ring *Patio de caballos:* The horse yard of the bullring *Patio de cuadrillas:* The yard in which the *matadors* and their *cuadrillas* wait for the bullfight to begin

Peña taurina: A bullfighting club

Peón: Worker or labourer; synonym for the *banderillero*. *Peón de confianza:* The most trusted and usually most *banderillero* in the *cuadrilla*

Percance: An injury of any kind

Peto: The mattress-like protection worn by the *picador*'s horse

Picador: A bullfighter on horseback, armed with a lance or pic, whose job it is to test the bull's bravery, weaken its neck muscles and lower its head, so it can follow the cloth better. *Picar:* To pic the bull with the lance from horseback

Plaza (de toros): The bullring

Presidente: The authority of the bullfight, usually a mayor, magistrate or a police official, who presides over the *corrida*

Puerta de cuadrillas: The gate at which the bullfighters congregate before the *corrida* begins

Puerta grande: The main gate of the bullring, through which a triumphant *matador* may be carried out on shoulders

Puya: The metal tip of a *picador*'s lance. *Puyazo:* The thrust at the bull with the lance

Querencia: The favourite haunts of the bull on a ranch. Also, its tendency to seek refuge in a particular part of the *arena*

Quiebro: A feint, a dodging action

Quite: Drawing away. This may be artistic, performed by the *matador* with the *capote*, or life-saving, when a bull is drawn away from a *torero* (or horse) in danger. *Quite de la gorra:* When one of the bullring employees tosses his gorra (cap) into the ring to distract the bull's attention

Rabo: The bull's tail

Reconocimiento: The physical examination of the bull in the corrals by the veterinary surgeons

Rejón: A short lance. *Rejón de castigo:* Punishing lance equivalent to the picing. *Rejón de muerte:* Lance with a sword-like blade used for the kill.

Rejoneador The bullfighter who fights the bull from horseback. *Rejoneo:* Bullfighting on horseback

Robapalmas: Applause-stealer, usually a *subalterno* who tries to show off and receive an ovation, often frowned upon by the *matador*

Ruedo: The sand-covered ring or arena

Saludar: To take off the *montera* to acknowledge an ovation

Sardo: A bull with a cream-coloured hide

Semental: A seed or stud bull

Sevillano/a: A person or object from Seville

Sinvergüenza: Shameless person

Sobre: An envelope. The bribe a *matador* would give to the critics

Sobrero An extra bull, which may substitute for one rejected and is returned to the corrals

Sobresaliente: An extra *matador* who may be brought into action if one is injured; legally required in *corridas* with only one or two *matadors*. A *rejoneador* is obliged to include one in his *cuadrilla* in case he cannot kill the bull from horseback and chooses not to dismount and dispatch it with the *muleta* and sword

Sol: Sun, the sunny section of the arena, where the cheaper seats are found. *Sombra:* Shade, the shady side of the arena, with the more expensive seats. There may also be *Sol y Sombra*, in an intermediate price range, where the first bulls are usually viewed in the sun and then the rest in the shade

Sortear: To draw lots. *Sorteo:* The official ceremony in which lots are drawn to determine which *matador* will face which bulls. His representatives determine the order in which he will fight his bulls

Subalterno: A member of a *matador*'s team or *cuadrilla*

Suerte Luck. Also, the different aspects of the corrida and the diverse actions the *matador* can take, whether it be with the cape, *banderillas*, *muleta* or sword. Sometimes used to indicate the *tercios* of the *lidia*

Taleguilla: The trousers of the *torero*'s suit of lights

Taurino/a: Pertaining to bullfighting. Also, any professional member of the bullfighting world

Tauromaquia: The art and science of bullfighting

Temple Smooth control, particularly when using the *muleta*

Tendidos: The spectators' seating areas directly behind the *barrera* and *contrabarrera*. Also, the radially numbered sections of the bullring

Tentadero: The testing of young calves (usually cows) for bravery (also *tienta*); from *tentar*: to test

Tercero: The third *banderillero* of the *cuadrilla* who often places one pair of sticks in each bull and is usually in charge of giving the coup de grâce with the *puntilla*

Tercio: A third. The fighting of an individual bull has three *tercios*: the *tercio de varas*, the picing; the *tercio de banderillas*; and the *tercio de muerte*, the *faena* and kill

Testigo: Witness. The third matador present when the *padrino* bestows the *alternativa*

Tienta: See *tentadero*

Torear: To fight a bullfight or to perform. *Toreo:* The art and profession of bullfighting. *Toreo de salón:* "Drawing-room bullfighting"; training or practising bullfighting without a bull, "shadow bullfighting"

Torera: Female bullfighter

Torería: The special style and class of being a bullfighter

Torero: A bullfighter; any person who participates in the *lidia* of the bull: *matador, novillero, banderillero, picador, rejoneador*

Toril: The place where the bull enters the ring. *Torilero:* The person in charge of the *toril* gate

Torista: An *aficionado* more focussed on the performance of the bull, unlike the *torerista*, who is inspired more by the *toreros*

Toro, toro bravo, toro de lidia: The brave, fighting bull, *Bos taurus ibericus*

Traje: A suit. *Traje campero:* Country outfit. *Traje corto:* The country outfit of straight, high-waisted trousers and short jacket, usually in grey, black or navy blue, and worn with boots, rather than the bullfighter's slippers. *Traje de luces:* The suit of lights, the *toreros'* costume

Trapío: The physical, muscular appearance of the bull, which should be impressive, arrogant, radiating strength and power, with well-developed horns

Trastos: The tools of the trade

Tremendismo: A flashier, less orthodox style of fighting. *Tremendista:* A *matador* or *novillero* who fights in that style

Triunfador: The most successful *matador* in a single *corrida*, a *feria* or a season

Truenos: The folded newspapers used as earplugs, stuffed into the ears of the *picador*'s horse

Túnel: The "tunnel", when *toreros* are obliged to fight for less than the legally established fees

Vaquero: A ranch hand; literally, a cowboy

Vara, vara de picar: The *picador*'s lance; also, each entry of the bull to the horse

Veedor: The expert (usually a former *torero*) who visits bull ranches to scout out possible bulls for the major commitments of a *matador* or *impresario*

Verónica: The fundamental two-handed cape pass named after Saint Veronica

Bibliography

Books in Spanish

Abella, Carlos: *Historia del toreo*, three volumes. Alianza, Madrid, 1992
Agrupación Española de Ganaderos de Reses Bravas, Madrid, 1999
Aguayo, José F.: *Imágenes del cine español* Centro Cultural del Conde Duque,
    Madrid, 1996
Alameda, José: *Crónica de sangre* Editorial Grijalbo, México, 1981
Amorós, Andrés: *Toros y cultura* Espasa Calpe, Madrid, 1988
Arévalo, José Carlos, José Antonio del Moral: *Las Ventas, 50 años de corridas*
    Excma. Diputación Provincial de Madrid, Madrid, 1981
Asociación Nacional de Ganaderías de Lidia *Relación oficial* 1999 (and other years)
Biblioteca Nacional *La fiesta nacional* Madrid, 1973
Claramunt, Fernando: *Historia ilustrada de la tauromaquia* Espasa Calpe, Madrid, 1989
Colegio Oficial de Veterinarios: *Ley y reglamentos de los espectáculos taurinos*
    Madrid, 1997
de Bonifaz, Juan José: *Víctimas de la fiesta* Espasa Calpe, Madrid, 1991
de Cossío, José María: *Los Toros, tratado técnico e histórico*, twelve volumes.
    Espasa Calpe, Madrid, 1943-1999
Del Moral, José Antonio: *Cómo ver una corrida de toros* Alianza, Madrid, 1996
Díaz-Cañabate, Antonio: *Museo Taurino* Diputación Provincial, Madrid, 1970
Domecq y Díez, Álvaro: *Memorias. 80 años. Mi vereda a galope* Espasa Calpe,
    Madrid, 1998
    El toro bravo Espasa Calpe, Madrid, 1993
Dominguín, Pepe: *Mi gente* Editorial Piesa, Madrid, 1979
Durán, Manuel Blázquez, Juan Miguel Sánchez: Vigil *Historia de la fotografía taurina*,
    two volumes. Espasa Calpe, Madrid 1991
Feiner, Muriel: *La mujer en el mundo del toro* Editorial Alianza, Madrid, 1995
    Los protagonistas de la fiesta. Vol. 1. El toro, el torero y su entorno;
    Vol. 2. La plaza, el ruedo y los tendidos Editorial Alianza, Madrid, 2000
    De Lumière a Manolete. El cine taurino Editorial Sol y Sombra, Madrid, 2010
    ¡Torero! los toros en el cine Editorial Alianza, Madrid, 2005
    Toreros de plata Espasa Calpe, Madrid, 2004
Fernández Salcedo, Luis: *D. Antonio Miura y la novelesca ganadería que fundó*
    Asociación El Toro de Madrid, Madrid, 1999
Ganaderos de Lidia Unidos, 1998-99, Madrid, 1999
García Alfonso, José: *Actuación de los veterinarios en los espectáculos taurinos (Guía básica)*
    Egartorre, Madrid, 1990

García García, José: Luis *Espectáculos taurinos, funciones del delegado gubernativo real*
    Federación Taurina de España, Madrid, 1998
Laverón, Jorge: *La Tauromaquia de 'Antoñete' de los años negros al mito*
    Las Páginas del Tendido, Madrid, 1988
Martínez Novillo, Álvaro: *Baldomero* & *Aguayo* Turner, Madrid, 1992
Molés, Manuel F.: *El nuevo reglamento y la ley taurina* Ediciones Epsilon, Madrid, 1992
    Antoñete, el maestro El País, Madrid, 1996
Moreno-Manzanaro, José Luis: *Madrid en el toreo. Homenaje a los toreros de Madrid*
    Unión de Abonados de España, Madrid, 1994
Navas Gómez, Juan Carlos: *El toro de lidia* Ángel Carrasco Navarro, Madrid, 1995
Nieto Manjón, Luis: *Diccionario ilustrado de términos taurinos* Espasa Calpe,
    Madrid, 1987
Palacios, César, José María Moreno: *San Isidro* Ayuntamiento, Madrid, 1998
Ramón, José Luis: *Todas las suertes por sus maestros* Espasa Calpe, Madrid, 1998
Rodríguez Montesinos, Adolfo: *Entre campos y ruedos* Consejo General de Colegios
    Veterinarios de España, Zaragoza, 1991
Saíz Valdivielso, Alfonso Carlos: *La fiesta taurina* Proyección Editorial, Bilbao, 1972
Sánchez Vigil, Juan Miguel, Durán Blázquez, Manuel: *Antología de la fotografía taurina*,
    1839-1939 Espasa Calpe, Madrid, 1999
Sotomayor, José María: *Miura. Siglo y medio de casta (1842-1992)* Espasa Calpe,
    Madrid, 1992
Unión de Criadores de Toros de Lidia *Relación oficial* Madrid, 1998 (and other years)
Vila, Enrique: *Miuras, más de cien años de gloria y tragedia* Escelicer, Madrid, 1968
Villatoro, Ángel: *Antología taurina Mexicana* Biblioteca Nueva, Madrid, 1964
Zabala, Vicente: *La corrida* Secretaría de Estado de Turismo, Madrid, 1977

Books in English (see also Publications of the Club Taurino of London)

Bonet, Eduardo, et al.: *Bulls and bullfighting* Crown, New York, 1970
Chaves Nogales, Manuel, trans. Leslie Charteris: *Juan Belmonte, killer of bulls*
    Doubleday, New York, 1937
Conrad, Barnaby: *Matador* Capra House, Santa Barbara, 1952
    La fiesta brava Houghton Mifflin, Boston, 1953
    Barnaby Conrad's encyclopaedia of bullfighting Houghton Mifflin,
        Boston, 1961
    Gates of fear Bonanza Books, New York, 1967
Daly, Robert: *Swords of Spain* Penguin, New York, 1967
Feiner, Muriel: *Women in the bullring* University Press of Florida, Gainesville, 2003
Fulton, John: *Bullfighting* Dial Press, New York, 1971
Hemingway, Ernest: *Fiesta (a.k.a The sun also rises)* Scribner, New York, 1926
    Death in the afternoon Scribner, New York, 1932
    The dangerous summer Hamish Hamilton, London, 1960
Josephs, Allen: *Ritual and sacrifice in the corrida: the saga of César Rincón*
    University Press of Florida, Gainesville, 2002

Kehoe, Vincent: *Aficionado!* Hastings House, New York, 1959
Lapierre, Dominque, Larry Collins: *Or I'll dress you in mourning* Simon and Schuster, New York, 1968
McCormick, John, Mario Sevilla Mascareñas: *The Complete Aficionado* World Publishing Company, Cleveland, 1964
Smith, Rex: *Biography of the bulls* Rinehart, New York 1957
Tynan, Kenneth: *Bull fever* Longmans Green. London, 1966
Vavra, Robert: *Curro. Reflections of a Spanish youth* Vavra, Sevilla, 1975
  Bulls of Iberia Oliva, Sevilla, 1972
Verner, Jim *Tauromaquia of Pepe-Hillo* 2013
Wood, Tristán *How to watch a bullfight* Unwin, Ludlow, 2011